*MORE PRAISE FOR*

# FREEDOMNOMICS

"Despite abundant evidence from around the world to the contrary, too many of our nation's elites—including academics, journalists, politicians, and authors—claim that free enterprise does not work. Instead, they advocate increased government regulation and central planning. In *Freedomnomics*, John Lott dispels the myths and shatters such "conventional wisdom." Based on fact, not ideology, he demonstrates how free market principles produce the greatest success, whether it involves business, labor, crime control, or public policy. This book is essential to those who seek to understand liberty."

—Edwin Meese III, former U.S. attorney general
under President Reagan

"*Freedomnomics* is a terrific exposition of matters pertaining to political economy—the interaction of politics and economics. Truly, this is a perspective that is enlightening and worthy of presentation. As Thomas Jefferson once uttered, 'the price of freedom is eternal vigilance.' John Lott has meaningfully contributed to the necessary vigilance toward the preservation of freedom with the tales of his professional journey."

—John Raisian, Director and Senior Fellow,
Hoover Institution, Stanford University

# FREEDOMNOMICS

# FREEDOMNOMICS

## WHY THE FREE MARKET WORKS
### AND OTHER HALF-BAKED THEORIES DON'T

## JOHN R. LOTT, JR., PH.D.

*Since 1947*
**REGNERY**
**PUBLISHING, INC.**
*An Eagle Publishing Company • Washington, DC*

Library of Congress Cataloging-in-Publication Data

Lott, John R.
  Freedomnomics / John Lott.
    p. cm.
  ISBN 978-1-59698-506-3
  1. Free enterprise. I. Title.
  HB95.L68 2007
  330.12'2—dc22

                                        2007011502

Published in the United States by
Regnery Publishing, Inc.
One Massachusetts Avenue, NW
Washington, DC 20001

www.regnery.com
Distributed to the trade by
National Book Network
Lanham, MD 20706

Manufactured in the United States of America
10 9 8 7 6 5 4 3 2 1

Books are available in quantity for promotional or premium use. Write to Director of Special Sales, Regnery Publishing, Inc., One Massachusetts Avenue NW, Washington, DC 20001, for information on discounts and terms or call (202) 216-0600.

*To Milton Friedman,*
*not only among the greatest economists of all time, but also*
*the heroic, often lone champion who fought for freedom with*
*gusto and a smile on his face. He helped many understand*
*how freedom makes us better off.*

# CONTENTS

# Introduction

> It is not from the benevolence of the butcher, the brewer, or the baker, that we expect our dinner, but from their regard to their own interest. We address ourselves, not to their humanity but to their self-love, and never talk to them of our necessities but of their advantages.
>
> —Adam Smith, *The Wealth of Nations*[1]

The free market works. This notion was clear to Adam Smith in the early days of capitalism, but since then it has come under a great deal of skepticism. These criticisms are nothing new, of course. As far back as 1848, Karl Marx published a Communist Manifesto, advocating an alternative economic system that would replace the market with state planning. Communism was adopted in countries ranging from Russia to North Korea, but somehow the outcome was always the same—mass shortages. Most Communist regimes eventually scrapped their dysfunctional economic system, if their populations didn't rise up and do it for them. Today, there are only a few remaining Communist countries, and the only ones that have any kind of economic success—like China—are the ones that are reestablishing free enterprise.

Meanwhile, countries that stuck with the free market have prospered. There is a simple reason for this—as Smith observed, the free market is based on the pursuit of economic self-interest. The market acknowledges that people's behavior is largely determined by incentives, whether in the form of carrots or sticks. Allowing people the freedom to improve their own economic condition helps to make society wealthier overall. Smith understood that free trade takes place because both parties in an exchange profit from it. Whether a person buys a new car, a computer, or a movie ticket, the customer values the good he purchases more than the money that he pays for it. The seller, for his part, values the money that he receives more than the product.

Yet, despite its proven success, a profound distrust of the free market has spread even among the citizens and governing elites of wealthy, free nations. In the United States, politicians convene hearings to rail against oil companies, accusing them of ripping off consumers and insisting on the need for price controls or higher taxes on the firms' profits. Newspapers denounce "corporate greed," arguing that the only thing keeping any big company from turning into another Enron is the watchful eye of government regulation. The general public grumbles that high medicine prices mean that drug companies are getting rich at their expense.

As a telling example of the prominence of this view, the book *Freakonomics* achieved phenomenal popularity, selling over a million copies. In it, authors Steve Levitt and Stephen Dubner purport to unveil the "obfuscation, complication, and downright deceit" that pervades our everyday life.[2] Naturally, suspicion of corporations is a paramount theme. But the authors' misgivings go much further. They see experts such as doctors, funeral directors, and life insurance agents as unscrupulous sharks looking to cash in on their expertise by swindling their own clients. "If you were to assume that many experts use their information to your detriment, you'd be right," they warn.[3] The pair even compare real estate agents to members of the Ku Klux Klan. In their world, almost everyone—from teachers to Sumo wrestlers to politicians—is cheating or lying to somebody. Whether it is Levitt and Dubner or Michael Moore, popular authors have found plenty of buyers for the argument that nearly all corporations are committing crimes.[4]

But are free market economies really based on fleecing the consumer? Is the U.S. economy truly just a giant, Hobbesian free-for-all that encourages duplicity in our everyday transactions? Is everyone from corporate CEOs to your local car salesman really looking to make a buck at your expense?

The analysis presented in this book, based on dozens of economic studies spanning my entire career, hardly fits in with the conventional wisdom these days. Sure, some people will always lie or cheat—that's just human nature. But a close study reveals that these problems are by no means systemic in the market—in fact, they're relatively rare. For every Enron, there are thousands of companies of all sizes in America that play by the rules, simply trying to make a profit by supplying people with something they want. As we shall see, there is a reason why gas prices spike even before a natural disaster hits, why monopolies exist in our economy, and why liquor is so expensive at bars and restaurants. The answer is a little more complex than "corporate greed," but all these examples are really just instances of a free market acting efficiently.

This reflects one great benefit of a free market—it creates incentives for people to behave honestly. Consumers don't like to be cheated—when they think they're being swindled, they take their business elsewhere. Companies and individual entrepreneurs who treat consumers right, however, stand to make big profits from satisfied, repeat customers.

A major deterrent to cheating, often overlooked by critics of the free market, is the importance of maintaining a good reputation. When a company commits fraud, most of its lost revenue stems from its damaged reputation—not government fines or legal actions. So even without the threat of criminal charges, there are big incentives for corporate shareholders to keep their executives and accountants honest. As technology improves, companies are developing incredibly inventive ways to profit from their reputations. For example, consider eBay, the Internet auction site. Even in its anonymous forums, sellers develop reputations by allowing customers to rate their transactions. Studies show that having a good reputation allows an eBay seller to charge higher prices.[5] Whether on-line or on the street, there is money to be made by behaving honestly.

Reputations keep people honest in all kinds of realms besides business. This is even evident among politicians—possibly one of the few professions that popular opinion holds in lower esteem than corporate executives.[6] Conventional wisdom holds that politicians en masse are subservient to special interests that provide the money to ensure their re-election. But do politicians really base their votes on the wishes of their donors? If that were the case, shouldn't we see retiring legislators in their last term break away from special interests, whose money they no longer need for re-election?

Yet, we do not see this at all. Politicians tend to vote the same way throughout their career regardless of the onset or ending of donations, even in their final terms. Could it be that politicians, deep down, believe in the "special interests" they support? Is it really impossible to imagine that a congressman from Michigan supports the automotive industry not because of its donations, but because he actually believes that the industry is critical to America's future?

In discussing campaign financing, most observers bemoan the problem of "too much" money in politics while avoiding the really key question: Why are so many individuals and interest groups sinking so much more money into politics than before? The answer is that the government is spending much more than it did previously. With so much government money at stake, a lot more people are going to try to influence how it's spent.

This leads to another interesting question: What has caused the skyrocketing growth in the size of government over the last century? Believe it or not, women's suffrage appears to be the biggest factor.

Granting women suffrage explains at least a third of the expansion in the size of government.

Misunderstanding incentives—those that make companies charge high prices, keep firms and politicians honest, and encourage politicians to vote in certain ways—frequently leads to demands for more government regulations. Since the market seems to be failing, the government is asked to step in and make things "fair." But government intervention often only succeeds in making things worse. From campaign finance laws to rules for gaining a professional license, government regulation tends to hinder free competition. This often reflects the unique incentives that the government itself has. For example, because government-run firms frequently are more interested in market share than profits, they are more likely than private firms to engage in predatory pricing.

Crime is another subject where this book will draw some unconventional conclusions. Criminals have something in common with everyone else—they make decisions based on incentives. Analyzing these incentives gives us a good indication of what policies will work in fighting crime. This approach helps to explain one of the great riddles that bedevil criminologists—what caused the dramatic fall in crime rates in the 1990s? The answer lies in a mix of policies—the more frequent use of the death penalty, higher arrest rates, and the spread of concealed-carry laws. Perhaps more surprising are the policies that didn't work—gun control bills and "broken windows" policing methods had negligible effects, while the adoption of certain kinds of affirmative action programs in police departments actually had a detrimental effect. What's more, contrary to a well-publicized argument in *Freakonomics*, legalized abortion was not the single biggest factor in reducing crime in the 1990s. Instead, this book will demonstrate that by increasing the number of out-of-wedlock births, abortion significantly *increased* crime.

## Incentives in Academia: a Personal Experience

I have been amazed by the constant resistance in academia to the idea that free market policies make people wealthier. If we look at the incentives of academics, we find that there's an understandable reason for their viewpoint: much of the funding for universities—even for private schools—comes from the government. Academics often find the amount of their funding directly tied to the size of government. If an academic—especially at a state university—were to advocate small-government policies such as tax cuts, he'd be read the riot act. Faculty and administrators feel directly threatened by such policies, fearing they will lead to reductions in other government programs, including funding of universities.

Toward the beginning of my academic career, when I was briefly affiliated with Montana State University in Bozeman, I saw firsthand the conflict of interest between academics' private interests and the best public policy. My wife—also a new Ph.D. in economics—and I had managed to find jobs in the same place. Soon after we moved to Bozeman in May 1986, Constitutional Initiative 27, which would have abolished property taxes in Montana, was put on the ballot. The vote was set for November, but the measure immediately elicited all kinds of horror stories in the press claiming that, if approved, the initiative would virtually eliminate Montana's state and local government. The state superintendent of public schools warned that it would force the closure of all the state's elementary schools. The governor and other top state officials resorted to similar jeremiads, releasing reams of statistics and twisting the data to support totally false claims such as the contention that Montana already was the lowest taxed state in the nation. In light of the barrage of criticism, most people, including myself, assumed the initiative would go nowhere.

But the facts were quite different from the fantastic declarations of public officials. The elimination of the property tax in 1984 would have left state and local government treasuries with at least $2 billion to spend—23.7 percent of personal income in the state. Thirty-five other states did quite well spending even less than that ratio. In fact, the state would have been left with even more money than that since income tax revenues would have risen when people and corporations lost their property tax deductions.

I could see that the statistics being bandied about in the press were misleading, but no one was challenging them. Initially, I decided to get involved only by writing an op-ed piece, which appeared on July 13, 1986, in the *Great Falls Tribune* and *The Montana Standard* (Butte). Until then, I hadn't had any contact with the four sisters who were primarily responsible for putting the initiative on the ballot. But after one of them, Naomi Powell, contacted me, I agreed to get more involved.

I went to Helena to talk to Frank Adams, a former newspaperman who was writing the ballot statement for the initiative. Then I met with the four sisters and some of their supporters in the small western Montana town of Corvallis. I quickly realized part of the reason why the initiative was having so many problems: the press was relentlessly attacking the sisters as "John Birchers" and as members of other sinister groups. Reporters were also angered by the sisters' inability to answer immediately some of their more complex economic questions—the sisters often had to delay their replies until they could do some more research.

Having retired with their husbands to the Bitterroot Valley, the sisters ranged in age from their late fifties to late sixties. Living on fixed incomes, they had felt the squeeze as the cost of living, especially their property taxes, had risen. The sisters were hardly wealthy—the furniture in Naomi's well-kept house was old and worn, and the windows had cracks that were mended with tape. They had spent much of their life savings trying to get the initiative on the ballot, traveling around the state and bedding down in sleeping bags while collecting signatures. The initiative, while not perfect, was pretty good—the effort struck me as an example of everyday Americans identifying a problem and trying to solve it. Collecting 50,000 signatures was not a problem. Ensuring the initiative received a fair hearing, however, was another story.

In hindsight, it was really the unfairness of the campaign against the initiative that prompted me to get more deeply involved in the effort. The fact that Naomi had my op-ed piece taped to her refrigerator door and told me, with tears in her eyes, that she would read it whenever people attacked her group or when they ran into other difficulties, probably didn't hurt either.

Initially, I agreed to handle "number-type questions" from the media. But I quickly found that all press inquiries were being routed in my direction, and that I had become the unofficial (and later official) spokesman for the initiative. I viewed my primary role as just getting the correct numbers out to the press, although I ended up talking to some legislators and other individuals about the benefits of lower taxes. By early August, I had become a regular on the state-wide Montana Television News Network.

Newspaper editorials began attacking my involvement as soon as my op-ed first appeared. By late August, I learned that the Commissioner of Political Practices had come close to filing felony charges against me for ostensibly violating a law forbidding state employees from engaging in political campaigns. I had no idea that such a law even existed, but fortunately for me, I wasn't on a state salary at the time because I was scheduled to go on leave at the Hoover Institution at Stanford University the following academic year. Learning of this, the commissioner's office dropped its investigation of me. Curiously, no one threatened to prosecute the host of state-salaried academics and other state employees who were energetically campaigning against the initiative.

During August, I also began hearing complaints about my activities from the Montana State University administration. The chairman of my department repeatedly told me that the dean didn't want me to continue publicly advocating the initiative. But I continued my work anyway, helping Frank Adams, who had also become an official spokesman for the initiative, send out a flurry of press releases. Before

I left for Hoover, I helped to convince several prominent Montana political figures to endorse the ballot measure.

I left Montana in late August, but I agreed to remain a spokesman for the initiative and to return to the state in September and October to participate in several televised debates. When I first came back on September 19, I found my colleagues in the Economics Department in a state of panic. Several faculty members hollered at me that I was destroying the department because the university was going to punish it for my involvement in the initiative. I learned from the department chairman that there really was some truth to this—the university president and other administrators were calling him and threatening to cut the department's funding if it did not get me to "shut up."

On September 22, the day of my first TV debate, I spent a few hours in the chairman's office listening to him describe the threats that my actions were posing to the department. He told me that while my analysis of the effects of property taxes was economically sound, it was best not to say anything about such a sensitive topic. I reluctantly agreed to skip that night's debate, for which a local businessman filled in for me. Ironically, his opponent was a political science professor from the University of Montana.

I returned to Hoover, but over the next few weeks I continued talking to the press about the real economic implications of cutting property taxes. I flew back to Montana on October 9 to participate in a debate that evening with some state senators. When I arrived in Bozeman the next morning, I found the department chairman in a state of near-apoplexy. He demanded to know if I had really stated during the debate that public school teachers were overpaid. When I told him that I had, he related how incredibly upset the dean was, and that he was unsure what the consequences would be. Given the pressure facing the department, I went back to Hoover and refrained from scheduling any additional appearances in Montana.

Constitutional Initiative 27, which would have abolished property taxes in Montana, was defeated on November 4, receiving 46 percent of the vote. However, we took some measure of consolation that a parallel measure designed to freeze property taxes, Initiative 105, passed by a comfortable margin.

Things didn't quiet down for me after the campaign ended. In the department evaluations conducted at Bozeman at the beginning of 1987, I received the department's lowest ranking in the category of "outreach," which deals with communicating with the nonacademic community. On a zero to four scale, with zero being the lowest score, I got the department's only zero. I'm typically not overly concerned with that ranking, since I usually concentrate more on my teaching, research, and publications. However, given that my high-profile activities in support of Initiative 27 had made me one of the best known economists in the state and, more importantly, my research had gotten some national attention, I was a little surprised. The ranking was obviously a form of punishment for my politically incorrect activities supporting the abolition of property taxes.

As a final bit of collective punishment, I was told that the method used to rank the department relative to other departments had been changed. The new method would likely end the department's ranking as the best department in the School of Agriculture, an event that could result in a cut in department funds. The chairman told me that the dean would consider returning to the old method if department members— especially me—behaved themselves in the future. The administration was particularly concerned over reports that there would soon be another ballot initiative on property taxes. The chairman asked me to promise not to talk to the press anymore about the issue. I declined, arguing that if the press were to publish more misleading statistics and I were asked about them, I would feel obligated to set them straight.

Perhaps I had been naïve, but I was surprised by the vehemence with which people who receive their income from taxes fought to protect that largesse. While administrators at Montana State University would constantly extol academic freedom, they would not let something that trivial prevent them from doing whatever they believed necessary to protect their jobs. The experience convinced me that there's an inherent inconsistency between publicly provided education and academic freedom. Even when people do not try to silence dissent as overtly as my former colleagues did, the fact that professors and administrators receive their income from taxes cannot help but color their opinions on issues touching on the free market or the size of government.

## Learning by Doing

Aside from concerns over their own salaries and jobs, there is another reason why so many academics are skeptical of the free market: too many of them spend their whole lives in academia. Many go straight from college to graduate school and then spend the rest of their lives teaching in the ivory towers, where their output is primarily evaluated by other academics. Academia is about the only profession that consumes its own output. It's as if car companies limited their auto sales to employees of other car companies. This tendency keeps academics too concentrated on theory and not enough on real world practicalities. Think about it: academic research about how an industry operates is refereed by other academics. Neither the author nor the referees may have had any actual experience in the industry.

I have spent much of my own career in academia, but one of my most educational experiences was my service as the chief economist at the United States Sentencing Commission during 1988 and 1989. The Commission, which set the criminal penalties for individuals and firms who violated federal law, offered me an inside view into the criminal justice system. It gave me a better understanding of how prospective penalties affect criminal behavior. I began to see that debates among economists in academic journals could be quite removed from the real world. Sometimes, neither the authors nor the referees nor the journal editors really understood the institutions they were discussing.[7]

Focusing so intensely on theory, economists too often take on the role of central planners. They identify the "right" prices that companies should charge and the "right" policies they should adopt without considering why market incentives haven't encouraged firms to take these measures on their own. A greater problem, though, is that some economists try to pinpoint the subsidies or taxes that should be applied to goods to ensure that the "right" amounts are sold.

But as Milton Friedman noted, a tax that might work in theory is difficult to make succeed in practice. Friedman and his wife Rose observed: "Government is one means through which we can try to compensate for 'market failure,' try to use our resources more effectively to produce the amount of clean air, water, and land that we are willing to pay for. Unfortunately, the very factors that produce the market failure also make it difficult for government to achieve a satisfactory solution....Attempts to use government to correct market failure have often simply substituted government failure for market failure."[8]

We should remember the gasoline shortages of the 1970s that accompanied government price controls. People may complain about paying a lot for gas today, when the market determines prices, but at least we know that we're unlikely to find a gas station completely out of gas or, as we often saw during price controls, a lack of gas in all the gas stations in an entire area.

Central planning has its appeal. After all, it's hard for many people to comprehend how the seeming chaos of markets, with millions of separate decision makers, can somehow translate into economic efficiency. But economic freedom has its advantages. The key is to allow firms to set prices that accurately reflect all their costs and their customers' preferences. Analysts and politicians can study trends for years without being able to account for all the factors that go into a single price. Planning accurate prices is near-impossible, and when the government gets them wrong, the results are shortages, black markets, or other harmful market distortions. Simply put, freedom better ensures that people get what they want. As Adam Smith noted, prices create incentives for people to meet the needs of others. Despite all the various guises in which central planning has been attempted, it is no real surprise that free economies work best.[9]

# 1 Are You Getting Ripped Off?

## Speculators, Price Gougers, and Other Good People

"My constituents think someone rigged the price [of oil] and some-one—them—is getting ripped off."[1] So thundered Republican Senator Pete Domenici at one of two Senate hearings convened to grill oil company executives about the steep rise in oil prices following Hurricane Katrina. Accused of price gouging and "unconscionable profiteering," oil executives faced the "bipartisan wrath" of furious senators, which surely reflected the genuine anger felt by many of their constituents at rising gasoline prices.[2] Some senators offered half-hearted objections that the oil companies might not really be the pillaging Mongol hordes as they were described. But no one on the panel seems to have made the really vital argument—what if, by dramatically raising prices during Hurricane Katrina, the oil companies were doing a good thing?

Many people cite corporate greed or monopoly power as the only possible explanation why gas prices began rising even before Hurricane Katrina hit land and disrupted oil production in the Gulf of Mexico.

After all, why should prices at the pump increase before a company's costs have gone up? Some take this argument even further, claiming that prices should not have risen even after Katrina hit.

Let's consider the more difficult questions—why would prices rise before Katrina's effects were actually felt? And how can this possibly be a good thing? Before analyzing the behavior of oil companies, let's look at the motivations of individual consumers and speculators. If a powerful hurricane is forecast to hit land in a week, and people expect that gas prices are going to rise after the storm hits, then the difference in the price today and the expected post-hurricane price creates the opportunity for consumers to save money today by filling up their tanks when gas is cheaper. Speculators do the same thing. They profit by buying gas when it is cheap and selling it for a higher price after the hurricane. What's more, by doing so, these speculators are performing a valuable economic service—they are removing gas from the market at a time when it's plentiful and adding it at a time of shortage later.

Oil company executives reason the same way. By raising gas prices before a hurricane, they reduce the demand for gas and are left with a bigger supply, which they can sell after the hurricane for a higher price. The downside of this action, of course, is that everyone has to pay more for gas before a hurricane hits. But no one talks about the upside—after the hurricane, when gas supplies are severely reduced due to the damage to production and supply lines, oil companies are sitting on increased inventories resulting from the pre-hurricane price hike. These inventories then hit the market right when they're most needed. And this extra supply at such a crucial time helps minimize the overall price increase.[3]

In other words, by raising prices before the hurricane hits, oil companies keep the post-hurricane price hike much lower than it would be otherwise. So, from an economic perspective, oil companies should raise prices before a hurricane until the price reaches the expected post-hurricane price. At that point, there will be no more profits to be made from this speculation, and there will also be additional inventories to help cover the expected post-hurricane shortages.[4]

If the damage from the storm is worse than anticipated, prices will continue to rise. But in the long term, the higher prices will help accelerate the affected area's energy recovery. After a hurricane, gas prices rise because the supply shrinks, and prices will begin falling once the supply improves. Rising prices in the short term actually help reduce prices in the long term by increasing supply. They do this in two ways. First, higher prices create a strong profit incentive for companies to find whatever ways they can to rush supplies into the area. The more profit to be made in a given area, the harder and faster people will work to transport gas there.

Secondly, temporarily high prices reduce demand. They encourage people to car-pool, use public transport, and take other unusual steps. Indeed, this kind of economizing was seen throughout the country as gas prices rose nationwide after Katrina.[5] Naturally, the poor will feel more pressure to take these kinds of steps than the better-off. This, at first glance, seems unjust. But the poor, like everyone else, will benefit when temporarily high prices result in increased gas supplies, ultimately leading to a faster reduction in prices.

Temporarily higher prices assist energy recovery in other ways as well. The prospect of higher prices after a hurricane gives oil companies an incentive to set aside more gas as a reserve for such a contingency even before a specific hurricane is forecasted. Storing gas is costly, and if we want gas companies to bear those costs, we had better compensate them.

Thus, we see that one need not resort to corporate conspiracy theories in order to explain Katrina's effect on gas prices. The U.S. oil industry was no more monopolistic when gas prices rose just before Hurricane Katrina than it was two weeks earlier when prices were lower. Neither did the companies suddenly become greedier. They were simply reacting to the ever-present forces of supply and demand. Some may argue Katrina was merely a pretext for U.S. oil companies to raise prices, and that they jumped the gun by hiking prices before the storm actually hit. But if there were really no justification for the higher prices, then why did oil prices rise worldwide after the hurricane? The simple, non-conspiracy explanation is that we live in a world market for gas and the loss of Mexican Gulf production means less total oil for the world to spread around.

But the senators who conducted hearings about gas prices seemed more interested in finding a politically-attractive scapegoat than evaluating the complex factors involved in determining gas prices. In fact, Senator Byron Dorgan freely admitted this, declaring, "None of us knows much about pricing....But we see the pain of the consumers, and we see the gains of the companies."[6] So the senators considered various measures to put an end to "price gouging;" that is, to stop the temporary rise in prices during disasters that is so crucial to helping energy supplies recover.

One such proposed measure was used to ill effect during the oil crunch of the 1970s—price controls. But instituting government price controls would have the precise opposite effect of the one intended. Without the prospect of high prices and high profits after a disaster, gas companies won't store as much gasoline. Thus when disasters hit there would be much bigger shortages. The end result is easily predictable: artificially cheap gas available only to those people willing and able to wait all day in line to get it. Ironically, the cost of this waiting (in terms of the money people could have made if they had been working during that time) would probably more than wipe out the savings that consumers would reap from the controlled gas prices.

The argument for "price gouging," and against price controls, also applies to other goods and services. For example, stamping out price gouging by hotels would simply result in a larger number of people being left homeless after fleeing a storm. No one wants people to pay more for a hotel, but we also want everyone to find some place to stay during emergencies, when hotels quickly reach capacity. As the price of a hotel room rises, some people will inevitably decide to share a room with others. A family that usually gets one room for the kids and another for the parents may choose to crowd together in one room rather than pay for another expensive room. At high enough prices, friends or neighboring guests may share quarters as well. The more people double up in this manner, the more rooms are freed up for other families and people who otherwise may be left with no place to stay.

We economists may dispute many theories amongst ourselves, but we all agree on two things: first, that when demand rises or supply decreases, prices will rise; and second, that price controls result in shortages. This, of course, was the outcome of the gasoline price controls instituted in the 1970s. Americans waited in lines for hours to fill up their tank due to chronic shortages, which instantly disappeared as soon as the price controls were removed. So why does this debate over price controls never end?

One problem is time lags. People see the short-term effects of controls in keeping prices low, but it is only later that the pernicious effects of shortages set in. People naturally find it easier to make connections between events that occur closely in time. Imagine if a day elapsed between the striking of a match and the resulting fire. Some people would fail to associate the two incidents. Many other events would have occurred during the intervening twenty-four hours that could seem to explain the fire.

Suppose that tomorrow the government capped gasoline prices at their current price. Surprisingly, the controls would temporarily increase the amount of gas for sale. As previously mentioned, gas companies hold extra supplies because of the possibility that prices will rise in the future. The greater the chance of future higher prices, the more gas that companies will store. But when price controls are imposed, firms no longer have any expectation that prices will rise. In turn, they no longer have any reason to hold these inventories and thus begin selling them off.[7]

When controls are imposed on gas prices, consumers quickly see that prices are kept low and supply increases. It's only once those extra supplies are used up—and this could take months or even a year—that shortages set in. Companies do not instantly dump all their gasoline on the market when controls are instituted because prices would then fall even below the controlled price.

Because of this delayed effect, companies—not price controls—are blamed for later shortages. This is evident in the coverage by the three television networks of the gas shortages of 1973-74 and 1978-79. The U.S. government was discussed as a cause of the first oil crisis 18 percent of the time and 19 percent in the second, while the oil industry was discussed 32 and 41 percent of the time, respectively.[8]

And gas isn't the only product facing constant calls for price controls. The current debate over pharmaceuticals is another example. This industry is subject to price controls in every industrialized country in the world except for the United States. For years, Americans have enviously eyed cheap drugs just over the border in Canada, where strict price controls and a socialized healthcare system allow for the sale of drugs at nearly half the U.S price.

Americans are now demanding access to these cheap drugs, and many state governments, such as those in Illinois and Minnesota, have pushed to have these price-controlled foreign drugs resold in the U.S. This essentially exports the Canadian price controls to us.

U.S.-based drug companies spend vast sums to develop new drugs, and Americans pay high prices for them. Once developed, drugs are reasonably inexpensive to manufacture, and companies are willing to sell the medicines abroad at a price that merely covers the cost of manufacturing and distribution.

Meanwhile, Americans cover the research and development costs through our high prices. Incredibly, Americans, who comprise just 5 percent of the world's population, account for 50 percent of the world's spending on drugs. In effect, the U.S. is underwriting the cost of a critical chunk of the world's R&D on drugs. Perhaps this is not "fair," as many other industrialized nations could bear to pay higher prices and thus help cover these costs. But if U.S. drug prices dropped sharply as a result of re-importation, drug companies would simply stop making many new drugs.[9]

Allowing price-controlled drugs to be sold in the U.S. would instantly lower the price of drugs, causing pharmaceutical companies to cut back on inventing new medicines.[10] Those that just started to be developed will be shelved, but many close to completion will be finished. It may take some years before new drugs completely stop being introduced. And when it becomes apparent that there are few new drugs being produced, who will people blame? Most likely, the harmful role of government price controls will be overlooked. Instead politicians, editorialists, and much of the public will rush to vilify drug companies for allegedly not doing their job.

Here is another prediction: it will be unusually difficult to get rid of any pharmaceutical price controls.[11] Abolishing future price controls would mean that people would have to accept higher prices for drugs as soon as controls are removed, but it would only be years later, perhaps a decade or more, before brand-new drugs start reaching the market again. Drug companies may even have to reconstitute their laboratories. Worse, pharmaceutical companies may not be willing to start new research out of fear that price controls will be re-imposed in the future.

To conclude, although consumers may feel that they're being ripped off when they see gas prices spike after a hurricane or realize that drugs are being sold far cheaper in foreign countries, there are in fact very subtle market mechanisms at play that increase supplies and eradicate market distortions. In these situations, the free market is working, and it's ultimately working far more efficiently than any government-mandated controls would.

Ben Stein, the actor and economist, perhaps summed it up best when he wrote, "Yes, I loathe the speculative premium in energy prices. Yes,

I wish that I did not have to pay as much when I fill up my car. But the idea that there is a conspiracy at work, the idea that Congress can make it better by regulation—that's insanity. To let the free market, the best economic idea of all history, work its magic—that's good sense."[12] And indeed it is.

## How Monopolies and Price Discrimination Help Save Lives

Now let's focus on whether consumers are being ripped off by the pricing of some everyday products. Many people, when they feel they're being charged "too much" for an item, will instinctively denounce "corporate greed"—these corporations just can't seem to get a break. Of course, it's a bit mysterious how a corporation could charge unjustifiably high prices when a competitor could easily steal their sales by undercutting their prices. The most common retort to this observation is to cite corporations' alleged "monopoly power." To paraphrase H. L. Menken, such answers are all too frequently simple, neat, and wrong.[13] "Monopoly power" is really just another form of corporate conspiracy theory.

Contrary to popular opinion, monopolies are rare and difficult to maintain, and the few real monopoly situations that exist tend to benefit consumers; in some cases, such as with pharmaceutical companies, they literally save lives. What's more, the kind of allegedly nefarious pricing schemes that monopolies employ—such as price discrimination—often increase the availability of products or services and spur innovation.[14]

"Price discrimination" is a malevolent-sounding phrase used by economists to describe certain pricing anomalies. Price discrimination is said to occur when a firm charges various people different prices for the same product or service, and these price differences can't be explained by differences in production costs. Price discrimination in certain instances allows firms to maximize profits by charging the highest prices to consumers who most value a product and are willing to pay the highest prices for it.

So is this necessarily a bad thing? Price discrimination frequently allows firms to produce more and increases society's total wealth. This is especially true for monopolies that make large investments in research and development or in infrastructure; if they are not allowed to price discriminate, the firms will simply have to charge a uniform high price in order to recoup their R&D costs. This would place their product out of reach for the poor or others who can't pay the high price.

Take pharmaceuticals again. Producers are given temporary monopolies in order to launch new drugs. Medicines are very costly to develop, test, and get approved, but cheap to manufacture. And once a drug is put on the market, it's easy for other firms to reproduce it. If any company were allowed to copy another firm's drugs, the original manufacturer would never recoup its R&D costs. Without the profits they can gain from their temporary monopolies on new drugs, companies would not be able to invest millions of dollars to develop new ones. So without monopolies, we would no longer get many new drugs, including the most vital, life-saving medicines.[15]

Let's look at Reyataz and Emtriva. These drugs stop HIV from replicating and thus help to prolong HIV victims' lives—often for many years. Many Americans can afford to pay a lot for these drugs; indeed, rich HIV sufferers would probably be willing to pay almost anything for them. But poor Americans and much poorer Africans can only pay very little for the drug, while others can probably afford some mid-level price. When manufacturers lower the drugs' price for poorer HIV victims, they are engaging in price discrimination. Although it might not seem "fair" to charge different customers various prices for the same drug, price discrimination is clearly a good thing here; poor victims can get their drugs, while the companies can still make a profit by charging higher prices to wealthier sufferers.

The inherent problem with price discrimination, however, is that customers buying a product at a cheap price can profit by reselling it to those being charged a higher price. This is a problem faced by manufacturers of the aforementioned HIV drugs, which are sold cheaply in Africa but then sometimes resold in Europe, the U.S., or other countries where the drugs are sold for more. This is an important downside of lowering prices for poor consumers; drug companies risk creating competitors from among their own customers and thus reducing their profits on new drugs.

Other industries in which monopoly situations are created through the use of patents or copyrights face similar problems—monopolies are simply difficult to sustain, even when firms' monopoly positions are legally protected. The publishing industry is a case in point. This industry functions similar to drug manufacturing—publishers must pay much more for the development of a book (the writing, editing, and marketing) than they do for the printing of each book, which may only cost a few dollars per copy. Although a book, once on the market, would be easy for a competitor to reproduce, publishers are protected from this competition through copyrights.

Ever wonder why a hardcover book is so much more expensive than its later paperback edition? It's not the difference in printing costs, which is minimal. Part of the answer is that those most keen on buying a book will want it as soon as it is released, and will be willing to pay a higher price for it. But another, less apparent factor is that by the time a paperback edition comes out, there is already a secondary market in the resale of the hardcover edition. Readers who want the book are already paying less than the bookstore price by buying it second-hand. So the publisher must lower the price of its later editions in order to compete with the new market created by its own customers. Thus, even monopolies face competition.

Such secondary markets are particularly evident on university campuses. Any college student knows how easy it is to avoid paying monopoly prices for textbooks. You may see a lot of new copies when a textbook is first assigned, but by its second semester in use, many—if not most—of the books in use will be resold ones from the previous semester. While it might be pleasant to imagine students keeping textbooks their entire lives and eagerly refreshing their knowledge every few years, this seldom is the case; the vast majority of students resell their books as soon as their course ends. This creates large, extremely well-organized markets for secondhand books that sell well below the original price. And these secondary markets have really exploded in recent years thanks to Amazon.com and myriad other websites that create national— and even international—marketplaces for these transactions.

Monopolies are often forced to compete with these secondary markets, but sometimes the firms find ways around them. Take a totally different example. Allerca is a small California biotech company that has developed a hypoallergenic cat—that is, a feline genetically designed not to produce the protein that makes some people itch and sneeze. These cats cost $3,950 (plus a hefty $900 for shipping). In order to forestall the creation of a secondary market by customers who buy the cats and then breed them themselves, Allerca simply neuters all the cats it sells. Like pharmaceuticals, given the high cost of developing these cats, competition from a secondary market would eliminate the incentive to develop animals like these in the future.[16]

Although monopolies and price discrimination can both have beneficial effects, differences in prices don't always—or even normally— indicate that either of these situations is occurring; price differences are frequently attributable to differences in quality or costs that may be invisible to consumers.

Not long ago, some neighbors of mine contracted to have their driveway repaved. A few days before the job, the paving company owner came to the neighborhood to see if he could line up more business. He offered to do my driveway for $2,000, but I wasn't interested. The neighbors across the street agreed to pay $2,100. Then, on the day of the paving, the paver unexpectedly rang my doorbell again and offered to do the job for only $1,200. I haggled him down to $1,000.

Was the paver engaging in price discrimination? It might seem so, since I was charged a lower price than our neighbors for the same service. But what goes unseen here is the likely difference in cost for the paver to add my driveway to his list. It was well over ninety degrees, and the owner wanted to let his employees go home early before they were overcome by the heat. Since he didn't have time to take all his equipment to another job in a different neighborhood, he offered to pave my driveway at a lower price so he could have one more job before sending everyone home. It would not cost him much to add one more job in the same neighborhood, and without it he would be stuck with the extra asphalt.

Here's another example of pricing that seems discriminatory but is not. My family and friends who frequent restaurants with me have to endure my annoying habit of asking restaurant owners and managers why they do things the way they do. A restaurant near my house charged a couple dollars more for a special takeout Thanksgiving meal for two than they did for two single portions of the same meal. Is this price discrimination targeting customers so blinded by love that they can't see they will save money by buying two single portions? Hardly. The owner explained that the meal for two includes more than twice as much food as the single portion. The meal is usually ordered by a couple, and the man typically eats more food. It wouldn't make sense to increase the size of single portions because the price would have to be raised, and customers won't want to pay more for extra food they don't need.

It may seem that price discrimination is also at work in the sale of colas. It's an interesting anomaly that colas tend to be priced at or below the cost of seltzers. For instance, on Amazon.com, six-packs of Seagram's Seltzer Water in 12 fl. oz cans recently cost $3.85. The drink is produced by Coca-Cola,[17] which sold its Diet Coke in the same size six-pack for just $1.99.[18] Why on earth would Diet Coke, with its added flavoring and sugar substitute, sell for less than seltzer, which is merely carbonated water? Was this just an anomaly?[19]

Could this be price discrimination? Are seltzer drinkers being charged higher prices in the belief that they tend to have higher incomes than cola drinkers? This is unlikely; if big profits can be made on purely carbonated water, we should expect other firms to have entered the market, eventually driving down the price. The real, although not readily apparent, explanation is that water quality and carbonization levels have to be higher when pure seltzer is not masked by cola flavoring.[20]

Now that we've established that high prices aren't always attributable to omnipresent, sinister monopolies or to unfair price discrimination, let's take a look at some expensive items that are the subject of particularly frequent consumer complaints. Are these cases of price discrimination, monopoly power, and corporate greed? Or, can market forces explain these pricing schemes?

## Why Are Dinners and Liquor So Expensive in Restaurants?

Are you curious why restaurants charge substantially higher prices for dinner than for lunch? While the size of the dinners are often slightly larger, meal size alone cannot explain the price difference. The knee-jerk answer is that restaurants charge more for dinner simply because they can. In a sense, this is true; restaurants, like any business, will charge the highest price the market allows in order to maximize profits. But if this holds true for dinner, why not for lunch?

This may seem like another case of price discrimination—supposedly, dinner customers are charged more because lunchtime diners typically work near the restaurants they frequent and are more familiar with the local eateries than are dinner customers, who more often travel to other neighborhoods to dine. Thus lunchtime customers could more easily switch to another establishment if a restaurant raised its lunch prices. But this explanation doesn't work, for dinners are more expensive than lunches even in cities such as New York City and

Washington, D.C. where dozens of restaurants are crammed into a few square blocks, with prices posted at the front door.[21] It is easy to compare prices in these neighborhoods, and finding the cheaper dinners is not a problem.

So if price discrimination is not at work, and monopolies clearly are not functioning in areas with so many restaurants, how do we explain the price difference? There is a simple answer totally consistent with competitive markets: dinner patrons linger over their meals longer than lunchtime customers, who usually face more severe time constraints.[22] In addition to the cost of the food, the price of a meal has to cover the rental cost of the table. The more leisurely the pace at which people enjoy a meal, the more money a restaurant loses by not selling meals to additional customers at that table. Anyone who regularly frequents restaurants has surely come across waiters who subtly rush patrons with little maneuvers like clearing the table before all the diners have even finished eating. In the restaurant business, time is money.

This time cost of the table also explains why certain kinds of drinks are so much more expensive in restaurants than in stores. Restaurants charge particularly high prices for coffee, tea, and wine because people either linger over these items or linger longer over meals that include them. The mark-up is highest for beverages that people linger over longest. That's why wine typically has a larger absolute mark-up than beer, and why both have larger mark-ups than soda.[23]

Alcohol and coffee also have other costs. Restaurants typically stock all types of liquor, incurring real inventory costs. They also have to throw out many cups of coffee over the day to insure freshness. All these are real costs, just as much as the cost of the alcohol or coffee itself.

The high price of liquor at restaurants has created a popular perception that restaurants break even on food and make huge profits on alcohol. This seems to imply that restaurants have to compete in food service, but can charge whatever they want for drinks. Although restaurants often do break even on meals, their high alcohol prices do not reflect a lack of competition. Restaurants might appear to rake in the money on booze, but drinks also comprise a large part of their costs; that is, the cost of providing a place to linger over a drink.

## Why are Last-Minute Airline Tickets So Expensive?

Does price discrimination explain why travelers flying on short notice must pay more for a plane ticket than those who book their trips in advance? The Southwest Airlines website clearly shows the relationship between ticket prices and how far in advance a ticket is bought.[24] A one-way flight from Philadelphia to Chicago on December 12, 2006, ranged from $109 for a non-refundable promotional fare purchased twenty-one days in advance to $168 for a ticket bought on the day of the trip. Waiting to buy your ticket until the last day thus raised the ticket price by 54 percent.

### Ticket Prices on Southwest Airlines

| Type of Fare | Price of one way fare from Philadelphia to Chicago's Midway Airport on December 12, 2006, if purchased on November 12, 2006 | Required number of days to purchase in advance | Refundable |
|---|---|---|---|
| Promotional | $109 | 21 days | No |
| Advance Purchase Fare | $120.93 | 14 days | No |
| Special Fare | $158 | 7 days | No |
| Refundable Anytime | $168 | 1 hour | Yes |

It may seem that short-notice travelers are charged more because they are more desperate to fly at a particular time than those who make more leisurely plans. But this would need further explanation: exactly how could airlines charge excessively high monopoly prices when numerous competitors exist and the cost of checking fares is so low? Short-notice travelers can consult Orbitz, Expedia, or other websites that compare ticket prices, or simply call someone who specializes in comparing rates—a travel agent. But the large discrepancy in fares for short-notice and advance-notice travelers exists despite the ease and low cost of shopping around for different fares. This should give us pause before immediately assuming price discrimination.[25]

What airlines are doing, in fact, is charging extra for a particular service—providing a ticket at the last minute. In order to provide this service, airlines must keep "inventories" of seats that are still available at the last minute. As a result, some of these seats can go unsold, and the airlines must be compensated for this loss. This is no different than any other business that stocks inventories—grocery stores, for example, buy more milk than they need in order to ensure that they will not run out. Stores have to throw away unsold milk, and this cost is factored into the price. But consumers are willing to pay a little more if it means that milk will always be available.[26]

Airlines can easily sell discounted advanced tickets, to the point that they limit the availability of these offers. For airlines to be willing to hold seats for last-minute travelers, they must earn the same revenue from these seats as they do from seats purchased in advance. Just take a simple numerical example from our table for Southwest. Suppose, on average, that just over one-third of the seats set aside for last minute travelers go unsold; assuming that all these tickets could have been sold at the advanced discount "promotional" price. In that case, the last-minute tickets would have to sell for over 50 percent more than the discount price in order to justify offering the last-minute tickets at all.

## Why Does the Price Spread Between Full and Self-Service Gas Vary?

Let's look at one last example of alleged price discrimination. Full-service and self-service gas pumps sell the same gasoline—full-service costs more due to the extra service, not to a difference in gasoline quality. One might expect that the price difference between full-service and self-service gas would be the same for each grade of gas; if a gallon of full-service, regular unleaded costs twenty cents more than a gallon of self-service regular unleaded, then a gallon of full-service super unleaded should cost the same twenty cents more than its self-service counterpart. But this is not the case—the absolute price spread is larger for regular gas than for supreme. AAA reports that for the week of September 25, 2006, the price spread in Rhode Island between full and self-service regular unleaded was five cents per gallon more than it was for the highest octane unleaded.[27] Another survey showed that out of sixty-five U.S. cities, fifty had a substantially larger difference for regular unleaded than for premium unleaded (the difference usually being at least at five cents).[28]

Take a look at prices at your local gas station and you will probably find this disparity. The chart below shows the price differences between full-service and self-service gas at a Sunoco station that I frequent, where regular unleaded had a sixteen-cent spread, while Ultimate only had a twelve-cent spread.

## Gas Prices at Sunoco Gas Station at the Chesapeake House Service Plaza off I-95 in Maryland on August 30, 2006

| Grade of Unleaded Gasoline | Self-Serve Price | Full-Serve Price | Difference |
| --- | --- | --- | --- |
| Regular | $2.819 | $2.979 | 16 cents |
| Mid grade | $2.939 | $3.079 | 14 cents |
| Premium | $2.979 | $3.109 | 13 cents |
| Ultimate | $3.019 | $3.139 | 12 cents |

So what explains this discrepancy? Are individual gas stations exercising monopoly power? This hardly seems possible; with so many stations showing clearly marked prices, competition is fierce. But aren't lower-income customers—who are more likely to purchase regular than premium unleaded—getting swindled?

Once again, what looks like a rip-off is really just the complex workings of an efficient free market. The hidden factor here is that full-service regular gas customers typically buy less gas than those purchasing full-service supreme.[29] Consumers of supreme gas tend to have more expensive cars and are generally wealthier than consumers of regular gas. The "time cost" of visiting a gas station is thus higher for supreme consumers—they are losing more money by not working while gassing up their cars. Supreme customers therefore try harder to minimize the time they spend at gas stations. One way to accomplish this is to wait to buy gas until the tank is low and then fill it up completely. Customers of regular unleaded, being comparatively poorer, are likely to buy less gas at any one time and then bear the additional time cost of refueling in the near future. This is especially true in full-service stations, where less wealthy customers are more likely to buy just a few gallons in order to get the "service"—having the attendant wash the windows, check the oil and air pressure, etc.[30]

Since gas stations sell less full-service gallons per customer of regular gas than of supreme, they need to make up the difference by adding a higher premium to regular gas.

## Predatory Pricing—Not as Easy as it Seems

One commonly discussed and particularly vicious method of maintaining a monopoly is through predatory pricing.[31] This occurs when a firm slashes prices below its own cost of production, usually in an attempt to drive competitors out of business. A predatory firm doesn't prevail due to the merits of its business plan; rather, its success depends on its willingness to lose money temporarily in order to shut down its competitors. Though cases are rarely serious enough to reach a courtroom, they certainly get attention when they do. Take the cases of Brown & Williamson cigarette makers and American Airlines: both faced high-profile court hearings over predatory pricing in the 1990s.[32]

This kind of publicity strengthens a common misperception that powerful corporations can engage in predatory pricing at will whenever they feel threatened by a competitor.

It seems perhaps that our entire economy is not really based on free competition, but rather on the overwhelming power of a few monopolies that can prevent other companies' entry into the market. However, to the contrary, the strategy of predatory pricing is so riddled with contradictions that it actually ends up creating new incentives for competitors to join the market.[33]

Even under the best of circumstances for monopolists, predatory pricing is difficult. For predation to work, a predatory firm must not only slash prices, but also expand its output at this low price. If it does not expand production as it lowers prices, the firm will not be able to steal sales from its competitors. According to many economists, even if predators succeed in driving away competitors, the fruits of victory will prove short-lived. To merely recoup its losses from predation, after competitors are driven out of the market a predatory firm has to raise prices even higher than the price had been before the predation effort. But raising prices that high lures new firms into the market, which can easily undercut the predator's new prices. This then forces the predator to slash its prices yet again in order to drive these new entrants from the market.[34] This Ferris wheel of lowering and raising prices makes little economic sense.

In addition, because the predator has to expand its output to hold down prices, the losses incurred from predatory pricing easily exceed any subsequent profits from monopoly prices. The losses to the predator also typically exceed the losses suffered by the victim firms that are driven out.

Furthermore, predation can be overcome by using a tactic employed over 130 years ago by the famous robber baron Jay Gould, whose maneuver, while not carried out against a predatory firm, still demonstrated why predation is so difficult and thus so rare. Firms have always been able to trade in other companies' stocks. In order to overcome the dominant position Western Union then enjoyed in the telegraph industry, Gould "shorted" Western Union's stock. Shorting involves borrowing shares in a firm's stock from a brokerage, selling them, and then repurchasing them later to return to the brokerage. When you short a company's stock, you are betting that the stock price will fall sometime after you borrow and sell the shares, so that you can buy them back later for a lower price and pocket the difference. In Gould's case, he shorted Western Union's stock and then set up his own telegraph lines to compete against the company, making a bundle as Western Union's stock fell. Gould and his partner made a million dollars each just on the stock deal.[35] Not bad for the 1870s.

And this tactic is doubly effective against a predator. Suppose a predator has convinced everyone that it is willing to lose whatever money is necessary to drive out any firm that dares enter its market. Precisely because it is believed to be willing to lose a lot of money, it should never have to lose any; no one would even consider entering its market. While one might think that this strategy will keep firms from entering, actually the exact opposite is true; potential competitors have been given an additional incentive to enter the market because they can make extra cash by shorting the predator's stock. The more the predator loses from the entry of the new firm and the slashing of its own prices, the more the new firm profits from the lost value of the predator's stock.[36]

The irony is that the more committed the predator is to bear whatever cost is necessary to wipe out any potential competitors, the more profitable it is for a new firm to enter the market. In other words, the exact strategy needed to make predation profitable actually ensures its failure.

## The Failure of Some Typical "Market Failure" Tales

Stories of everyday market failure are easy to find in popular literature. Calls for public vigilance against unscrupulous business agents, various minor scams, and instances where the market somehow doesn't function properly have turned a tidy profit for a number of authors and economists. But there is often much more to these cases than meets the eye. Perceived rip-offs and alleged market failures oftentimes merely entail the market working in unexpected ways. Here are a few examples:

## A Sour Lemon Story

> A new car that was bought for $20,000 cannot be resold for more than perhaps $15,000. Why? Because the only person who might logically want to resell a brand-new car is someone who found the car to be a lemon. So even if the car isn't a lemon, a potential buyer assumes that it is. He assumes that the seller has some information about the car that he, the buyer, does not have—and the seller is punished for this assumed information.
>
> And if the car *is* a lemon? The seller would do well to wait a year to sell it. By then, the suspicion of lemonness will have faded; by then, some people will be selling their perfectly good year-old cars, and the lemon can blend in with them, likely selling for more than it is truly worth.
>
> —*Freakonomics*[37]

Nice story—except that it's wrong. In fact, the widespread perception that a new car loses substantial value as soon as a buyer drives it off the lot is really just a myth, as we shall see.

In a market economy, if anomalies like the well-known lemon problem described by Levitt and Dubner occur, they inevitably create a financial incentive for entrepreneurs to solve them.[38] Suppose you buy a car for $20,000 and decide for whatever reason to resell it quickly. Assuming nothing is wrong with the car, you have a $20,000 car with just a few miles on it, but according to Levitt and Dubner you can only sell it for $15,000 because buyers believe that people only try to sell a new car so quickly when there's something seriously wrong with it. What do you do? Do you really sell the car for a $5,000 loss?

Here is the real question: can you convince someone for, let's say, $4,000 that there is nothing wrong with your car? What about for $500? Could you hire the car's original manufacturer to inspect the car and certify that it's in brand new condition? If you could do this for $500, and inform potential buyers about the certification in your advertisements, you could likely sell the car for the full $20,000, earning for yourself $19,500—not $15,000.

There are, in fact, lots of other possible solutions. For example, car manufacturers also allow warrantees to be transferred to new owners. Whether the warrantee is for three years/36,000 miles or five years/60,000 miles, a person who buys a lemon will not be stuck with it, even if he is the second owner. Furthermore, some places allow you to return a used car for a full refund. For instance, *CarSense*, a certified used car dealer in the Philadelphia area, offers full refunds for cars returned within five days of purchase.[39] And of course, these resale companies want to maintain a reputation for screening out any problematic cars.

Luckily for us, the lemon thesis can easily be tested. I analyzed the prices of fifty-five certified used cars—all 2006 models—in the Philadelphia area, comparing the manufacturers' suggested retail price (MSRP) for brand new cars with the certified used price and the Kelly Bluebook price.[40] The Kelly Bluebook price "reflects a vehicle's actual selling price and is based on tens of thousands of recent real sales transactions from auto dealers across the United States."[41] I looked at forty used cars that were less than a year old, all with about 15,000 miles on them. These were chosen to divine what used cars sell for when they are about a year old. An additional fifteen used cars had been driven less than 5,000 miles on them, averaging 3,340 miles.

One thing immediately became clear: used cars with only a few thousand miles on them sell for almost the same price as when new.

(See table on pages 38-39.) The certified used car price was on average just 3 percent less than the new car MSRP. And it was 3 percent higher than the new car Bluebook prices. The Kelly Bluebook further indicates that the private-transaction used car price was only 4 percent less than the new car Bluebook prices.[42] One explanation for such a small discount on private transactions—in which buyers can't even rely on a brand name dealer's certification—is that manufacturer warrantees still protect buyers.

I called Kelly Bluebook to check if the sample I had was representative and was told that a study of all the cars in their sample would have yielded a similar result; there is surely no 25 percent drop in a car's price as soon as you drive it off the lot. Even more damning, the price of these virtually new cars occasionally rises even above the MSRP. The Kelly Bluebook representatives claim that in order to maintain strong resale price values and prevent customers from feeling as if the dealer is taking advantage of them, manufacturers often ensure that dealers cannot sell their cars—even the most popular models—at more than the MSRP.

If the lemon thesis had been correct and "the seller would do well to wait a year to sell it," as Levitt and Dubner claim, then used cars that are about a year old should not sell for much less than those with only a few thousand miles on them. But, indeed, they do sell for a lot less. Cars that are a year old have substantially lower prices. The certified used car price for these older cars was 14 percent lower than the new car MSRP and 8 percent lower than the new car Bluebook prices.

## Are Real Estate Agents Really Like Klansmen?

Agents are often better informed than the clients who hire them and may exploit this informational advantage. Real estate agents, who know much more about the housing market than the typical homeowner, are one example.

Because real estate agents receive only a small share of the incremental profit when a house sells for a higher value, there is an incentive for them to convince their clients to sell their houses too cheaply and too quickly...we find homes owned by real estate agents sell for about 3.7 percent more than other houses and stay on the market about 9.5 days longer, even after controlling for a wide range of housing characteristics.

—Steven Levitt and Chad Syverson[43]

## Do Car Prices Plummet as Soon as They Leave the Show Room? Looking Suggested Retail Price with Kelly Bluebook Prices and Certified Used Prices

| Car Make and Model (All 2006) | Mileage | Transmission | Engine | Drive | Features | MSRP |
|---|---|---|---|---|---|---|
| Ford F150 SXT Supercab 5 1/2 | 3,841 | Automatic | 8 cyl | 2WD | Standard | $26,300 |
| Ford Focus Zx4 Sedan S | 4,873 | Automatic | 4 cyl | 2WD | Standard | $14,295 |
| GMC Canyon 4x4 Crew Cab SLE | 1,143 | Automatic | 4 cyl | 4WD | Standard | $24,960 |
| Toyota Tacoma 4x4 Doublecab | 4,483 | Automatic | 6 cyl | 4WD | Standard | $26,460 |
| Toyota Avalon Sedan XL | 3,928 | Automatic | 6 cyl | 2WD | Standard | $27,395 |
| Volvo S40 2.4i | 3,141 | Automatic | 5 cyl | 2WD | Standard | $24,735 |
| Mercedes-Benz ML 350 SUV | 2,673 | Automatic | 6 cyl | 4WD | Standard | $40,525 |
| Mercedes-Benz R350 Wagon | 3,388 | Automatic | 6 cyl | 4WD | Standard | $48,775 |
| Honda Civic EX Sedan | 3,998 | Automatic | 4 cyl | 2WD | Standard | $19,055 |
| KIA Optima LX | 3,160 | Automatic | 4 cyl | 2WD | Standard | $18,240 |
| KIA Amanti | 2,653 | Automatic | 6 cyl | 2WD | Standard | $28,675 |
| Saturn VUE 2.2L | 3,974 | Automatic | 4 cyl | 2WD | Standard | $19,345 |
| Nissan 350Z | 4,221 | Manual | 6 cyl | 2WD | Standard | $28,265 |
| Nissan Pathfinder 4x4 | 2,030 | Automatic | 6 cyl | 4WD | Standard | $28,050 |
| Nissan Altima 2.5 S | 2,597 | Automatic | 4 cyl | 2WD | Standard | $20,715 |
| Averages | 3,340 | | | | | $26,386 |

Some of us probably feel cheated in life. After all, many experts know more about whatever product or service we are buying from them than we do. Whether it is doctors or lawyers or auto mechanics, we seem to be at the mercy of specialists who have the ability to dupe us.

In *Freakonomics*, Levitt and Dubner portray America's free market as a cut-throat environment in which consumers are constantly swindled by so-called experts. Habitually attributing economic anomalies to some kind of scam, the pair don't seem to realize that market forces exist that punish dishonest behavior. Their distrust of the market is

## at Used Cars Being Sold with about 3,000 Miles (Comparing Manufacturer for the same 2006 models on September 27, 2006)

| Kelly Bluebook New Price (actual transaction price of new cars) | Kelly Bluebook Used Price | Certified Used Price (source: Yahoo Auto) | Kelly Bluebook Trade-in Excellent Condition | Kelly Bluebook Private Party Sale Value | Certified Used Price/Kelly Bluebook New | Private Party Sale/Kelly Bluebook New |
|---|---|---|---|---|---|---|
| $23,974 | $25,820 | $21,595 | $17,075 | $21,365 | 90% | 89% |
| $13,734 | $14,215 | $14,387 | $11,475 | $12,495 | 105% | 91% |
| $23,033 | $26,470 | $22,366 | $20,100 | $23,210 | 97% | 101% |
| $24,644 | $29,125 | $26,855 | $25,250 | $27,125 | 109% | 110% |
| $25,155 | $26,350 | $24,995 | $22,525 | $24,435 | 99% | 97% |
| $23,561 | $26,885 | $23,681 | $22,800 | $24,790 | 101% | 105% |
| $38,120 | $42,410 | $46,995 | $36,300 | $39,255 | 123% | 103% |
| $45,869 | $47,775 | $47,722 | $43,275 | $45,525 | 104% | 99% |
| $18,790 | $21,455 | $20,995 | $18,625 | $20,025 | 112% | 107% |
| $17,250 | $13,655 | $16,900 | $9,200 | $12,385 | 98% | 72% |
| $26,714 | $23,100 | $20,659 | $16,100 | $19,520 | 77% | 73% |
| $18,380 | $21,600 | $18,995 | $16,325 | $18,930 | 103% | 103% |
| $27,004 | $27,260 | $30,995 | $23,675 | $25,465 | 115% | 94% |
| $26,803 | $29,385 | $28,665 | $22,475 | $25,890 | 107% | 97% |
| $19,900 | $20,315 | $19,978 | $16,750 | $18,480 | 100% | 93% |
| $24,862 | $26,388 | $25,719 | | | 103% | 96% |

especially evident in their discussion of real estate agents. (Dubner once wrote an article on Levitt entitled "The Probability that a Real-Estate Agent is Cheating You.")[44] Levitt and Dubner are certainly entitled to their opinion, but in asserting that "the Ku Klux Klan [is] like a group of real-estate agents" because both groups use the "principle" of "fear" to take advantage of others, they push the rhetorical boundaries beyond what is tasteful.[45]

Are real estate agents really ripping off their own clients? Levitt and Dubner provide an anecdote by an anonymous Mr. K to illustrate how realtors cheat the sellers they represent by refusing to maximize the sale price of their homes:

> [K] was prepared to offer $450,000 but he first called the seller's agent and asked her to name the lowest price that she thought the homeowner might accept....The agent told K, "Let me say one last thing. My client is willing to sell this house for a lot less than you think." Based on this conversation, K then offered $425,000 for the house instead of the $450,000 he had planned to offer. In the end, the seller accepted $430,000. Thanks to *his own agent's* intervention, the seller lost at least $20,000.[46]

It's hard to see why real estate agents would deliberately depress bids. What can the agent gain from encouraging bidders to lower their offer? A lower bid means less money for everyone, including the agent. If agents are lowering the asking price solely to make a faster sale, then this is a poor example; the lower bid didn't help sell the house any faster, since "K" was, in fact, willing to pay a higher price.

Assuming this story is completely true, a far more likely explanation for the agent's actions is that she thought that the buyer was unwilling to make a higher bid. There is no way the agent could have known K was willing to bid up to $450,000, and perhaps she wasn't sure whether K would even bid at all. There are many other possibilities; maybe the seller was under pressure to sell quickly and there were no other likely buyers. Perhaps the agent knew that other houses in the neighborhood would soon go on sale and would depress the price of K's home. Or, K may have simply been a good negotiator in this transaction. But that doesn't mean the agent was chiseling her client for her own benefit.

Consider this true-life example. With a growing family a few years back, my wife and I were considering adding on two bedrooms to our existing house. But we were not sure and thought it might possibly make more sense to sell our house and buy a larger one. So we went for advice to an agent with the local Patrick D. Welch real estate office.

Now, if you believe Levitt and Dubner's view of realtors as Klansmen-like swindlers who are out to make a fast buck, you would probably expect the agent to have recommended that we allow her to sell our house and find us a new one—a potential for two commissions. But instead, she told us, "I'd love to sell your house, but you'll have a lot fewer hassles by putting on an addition." She did not receive a commission or even charge a fee for her advice. And there is a market incentive for this kind of honesty—her actions enhanced her reputation and that of her employer as honest and reliable realtors. These reputations are extremely important for professionals such as real estate agents, who get many clients through recommendations from previous clients. And the importance of these reputations helps prevent experts from cheating their customers. If Levitt and Dubner could discover that the real estate agent selling the house to K was underselling her clients' houses, odds are that other people have found that out, too.

Levitt and Dubner's core argument is that realtors encourage their customers to "sell their houses too cheaply and too quickly," while the agents themselves, when selling their own houses, leave them on the market longer and earn on average an extra $6,000-$10,000 on the sale of a $300,000 house. At first glance, this seems like a lot. But in reality, the difference is only 2 to 3.3 percent.[47] This indicates that if a realtor lives in a home for even just a few years before selling it, the extra return she gets on the sale for being a real estate agent is merely a little over 1 percent per year.

True, realtors typically earn a lowly 3 percent commission when selling someone else's home but keep virtually all the revenues when selling their own homes, and this gives them a greater incentive to get the maximum price for their own abode. But one would still expect realtors to make more money selling their own houses simply because—as experts—they probably found a good deal when they originally bought them.[48] Given all the time that realtors spend getting their license, learning the business, and spending every workday looking for bargains, a 2-3 percent higher price actually seems quite low. If anyone spent years looking at houses, they would also occasionally come across some great deals.

In addition, real estate agents know better than most people what improvements will boost a house's value. While they do make these suggestions to their clients,[49] realtors are more likely than their clients to take their own advice.

Finally, the cost for a real estate agent to sell her own home is probably significantly less than the cost of selling a client's home simply because the realtor knows her own schedule. The agent does not have to coordinate with the seller on things like the timing of showing the house.

Similar advantages accrue in any profession with specialized knowledge; it's not an indication that clients are being cheated. Don't we expect doctors to obtain the top medical treatment for themselves simply because they know who the best doctors are and are better able to evaluate the medical advice they receive? Does this mean that patients who are not doctors are being treated unfairly?

Sellers of houses enjoy a competitive market among realtors. Realtors must compete against each other for clients based on their reputations, commission levels, and their recommended selling price for a given house. Sellers also have the option of selling the house themselves, without an agent. In short, home owners who sell through a realtor do so because this allows them to get the best price for their house.

## LoJack: A Weak Product in an Efficient Market

Some academics cite the poor sales of LoJack, a vehicle anti-theft device, as a textbook case of market failure.[50] LoJack is indeed an interesting idea—it's a small tracking device a manufacturer can hide in a car. If the car is stolen, the police can use the device to emit a radio signal that allows them to find the car. LoJack would seem to have an overall societal benefit—since criminals won't know which cars are protected, even cars without LoJack should benefit.[51]

But, as the argument goes, this creates a problem: you don't install the devices on your car, but hope other car owners will. That way, if auto thieves don't know which cars are protected, you benefit from the overall drop in car theft stemming from the presence of LoJack on some cars, while only other car owners bear the cost of installing the device. So in the end, no one installs it, because everyone hopes that everyone else will do it.

Is this a case of market failure? Not quite. If these devices worked, this problem would solve itself. For example, if only Porsche installed LoJacks on its cars, car thieves would learn to stay away specifically from Porsches, and thus only Porsche would reap the benefits of the device. The incentive, in fact, would be even stronger; thieves would pass up Porsches for other cars, meaning thefts of cars without LoJack would likely *increase* as thefts of Porsches declined. Rather than having too little of an incentive to install LoJacks, any single company would have too much of an incentive to do so.

So if the market is working properly, why aren't car manufacturers installing LoJack? The clear answer is that LoJack's benefits are greatly exaggerated. Most auto insurance companies give "no discount for

LoJack except in states where discounts are mandated."[52] Amy Kelly, a sales agent with GEICO insurance, points out that the device doesn't effectively deter theft because by the time a stolen, LoJack-protect car would be found, "it would [already] be wrecked."[53] Moreover, academic research was unable to confirm the benefits originally claimed for the device.[54] With $8.4 billion worth of cars stolen in 2002, car companies would love to have access to an effective anti-theft device. Reducing the rate of theft would make any car model very attractive to consumers by lowering insurance premiums and giving buyers confidence that their cars won't be stolen. In this case, the market works but the product doesn't.

## Court Regulation: Good Intentions, Bad Results

Anti-corporate hostility can be especially damaging when it's embraced by judges. If accused of wrongdoing, companies, like individuals, are entitled to a fair hearing in court. When such cases entail a lone individual squaring off against a company or corporation, judges are responsible for evaluating the competing claims and rendering an impartial judgment based on the evidence. As we will see from the following examples, however, judges can become overly-sympathetic to individual plaintiffs, especially the poor, the sick, or those suffering from other difficult circumstances.

It's human nature to want such plaintiffs to win their cases—who could possibly hope to see a "greedy" corporation with high-priced lawyers emerge victorious over a poor single mother or a critically ill patient? But in allowing their hearts instead of the law to decide such cases, judges fail to consider the larger economic consequences of their judgments. And these trends, ironically, often are most harmful to the poor, the weak, and the ill—in other words, the exact kind of people the judges are seeking to help. By assisting one individual, justices inadvertently harm a much larger number of people.

Take a well-publicized case from Washington, D.C.[55] A mother on welfare wanted to buy a $514 stereo system on credit from a store that had previously sold her such items as a bed, a washing machine, and four kitchen chairs. The store agreed to sell her the stereo but asked her to grant a lien on her previous purchases—if she proved unable to pay off the stereo, she would have to give the items back to the store. When the mother defaulted, the company turned to the courts to enforce its contract. The courts initially ruled in favor of the company, but on appeal a D.C. Circuit Court found it "unconscionable" that "with full knowledge that appellant had to feed, clothe and support both herself and seven children on [just her welfare payments], appellee sold her a $514 stereo set." The court thus invalidated the contract.

The ruling clearly assisted the woman by allowing her to keep her previous items. And the judges probably felt good after helping a poor woman take on a richer, more powerful company. But the judges don't seem to have considered the likely effect of their ruling on the store's other poor customers or on other stores that knew about the verdict.

Because the mother was on welfare, the store took a big risk by selling her a stereo. Without the assurance of collateral, the store would probably have refused to extend credit to the woman. Reclaiming the stereo in the event of a default was not a sufficient guarantee for the store because it may have been difficult and expensive to retrieve the unit, and it may even have come back damaged. The most sensible reaction to this verdict—for this particular store and others—would simply be to stop extending credit to poor people. And the people this would most harm, obviously, are the poor; poor people are big credit risks, but they are also frequently the customers most in need of credit. In this case, the market created a method—collateral—to help the poor gain access to expensive goods, but the courts effectively took it away from them—in order to help a single poor person.

Another important and particularly heart-breaking case involved an eight-month-old girl, Anita Reyes. She was diagnosed with polio two weeks after receiving a polio vaccine made by Wyeth Laboratories.[56] In 1970, Anita's father sued Wyeth, claiming Reyes contracted the disease from the vaccine. The court understood that Anita clearly had contracted the disease before she was vaccinated, as the strain she contracted differed from the strain used to make the vaccine. But it wanted to hold someone liable for the suffering of this poor little girl, so it ordered Wyeth to pay what amounted to over $850,000 in today's dollars.[57]

The court argued that *someone* had to be compelled to assist families such as Anita's "until Americans have a comprehensive scheme of social insurance," and that this someone should be the vaccine manufacturers. Judgments like this established a precedent that companies can be held liable for problems for which they are in no way responsible, just so that *someone* will pay for whatever problem has arisen.[58]

The court's desire to help out Anita's family was fully understandable. But once again, the decision had larger economic effects that harmed other disadvantaged people. When the courts began holding vaccine companies liable for large judgments unrelated to their products, the firms had to raise prices on their vaccines in order to cover these higher costs. And these liability costs are now enormous, accounting for over 90 percent of the price of childhood vaccines.[59]

The unfortunate economic reality is that by improperly favoring individual children like Anita, courts have forced the price of vaccines high enough that some poor families can no longer afford them; liability rule changes decreased the number of children getting vaccinated by an estimated 1 million.[60] Anita's family got paid, but other poor children are forced to go without vaccinations and are more likely to get the very disease that afflicted Anita.

Let's look at one last example of harmful court intrusions into the free market. This one involved workers' rights to sue their employers for job-related injuries.[61] Many jobs that are particularly dangerous include a premium to compensate for these risks; although the overall wages for such occupations may not be high, they are higher than they would be if the jobs were safe. For some occupations, such as policemen and firemen, the potential hazards are direct and immediate. For others, such as those that may expose employees to toxic chemicals, it may take years before the harm becomes evident.

Until the late 1970s, worker compensation insurance gave workers easy access to compensation for job-related injuries without having to hire lawyers. In exchange, lawsuits against employers were strictly limited. During this period, the salaries of American workers who faced the average occupational exposure to carcinogenic hazards—workers in industries such as tobacco manufacturing—included a "risk premium;" these higher wages over their lives totaled over $185,000 in today's dollars.[62] Not too bad, especially when you consider that the highest estimates that someone will get cancer from job-related exposures range from 0.004 to 0.016 percent.[63] But in the late 1970s, a legal change made it much easier for workers to sue their employers. As a result, firms no longer had to pay such high salaries to compensate workers for job-related risks. The risk premiums included in the wages for these jobs were either largely or completely eliminated, and salaries fell accordingly.[64]

This legal change created real economic imbalances for jobs—such as those that risk exposure to carcinogens—where illnesses only appear after a long period of time. True, employers were partly compensated for the lawsuits by the decline in wages. But workers who had been employed prior to this legal change had already been compensated for these risks with higher wages over many years. Allowing them additionally to sue their employers essentially compensated them twice for their risks. The end result was that workers were laid off and companies went bankrupt.[65]

Judges are usually smart people, but some of them have yet to learn an important lesson: the free market works.

# 2 Reputations

Reputations are a vital element of our economy and our society. They are infused in everything from the pricing of consumer goods to the management of political campaigns. But their importance is frequently overlooked by analysts, legislators, and even the general public. This poses some important problems, for misunderstanding reputations can have profoundly harmful consequences. In the political arena, it has led to the adoption of the McCain-Feingold bill and other campaign finance laws that inadvertently favor incumbents, lower the competitiveness of elections, and reduce voter participation rates. Overlooking the value of reputations has also resulted in the application of excessively high penalties for high-income criminals and for companies convicted of fraud.

The reason for these unexpected outcomes becomes clear if one applies a little economic analysis to the overall role played by reputations in our society. We intuitively understand how reputations work in many aspects of our lives, but we rarely consider how they affect our political and economic systems at large. And whether we look at political fund raising, criminal sentencing, or corporate behavior, we find that reputations permeate our decisions and actions in surprising ways.

## What Keeps Politicians and Businesses Honest?

What restrains politicians and businesses from acting dishonestly? A lot of people would answer: nothing. Periodic political and corporate scandals have created a popular image of politicians and businessmen as little more than a collection of cheats, liars, and crooks. However, while there will always be some dishonest people in any profession, the vast majority of American politicians and businessmen do not end up being frog-marched out of their offices in handcuffs before a gaggle of news cameras with their heads held low in shame.

Cynics will argue that many cheaters are simply getting away with it. This notion often stems from a general view of our political and economic systems as inherently corrupt; perhaps "the system" takes otherwise good people and subverts them, or perhaps merely allows the dishonest to flourish. Either way, we are habitually told that politicians and businessmen are not to be trusted. The popularity of books propagating this view—Michael Moore's *Stupid White Men*, for example, was the bestselling nonfiction book of 2002[1]—testifies to the widespread perception that our political and economic systems provide a welcome home to the irredeemably depraved.

What this argument fails to acknowledge is that in both politics and economics, there is a strong, omnipresent incentive to behave honestly. One might assume this refers to the threat of prosecution for dishonest conduct—surely, not many people want to go to jail or pay heavy fines. But what about lesser kinds of cheating not subject to legal sanctions? What incentives do politicians have not to break their promises? What keeps businesses from flooding the market with low-quality or unreliable products? As it turns out, there is a powerful incentive toward honest behavior that is built into our democratic political system and free market economy—that of maintaining a good reputation.

Let's begin by looking at businesses. High-quality products are usually more expensive than lower-quality varieties—think of the extra cost as a high quality "premium." This premium has to be even higher than the extra cost of materials and production incurred in making a high-quality item. The additional premium represents the charge for buying from a firm with a reputation for selling high-quality products.[2]

The future profits from this premium is what a firm stands to lose if it cheats its customers. For example, imagine if a reputable maker of deluxe, expensive sports cars suddenly begins selling cars that quickly break down. Customers may initially pay high prices for the new cars, but as word spreads that they are unreliable, the firm will lose its good reputation. The company will then have to lower its prices because customers will no longer pay the high-quality premium for a car they know tends to break down.

The potential loss of profits stemming from the loss of a good reputation helps keep businesses honest. This holds true so long as a business is concerned with its future profits. But if a reputable firm has some low-quality merchandise and is going out of business, it may decide to try to sell off these products for the same price as its high-quality versions; the firm is no longer worried that it will lose its reputation or its ability to charge the high-quality premium because it has no future anyway.[3]

This is where the incentives for firms to act honestly differ from those of politicians. Analysts usually assume that politicians have a similar motivation for honest behavior as companies do; politicians won't get re-elected if they break their promises, just like companies will lose sales if they cheat their customers. But there is a key difference between the incentives for firms and for people: firms can, at least theoretically, last forever, while people can't. Firms—unless they are about to shut down—will always face the potential loss of sales stemming from dishonest behavior. But politicians don't always have the incentive of re-election because eventually they will leave office one way or another.

This is called the "Last Period Problem," and it indicates a weakness in the conventional wisdom that politicians are kept honest only due to their desire for re-election. If a politician only keeps his promises in order to get re-elected, why would he keep them after he decides to retire? Suppose a politician announces during a campaign that his next term will be his last. Why would voters elect him to a final term in which he will no longer have the threat of re-election to keep him honest? The answer is: they wouldn't. And if he has no prospect for re-election to his last term, why would the politician keep his promises in his second-to-the-last term? The Last Period Problem thus unravels the supposition that a politician only governs with an eye to re-election.[4]

It may seem that three circumstances could resolve this predicament. Firstly, perhaps a politician could avoid the Last Period Problem by refusing to announce publicly that a forthcoming term will be his last (although this would not apply to the presidency, many governorships, and other public offices that are term-limited, or to House and Senate candidates who adopt voluntary term limit pledges). Secondly, a politician may hope to maintain his reputation throughout his last term in hopes of winning election to some other government position after his retirement, or securing employment as a lobbyist for some group that he "took care of" while in office. Finally, a politician may want to keep his reputation intact in order to pass it on to his children and assist their political careers.

To test these possibilities, I conducted a study of congressmen who retired in 1978. Nearly 40 percent of this group neither went into government service after retirement, nor went to work as a lobbyist, nor had children who went into politics, government, or lobbying.[5] Surprisingly, the retiring congressmen who did not have these incentives kept their election promises just as frequently as the retiring congressmen who had one or more of them.[6] Clearly, there is some other incentive at work that's keeping politicians honest.

The prospect of passing on a political reputation to others deserves a brief digression here. Might a politician stay honest in his last term in order to transfer his good reputation to other politicians? Popular former presidents, governors, senators, and congressmen frequently pop up at campaign rallies and political conventions to endorse current candidates. But a closer look reveals that politicians are not able to transfer their reputations wholesale to others. When Rudolph Giuliani endorsed Michael Bloomberg as his successor for New York City mayor, it was surely helpful, but it wasn't the same thing as having Giuliani run for another term. The same rule applies to Ronald Reagan's recommendation of George H. W. Bush and Bill Clinton's endorsement of Al Gore. People can't simply transfer their own reputation to others whenever it's convenient to do so.

This reflects another difference between businesses and politicians; firms can sell their reputations, but individuals can't. If some company buys out Campbell Soup, consumers won't feel the need to get to know the new Campbell owners before they decide whether to continue buying the soup. Customers will still pay for the product as long as the price and recipe remain unchanged and it continues to carry the Campbell name. It's the reputation a firm cultivates for its product—not a firm's personnel—that guarantees a product's quality. Retiring politicians cannot pass on their reputations in the same way.

There is, however, one instance in which politicians can bestow their reputation on someone else—they can pass it on to their own family members, especially their children and grandchildren. A successful politician's children begin their own political careers with an advantage; until they develop their own political record, they are generally associated with their parent's political reputation. Politicians ranging from former vice president Al Gore to President George W. Bush have used their forebears' political reputation as a launching point for their own political careers.

Because a politician's reputation can't be transferred outside his family, a politician's child who doesn't go into politics simply loses the benefits of this reputation. It's not like inheriting a family business, where a son or daughter could sell it off and use the proceeds toward some other line of business. Since going into politics is the only way a politician's child can exploit his parent's political reputation, it should come as no surprise that politicians' children follow their parent's careers at higher rates than most other professions: about 30 percent of politician's children follow their parent's profession, second only to the children of farmers.[7] By contrast, about 15 percent of sons of fathers from all self-employed licensed occupations follow that path themselves.[8]

We have already seen, however, that the prospect of passing on a good political reputation to one's children does not make a retiring politician more honest than others. Neither does the threat of re-election nor the hopes of securing a good job after retirement from politics. So what does keep politicians honest?

To answer this question, let's first analyze some professions that enjoy near-total job security. For example, with lifetime appointments, Supreme Court justices are removed from any equivalent of re-election pressures. If we look at the current justices with over ten years' experience on the court, nearly all of them rule in an ideologically consistent fashion—Justices Breyer, Stevens, Souter, and Ginsberg are reliable liberal votes, while conservatives extol the dependability of Scalia and Thomas. Only Kennedy is considered a swing justice.

Most people would have little difficulty explaining why the individual justices consistently vote either liberal or conservative—it's because they really believe in their political philosophy. When a president nominates justices, he looks for a judge who will provide a reliable vote for his political orientation. He analyzes potential nominees' career voting records and looks for other signs of an intrinsic commitment to shared

ideals. Judges may be able to hide or misrepresent their true philosophy in hopes of getting a Supreme Court nomination, but it is difficult
to do this over a long period of time. Supreme Court nominees will
usually have years of consistent rulings that testify to their reliability.
If a president nominates someone without a clear record, he risks getting burned. This was the case with George H. W. Bush's 1990 nomination of David Souter, a judge with little experience on the Appeals
Court who, after his appointment, became one of the Supreme Court's
most liberal justices.[9]

The tenure process among university professors works in a similar
way. Once a professor gets tenure, he has near-absolute job security. So
why would a professor continue to work hard once he gets tenure? The
answer is that tenured professors usually have an intrinsic interest in
teaching and research. A candidate for tenure who doesn't really enjoy
working may try to work just hard enough to get tenure in hopes of
having a minimal workload thereafter. But the period leading up to the
tenure decision, which typically lasts around five to seven years, acts as
a probationary period in which professors can pick up on subtle signs
that a candidate may not genuinely value his teaching and research.
Does a candidate spend his summers doing research or vacationing?
Does he like to talk about his academic interests or about television?
Ultimately, over time, candidates who value work will distinguish
themselves from those who do not, and it is these professors who tend
to get tenure.[10]

This same process helps to explain why professors are overwhelmingly liberal. Because tenure is for life, professors are reluctant to offer
it to conservative candidates whose politics may then annoy them for
decades. The probationary period leading up to the tenure decision
gives professors a chance to observe not only a candidate's work habits,
but also his political inclinations. Perhaps a candidate can hide his true
politics for a time, but can he do this for five to seven years? Candidates
who show conservative leanings in their research, social discussions, or

lifestyle choices can thereby be weeded out. The end result: studies show that 96 percent of registered voters among liberal arts professors in top-rated schools such as Harvard and Cornell are Democratic or Green Party members,[11] while 86 percent are Democrats at large state schools like the University of Texas and Penn State.[12] Thus the tenure process tends to result in the promotion of professors who are *both* liberal *and* hard-working.

The point here is that it might be easy to fake dedication to a certain political philosophy or to a good work ethic, but people who genuinely believe in these things, especially over a long time, will appear more convincing. Evaluators can typically distinguish between the two groups, and they will usually pick the latter to become Supreme Court justices or tenured professors. Justices offer consistent rulings after receiving lifetime appointments for the same reason that professors remain hard-working and liberal even after getting tenure—because both groups reached their positions as the result of a sorting process that eliminates insincere or uncommitted candidates.[13]

Politicians go through this same vetting process. A politician may be able to fake an allegiance to a set of principles. He may parrot the "right" slogans and even vote the "right" way in order to get re-elected. But voters, like presidents and faculty members, can distinguish between sincere and insincere politicians, especially over a long period of time. And they reward the sincere ones with their votes.[14]

Contrary to popular belief, politicians who get elected and re-elected tend to be the ones who show that they really believe in the positions they espouse.

Politicians from Kansas really do think that farmers are the backbone of America. Those from Detroit really do want to help the car industry. This is why politicians keep their promises even during their final terms—they don't promise to support certain positions merely in order to win re-election, but rather because they genuinely believe in those positions.

## Why Do People Donate Money to Political Campaigns?

People often point to political campaign financing as a prime example of the corrupt nature of the U.S. political system. Big corporations, wealthy individuals, and powerful political action committees (PACs) allegedly buy influence from politicians, who then focus on pleasing their big donors at the expense of the little guy. This outlook presupposes that when someone donates to a politician, he is hoping to affect the politician's votes in his favor—in effect, he's looking to "buy" the politician's votes.

Labor unions, business groups, lawyers, doctors, and a galaxy of special interest groups all regularly donate money to politicians. But the surprise here is that these contributions, in fact, do not significantly alter how individual politicians vote. What's more, donors do not expect them to do so.

The main evidence for the view of political donations as an exercise in vote-buying is that politicians tend to vote in line with the wishes of their donors. Very few people would deny this is true. But an analysis of donation and voting patterns reveals that donors support politicians for the same reason voters do: politicians intrinsically value policies, and donors give to candidates who share their values. Vote-buying is not occurring because individual politicians are not altering their votes based on donations.

Analyzing this dilemma is a bit tricky: how can we figure out whether donors are giving money to candidates because they want to affect the politicians' votes or because they agree with the politicians' values and positions?

One way to approach this dilemma is to take another look at retiring politicians. When politicians decide not to run for re-election, they no longer have to worry about adhering to donors' wishes in order to secure contributions for future elections. If donors are bribing politicians to vote differently than they otherwise would have voted, politicians should shift at least somewhat away from the voting interests of their donors when they no longer have to worry about losing these donations. But if donors support politicians based upon the politicians' genuine beliefs, there should be little change in politicians' voting patterns once they decide to retire.

Economist Steve Bronars and I examined the voting records of the 731 congressmen who held office for at least two terms between 1975 and 1990. We found that congressmen do continue their previous voting patterns after they announce their intention to retire, even when accounting for other explanations such as whether they will secure other jobs after their retirement from politics. Although retiring politicians only receive 15 percent of the amount of PAC contributions that they enjoyed in the preceding term, their voting pattern remains virtually identical; on average they only alter their position on one out of every 450 votes.[15]

Even politicians who raked in hundreds of thousands of extra dollars during their second-to-last term did not significantly change their voting patterns. Politicians consistently vote the same way over their entire careers, regardless of the onset or the end of donations from any particular interest group.[16]

This is not to say that cases of influence-peddling and outright bribery never occur. In 1978, for example, the FBI launched ABSCAM, a corruption sting that resulted in the conviction of one senator and six congressmen for accepting bribes from fictitious Middle Eastern businessmen. More recently, we have seen an unusual number of bribery cases: California congressman Randy "Duke" Cunningham was caught taking bribes from defense contractors; Louisiana congressman William Jefferson was investigated for allegedly accepting $400,000 in bribes in return for helping a telecom company secure business in Nigeria and Ghana (the FBI found $90,000 in cash in Jefferson's freezer); and most famously, lobbyist Jack Abramoff was convicted on corruption-related charges that implicated several congressmen and staffers including Ohio representative Bob Ney, who was forced to resign from office and later convicted of related charges.[17]

Everyone loves a good corruption story. The corrupt politician is an iconic image in American popular culture, and the torrent of headlines generated by stories like the Abramoff scandal reinforces this impression. But how pervasive is this problem? Do most congressmen engage in corrupt activities?

There is an interesting way to test this question. Until 1994, congressmen who had begun their first terms prior to January 8, 1980, could spend unused campaign funds as they pleased, with no restrictions. But congressmen elected after that date could only spend such funds to cover further campaign-related expenses or to pay for moving expenses back to their home district after retirement. So until 1994, a contribution to one of the earlier congressmen during his last term could easily represent a direct cash payment for services rendered; the congressman came through with the votes, and so a donor rewards him with a contribution that he can legally spend on personal luxuries. Yet, interest groups rarely donated money to these retiring congressmen during their last terms, and those donations that were made were almost entirely given before the politician announced his intention to retire.[18] This indicates the donations were intended for use in political campaigns, not as personal bribes.

The public perception of widespread corruption in our political system undermines confidence in the government, breeds cynicism toward our democracy, and results in demands for ever-greater regulations on campaign financing that actually restrict public participation in politics, as will be discussed below. Likewise, the belief that politicians sell their votes to the highest-bidding donors supports the notion that politicians don't really value policy outcomes, and that they only pretend that they do in hopes of raking in more contributions. The evidence, however, indicates that these views are misguided. Politicians do care strongly about policy outcomes.[19] They tend to vote consistently throughout their careers, regardless of donation patterns. And donors give to politicians who have developed a reputation, through their voting record, of supporting the donors' values. In short, the system generally works, in that the public gets the kind of government that it votes for.

## Campaign Finance Reform

> Clearly there is too much money being pumped into our
> political system and because of that, the public's perception
> is that the entire electoral process and governmental system
> is corrupted....If there is a consensus that there's too much
> money in the system, let's impose spending limitations.
> —Senator Joseph Biden[20]

Campaign finance reform is usually touted as a means to address political corruption and influence peddling. Indeed, the Supreme Court is so sensitive to this issue that it looks kindly on reforms that claim to eliminate even the "appearance of corruption."[21] The justices themselves have also recognized the Achilles heel of campaign finance reform: it tends to protect incumbents. Even Justice Breyer, who has consistently voted to uphold campaign finance regulations, has noted the risk of allowing legislatures to pass campaign finance reform that allows "incumbents to insulate themselves from effective electoral challenge."[22]

Incumbents usually have a financial advantage over their challengers in the form of campaign "war chests" built up during their terms. But they also have another crucial advantage that gains much less attention—they have an established reputation. Voters typically know an incumbent's key positions even before he spends a dollar in a re-election campaign thanks to his past campaigning and media coverage of his previous terms in office. Even if the challenger is a famous athlete or movie star, his reputation won't fully transfer to the political realm. Why? Because even if the person is well-known, he does not have an equally familiar history of making political decisions. Voters can predict how an incumbent will vote much better than they can divine the future votes of this type of challenger.[23]

This simple point is vital for understanding the problems created by campaign finance regulations.[24] Suppose that during a campaign, these regulations limited the spending by an incumbent and his challenger to $100,000 dollars each. If this money allows both candidates to reach a similar number of voters through TV commercials, direct mailing, and the like, the incumbent is left with a huge advantage because many voters are already familiar with his reputation from his previous terms. Imagine a race where political spending by both sides was reduced to zero—voters would still recognize the incumbent, while the challenger's positions would be largely unknown. The only factor that could eliminate this inequality is if the challenger already had a reputation as a result of holding some previous political office. Although challengers do frequently have prior political experience, the fact remains that challengers from all walks of life outside of politics are left at a huge reputational disadvantage when competing against seasoned politicians.[25]

Thus challengers benefit more than incumbents from each dollar of campaign financing because incumbents are already largely known.[26] In other words, for each additional dollar spent, challengers can convey much more new information about themselves than incumbents can.

Campaign contributions from individuals and organizations were strictly limited in 1974 by amendments to the Federal Election Campaign Act, which was largely a response to the Watergate scandal. Analyzing election data since 1946, the rate of incumbents' victories in federal races has risen since these regulations were passed; the re-election rate for House members has grown from 88 to 94 percent, while the rate for Senate members has increased from 76 to 81 percent.[27] Granted, factors aside from campaign financing may have contributed to this result, but the reforms clearly have not succeeded in making House and Senate races more competitive.

Contribution limits have had a similar effect on the local level. Looking at all the state senate races from 1984 through the beginning of 2002, I found that donation limits increase the average margin of victory by anywhere from 4 to 23 percentage points. The regulations double the probability that only one candidate runs for office, and they increase the chances that incumbents win re-election. Campaign finance regulations also tend to reduce the number of candidates who run for office by an average of about 20 percent.[28]

Limiting the size of individual donations always works to the advantage of incumbents. When the size of individual donations are restricted, candidates are forced to rely on a larger number of small donors. This benefits incumbents who, having previously run for office, begin a campaign with a much longer list of past and potential donors.

Presidential history may have been a lot different if our current limits on individual campaign donations had existed in the 1960s and early 1970s. In March 1968, President Lyndon Johnson shocked the nation by announcing he would not seek re-election. His withdrawal is usually attributed to his poor performance in the Democratic primaries against Senator Eugene McCarthy, who campaigned against the Vietnam War. McCarthy's candidacy heavily relied on just six big donors who bucked the party establishment and financed much of his campaign. Yet, McCarthy raised almost as much money—after adjusting for inflation—as George W. Bush did from 170,000 donors by the time of the first primaries of the 2000 campaign.[29] Under today's campaign finance regulations, McCarthy's insurgent campaign would have been impossible, leaving an easy re-nomination for Johnson despite strong opposition within his party to the Vietnam War.[30] Thus we see that campaign finance regulations help squelch dissenting voices within the parties and strengthen the position of the parties' leaders.

Another drawback to limits on individual campaign contributions is that they force candidates to begin fundraising long before a race begins as candidates need more time to assemble a large number of small donors. This trend further decreases the competitiveness of these races, for if a front-running candidate falters, it is extremely difficult for other candidates to enter the race at the last moment.

Limitations on individual donations to candidates are harmful enough. But the McCain-Feingold bill of 2002 worsened the situation by abolishing so-called "soft money"—non-federal accounts through which individuals could make unlimited contributions to national political parties.

Before McCain-Feingold, party funding was particularly important for those challenging incumbents and for the least-known candidates. To illustrate this point, let's look at both Republican and Democratic Senate and House campaigns from 1984 to 2000. During this time, the average Republican House incumbent received only about 2 percent of his money from the party, while the average challenger received almost 10 percent. For Democratic House candidates, the numbers were 2 and 7.2 percent, respectively. Indeed, during these nine campaign seasons, there was only one single case—Democratic Senate races in 2000— where incumbents received more money overall from their party than did challengers.

The conclusion from all this is straightforward—if we want to make campaigns more competitive by limiting donations and expenditures, we should place such limits disproportionately against incumbents. Of course, it would be extremely difficult to make campaigns "fair" through this method, since different incumbents have different levels of name recognition. Although incumbents are almost always more well-known than their challengers, their level of name recognition varies depending on the number of terms they have served, the amounts spent on past campaigns, and the amount of press attention they earn while in office.[31]

Contrary to all the evidence cited above, advocates of campaign finance reform claim that contribution limits actually make political races *more* competitive. This was argued by George Mason University Professor Thomas Stratmann in a legal brief submitted in support of McCain-Feingold for a court case challenging that law.[32] Stratmann maintained that campaign finance restrictions make races more competitive because they make it more difficult for better candidates to differentiate themselves from inferior candidates through advertising. Aside from the methodological problems of this theory,[33] it must be somewhat uncomfortable to argue that campaign finance regulations are beneficial because they make it more difficult for the best candidates to win elections.

Proponents of campaign finance regulations also claim that donation limits increase voter participation by removing the appearance of corruption from elections. California State Senator Debra Bowen summed up the conventional wisdom on the issue during her 2006 race for California Secretary of State: "One of the reasons that people don't vote is they think the big-moneyed interests run everything anyway, so what's the point?"[34]

But empirical evidence shows that campaign finance restrictions actually lower voter turnout by reducing the number of competitive races.[35] Limits on corporate donations to candidates diminish turnout by 4 percent, while limits on corporate PAC donations to candidates cut turnout by 6 percent. Limits on overall spending by the candidates have an even bigger effect, lowering turnout by 8 percent.[36]

Other analysts claim—somewhat quixotically—that campaign finance regulations are essentially harmless because donations don't exert any meaningful impact on elections; they're just wasted money. An extreme form of this argument appears in *Freakonomics*, in which the authors claim that "a winning candidate can cut his spending in half and lose only 1 percent of the vote. Meanwhile, a losing candidate who doubles his spending can expect to shift the vote in his favor by only that same 1 percent."[37]

If this were true, it would mean that nearly every congressman and senator—that is, America's most successful politicians—knows absolutely nothing about how to get elected. If fund-raising were really so futile that cutting expenditures in half would only cost candidates 1 percent of the vote, why do all these politicians spend so much time raising money? Why do they bother at all with their endless direct mail solicitations, fund-raising banquets, and the like? And how important is 1 percent of the vote to a politician? Consider this: in the 2006 Congressional elections, just eight seats out of 435 were decided by less than one percentage point, while only 35 races were decided by five percentage points or less.[38]

It seems that the next crop of presidential candidates will continue to belabor the notion that fund raising matters. *The Daily News* recently reported the leaked contents of a dossier outlining Rudy Giuliani's strategy for his 2008 presidential run. According to *The Daily News*, "At the center of his [Giuliani's] efforts: a massive fund-raising push to bring in at least $100 million this year, with a scramble for at least $25 million in the next three months alone."[39] Shortly after Barack Obama and Hillary Clinton announced their intentions to run for the Democratic nomination, the *New York Times* reported that both candidates aimed to raise $75 million just in 2007.[40] Apparently, no one has told Guiliani, Obama, or Clinton that all this fund-raising is a waste of time. Haven't they read *Freakonomics*?

Such counter-intuitive arguments notwithstanding, the vast majority of research confirms that contributions do affect political races. The studies also confirm that campaign contributions are much more important for lesser-known challengers than for incumbents.[41]

A final problem with restrictions on campaign financing is that their adoption inevitably creates momentum for ever more limitations on public participation in elections. Such restrictions are becoming increasingly ridiculous and oppressive. In the state of Washington, we get a glimpse of the kind of new regulations that McCain-Feingold inspires. There, a judge ruled that statements by two radio talk show hosts who supported an initiative to lower the gas tax had to be defined as political advertising and thus were subject to campaign spending restrictions. This would have limited the pair's conversations on the topic to fifteen minutes per week for the three weeks before the vote. The talk radio hosts ignored the ruling which, as of this writing, is before the state Supreme Court.[42]

## Why is Campaign Spending Increasing So Quickly?

Real per capita federal campaign expenditures for all candidates running for the House and Senate have risen 110 and 152 percent, respectively, from 1976 to 2006.[43] Over the same period, real per capita income grew by only 46 percent. The dramatic growth in campaign spending is clear, but in the public debate over this problem, we rarely hear anyone consider the real reason for this explosion in spending— campaigns spend more and more because the government keeps getting bigger and bigger.

The rise in campaign spending has sparked demands for reforms ranging from stricter limits on campaign expenditures to public financing of election campaigns. And concern over "excessive" campaign spending is not limited to the federal government. Since the passage of McCain-Feingold, many states have adopted campaign finance regulations limiting donations to state political parties and restricting contributions to candidates from parties, individuals, corporations, or unions.

All these proposals to reduce campaign spending invariably ignore the root cause of the problem. The reason why campaign financing keeps growing is because the government is constantly expanding its grip on the economy; the more that is at stake, the more people will spend to get their candidates elected.[44] One-hundred years ago, when federal government spending accounted for just 2 to 3 percent of GDP, government expenditures did not affect the average citizen so directly. Today, with federal government spending at about 20 percent of GDP,[45] much more is at stake when we select who will control the purse strings.

Nearly 90 percent of the growth in federal campaign spending from the 1970s to the 1990s can be explained just by the growth in federal government expenditures. Likewise, on the state level, states that saw the fastest growth in per capita government spending also witnessed the most rapid growth in per capita campaign spending. Indeed, the rise in state government expenditures explains as much as 80 percent of state legislative and gubernatorial campaign expenditures.[46]

Instead of addressing the growth of government, groups concerned by the rise in campaign financing inevitably advocate restrictions on campaign spending and contributions to candidates. But attempts to limit the amount of money in campaigns have failed quite extraordinarily, as we have seen. Campaign finance restrictions don't really decrease the amount of money in campaigns; they just change the avenue the money takes from the donor's wallet.

Due to campaign finance restrictions, many donors simply give their money to PACs instead of candidates. PACs are often portrayed by advocates of campaign finance reform as "special interest" groups that exert a malign influence on the political system. Proliferating quickly after the passage of the campaign finance reform regulations of the 1970s, they are sometimes perceived as vehicles used to avoid campaign finance restrictions. This is especially true in recent years, when a special type of political advocacy organization that is exempt from many campaign finance restrictions—so-called 527 groups—has multiplied quickly.

The proliferation of PACs was a natural reaction to campaign finance restrictions. People want to participate in the political process and to support the candidates they like. When new regulations restrict their ability to do this, they look for other ways. Generally, when given an option, donors prefer to give directly to candidates, not to intermediaries like PACs and 527 groups. Direct donations to candidates are more efficient, largely because McCain-Feingold greatly limits coordination between interest groups and the candidates they support. PACs and 527 groups thus sometimes create inconsistent messages for a candidate, or even worse, may push an agenda that differs from that of the candidate they support. But due to restrictions on direct donations to candidates, donors are left with little choice; they are forced to support PACs and 527 groups by default.

While utterly failing to counter the surge of money in politics, campaign finance restrictions have empowered PACs and 527 groups. This is evident in the campaign spending by billionaire George Soros, who spent close to $18 million advocating for campaign finance reform.[47] However, the adoption of McCain-Feingold has not removed Soros' own money from politics. Instead, he has given tens of millions of dollars to a variety of liberal PACs and 527 groups including Moveon.org and America Coming Together (ACT). These groups have largely taken over some campaign functions that the political parties used to control, such as advertising and get-out-the-vote drives.[48] (ACT raised and spent a hefty $200 million during the 2004 campaign alone.)[49]

As Soros himself demonstrates, since McCain-Feingold, money continues to pour in to political campaigns, even from some of the biggest advocates of campaign finance reform. But instead of going directly to political parties and individual candidates, the money is now being funneled through the less efficient auspices of non-party organizations.[50]

The empowerment of PACs and 527 groups by campaign finance restrictions brings a detrimental consequence that is frequently overlooked—it increases the number and intensity of negative political advertisements. Political commentators and newspaper editorials frequently complain that the proliferation of negative campaign ads breeds cynicism and depresses voter turnout.[51] Just before the 2006 November election, for example, CBS bemoaned that "This political season has already set records... in terms of the number of negative ads that we're forced to watch."[52] Such commentary, however, tends to ignore the relationship between the rise in negative ads and campaign finance reform. Candidates have been forced by campaign finance limits—and particularly by McCain-Feingold—to cede much of the responsibility for producing political ads to independent PACs and 527s. These groups are more able to run negative ads than candidates can themselves because these groups are less concerned about a possible backlash—if a PAC-sponsored ad is particularly offensive, the candidate that it is supposed to help can always claim that he has no connection to the commercial or to the group that produced it. This is not so easy to argue if the objectionable ad is produced by the candidate's own staff.

Annoyed that 527 groups still allow citizens a roundabout way to donate to their favored candidates, campaign finance reformers have introduced legislation to further restrict their activities, such as the 527 Reform Act of 2005. Even if approved, such "reforms" will not abolish money from politics; they'll just once again change its route. The National Rifle Association (NRA) recently foreshadowed how interest groups might react to all these restrictions when it looked into purchasing a TV or radio station. The group, perhaps, could thereby avoid myriad campaign finance restrictions by claiming the status of a media organization.

While campaign spending continues to grow rapidly, we must keep the overall figures in perspective. In 2004, total campaign spending for all House, Senate, and presidential candidates amounted to $2.17 billion while overall federal government spending was about $2.23 trillion.[53] Thus campaign expenditures totaled roughly one-thousandth of what the federal government spent. With trillions of dollars a year at stake, is that really too much to spend in debating how that money should be allocated? We must expect a lot of people will spend large amounts of cash to influence the selection of the people who control such huge amounts of money. But for those of you who think $2.17 billion is an outrageous sum, consider this: Proctor & Gamble spent $3.9 billion on advertising in that same year.[54]

## The Myth of Double-Giving

In the popular mind, one of the quintessential examples of influence-peddling is the phenomenon of "double-giving"—donors giving funds to both candidates in a political race to ensure that whoever is elected will be in their debt.

Judging by media articles and reports from various interest groups, the phenomenon of double giving is a widespread, cynical practice that illustrates the need for campaign finance reform. The AP reported that the practice "isn't all that unusual" in an August 2006 article entitled, "No need to choose sides, some donors give to both gubernatorial candidates."[55] According to the Center for Responsive Politics, "double-giving [by PACs] is the classic example of pragmatic political investment. It shows that there is little ideological content behind the contributions. They just want to give to the winner with the hope that it will pay off legislatively."[56] A study by Public Campaign, an advocacy organization for campaign finance regulations, found that "forty-seven companies and organizations that appear on the donor list of three or more presidential candidates gave at least $50,000 overall. Forty-five of these companies are playing the entire field, showing up on all four of the front-runners' donor lists."[57]

This indeed seems cynical. Not many donors can really believe that both the Democrat and the Republican candidate in a race are equally good. And even if this were the case, why would donors waste their money donating to both candidates instead of moving their donations to other races where politicians differed in a more substantial way? The only explanation for double-giving seems to be to buy influence.

Yet, this entire image of double giving is a complete myth.[58] In fact, it is impossible for corporations to practice double-giving in any federal races at all, since they are legally banned from donating to federal candidates whether in House, Senate, or presidential races. Similar restrictions also exist in many states for state elections.[59]

What is often lazily reported as "corporate" donations for a federal race is really the sum-total of donations by a corporation's individual employees. And there is a perfectly logical explanation why we would see corporate employees donating to both parties: most companies employ both Republicans and Democrats.

As for PACs, they almost never double-give. Ron Pearson of the Conservative Victory Fund reports, "I cannot think of one case, and I have carefully studied all the conservative PAC contributions, where a conservative PAC has simultaneously given to more than one candidate in a race."[60] Likewise, Ann Murry of the American Medical Association notes, "I couldn't say with complete certainty that we have never done that, but it sure would seem weird if we did." Indeed, there is certainly good cause for viewing double-giving as "weird." According to Chris Farrell, the director of the National Association of Retired Federal Employees' PAC, "contributions to both candidates in a race is the same as contributions to neither." The purpose of double-giving is ostensibly to ensure that whoever wins the election will feel indebted to the donor, but it's hard to imagine how a candidate could perceive such a debt to a PAC that had also given money to his opponent. As Farrell remarked, "it's not like these candidates are stupid."

Even in the few instances when PACs do double-give, the donations are usually not made for the cynical reason claimed by campaign finance proponents. Mary Anne Karpinsky of the Association of Trial Lawyers of American affirms that her organization only engages in double-giving "in one in a thousand races," and that "the only time that that occurs is if a particular candidate is a member." Similarly, Jim Tobin, the director of the National Association of Life Underwriters PAC, testifies that instances of double-giving by his PAC are "extremely rare," occurring "no more than 1 percent, maybe 2 percent of the time." This happens when "one of our members may be running for Congress and, even though he may not stand a chance, we feel obligated to give him some money so as to encourage other members to run in the future."

I interviewed representatives from many of the biggest PACs about this topic.[61] Most of them have rules forbidding double-giving; in the exceptional cases where they do double-give, it is almost always because one of their own members is a candidate. This held true whether the group was a trade, corporate, ideological, or labor PAC.

So where does this myth of widespread double-giving originate? Mostly, it comes from sloppiness in using the data, such as attributing corporate donations to the companies themselves rather than to their employees, as previously discussed. Additionally, double-giving is sometimes alleged when PACs simultaneously donate to both Democratic and Republican primaries. But this is not actually a case of double-giving, and there is nothing cynical about it; PACs simply seek to support candidates in both parties whose positions are closest to their own. And even in such instances, if the candidates supported by a PAC win both parties' primaries, PACs almost always limit their donations to one candidate in the general election. Unfortunately, this kind of sloppy reporting helps breed a general animus toward the entire political system and generates demands for new campaign finance laws, which in turn create far more problems than they solve.

## Individual Reputations and Crime

> A state judge on Monday sentenced former Tyco International Ltd. executives L. Dennis Kozlowski and Mark H.

Swartz to 8 1/3 to 25 years in prison for looting the company of hundreds of millions of dollars to pay for lavish parties, luxurious homes, and extravagances such as a $6,000 shower curtain.

In a case that came to symbolize corporate greed, state Supreme Court Judge Michael J. Obus also ordered Kozlowski and Swartz to pay nearly $240 million in fines and restitution. Kozlowski and Swartz were immediately taken into custody and led from a packed courtroom in handcuffs as family members of both men sobbed. The men are likely to serve at least part of their sentences in one of New York's 16 maximum-security state prisons.

—*Washington Post*[62]

A commonly heard complaint about our criminal justice system is that it favors the rich over the poor. With their ability to hire high-priced attorneys, wealthy defendants can allegedly "buy" a favorable verdict or at least secure a minimal sentence if found guilty. Very few people would disagree that a rich defendant has an overwhelming advantage over a poor one. But when we analyze the overall consequences a criminal faces after conviction, we find a surprising result: rich criminals face disproportionately high penalties.[63]

When people think about how criminals get punished, they tend to focus on prison terms. Perhaps financial penalties also come to mind such as fines, restitution, and legal fees. But for many convicted criminals, the most significant penalty is something else—their lost reputation. And it is through the loss of reputation that the wealthy really pay for their crimes.

Let's look at a statistical composite of two hypothetical people—in 1984, Jim made $17,000 per year working as a bank teller, while Brandon made $82,000 per year as a manager at the same bank. Aside from their jobs and income, both men are statistically identical—they are unmarried, forty-year-old, white male Californians with no criminal history. Let's say they were both convicted of committing the same crime—embezzling over $350,000 from the bank, the average amount stolen in these crimes.

According to statistics, their prison sentences would be very similar, with Jim spending around five weeks in jail, while the better-off Brandon would be locked up for five days less.

But the slightly shorter prison term is the only advantage that Brandon would receive from his wealth. On the downside, Brandon would face financial penalties far in excess of those applied to Jim. But the larger fine extracted from Brandon—$4,000 compared to $1,700 for Jim—is just the beginning. Brandon's main punishment comes in the lost earnings after he returns to work. While Jim can expect his income to fall from $17,000 before his conviction to just over $10,000 afterward, Brandon's income will plunge from $82,000 to a mere $4,700. Amazingly, after controlling for a variety of social and demographic factors, wealthier ex-convicts on average earn a *lower* salary after their conviction than poorer ex-convicts.

This crushing drop in income is especially evident with the richest ex-convicts. The average person convicted of insider trading in 1984 and 1985 made $365,000 a year prior to conviction versus $14,000 in the last year of probation or parole. If the legal costs and fines weren't enough to bankrupt them, around two-thirds of white-collar criminals get divorced, with their spouses getting 90 percent or more of their assets. (The normal property division rules don't apply when one spouse becomes a convicted felon.)[64]

Why would the conviction of a rich corporate executive depress his later income so dramatically? To begin with, after his conviction, he is highly unlikely to regain enough trust to be rehired to a job at his previous level. Although shareholders oversee the activities of a firm's top officers, it is impossible for them to monitor all of their executives' decisions. They must have some degree of trust in their officers' honesty. Although shareholders will probably learn of corrupt activities eventually, by then it may be too late to correct the problem. A CEO could embezzle huge amounts of money or do other irreversible damage to a company before his dishonesty is discovered.

For this reason, companies place a premium on their executives' honesty.

They, like most Americans, see the terrible price paid by companies like Enron, Adelphia, Tyco, Imclone, and WorldCom due to the dishonesty of a few corporate executives. Despite the headlines generated by these scandals, however, it should be noted that the overwhelming majority of America's 11,000-plus publicly traded firms are not run into the ground by their own corporate officers. Shareholders tend to find honest people to run their companies because it is in their own interests to do so.

This means they will be very hesitant to hire anyone with a criminal record. It is difficult enough to hide a criminal conviction, as probation or parole can last for years, and employers have to submit reports to an employee's case officer. But it's even harder for the wealthy to cover up a conviction; the richer and more powerful the man, the more publicity his trial is likely to receive, and thus the easier it is to discover his criminal past through something as simple as an internet search.

Even the relatively few rich ex-convicts who do secure a high-paying job after their conviction tend not to be successful. As Robert McCries, who studies the lives of indicted or convicted insider traders, notes, "Some of them do get back to [the securities industry], but they never shine with the luminance that they had during the time that they were previously operating. If they do re-enter the field, they find the community isn't ready to support them. They just generally don't do so well and after a period of time they tend to drop out....People avoid them....There are so many people to do business with, why must you do business with this person? That's the kind of harsh questioning that is raised."[65]

But how do we explain why rich ex-convicts' incomes fall even lower than those of poorer ex-convicts? It's because rich convicts not only get shut out of high-paying jobs, but they also have more difficulty finding lower-paying employment. Suppose that a successful lawyer is convicted of a crime and is disbarred. Unable to get hired to a different high-paying job due to his criminal record, he looks for a blue collar job. How would prospective employers view his application? Most likely, they'll think he is vastly over-qualified, that he will quickly grow bored with the job, and that if he's hired he will continue looking for a higher-paying job. The lawyer's prestige and experience—the very things that made his resume so impressive—now work against him. If an employer of manual laborers had to choose between two convicted criminals, he would likely prefer one with a blue collar background to someone with vastly higher credentials. In the case of Robert Chestman, a stock broker convicted of insider trading, his conviction made it so difficult to find work that he simply went to jail pending his appeal.[66]

Let's look at the fate of Peter Bacanovic, a key player in what is perhaps the most highly-publicized white-collar crime prosecution of the last decade—the Martha Stewart case. Bacanovic was a stockbroker for both Martha Stewart and Samuel Waksal, the CEO of biopharmaceutical company ImClone. When the FDA refused to approve one of ImClone's key drugs, Waksal and his daughter sold their own ImClone stock before the FDA decision became public. Informed by Bacanovic of Waksal's stock sale, Stewart sold off her own ImClone stock. Although Waksal was eventually sentenced to over seven years in jail for insider training, neither Stewart nor Bacanovic were charged with any crime related to Stewart's stock sale which, in the end, appears to have been legal. But they were both convicted of lying to regulators about the sale.

Bacanovic was sentenced to five months in prison and five months of home detention. This sentence was widely publicized in the press, which rarely explored the additional penalties Bacanovic had to suffer due to his loss of reputation. Bacanovic was fired by Merrill Lynch in October 2002, when he was first charged, and has been unemployed for the four years since then.[67] Furthermore, there is no chance that he can re-enter his former occupation, as he is barred for life from even associating with stockbrokers or investment advisers. It is also doubtful that he can ever obtain any type of professional license. His criminal and civil fines totaled $79,645—for lying about a stock sale that earned him all of $510.[68]

Like the case of Bacanovic, it is common, indeed usual, for people to lose their job as soon as they are charged with a crime. This tendency is not confined to companies, as borne out by the 2006 lacrosse rape scandal at Duke University. Three Duke lacrosse players were charged in April and May 2006 with raping a stripper during an off-campus party. Despite the players' vehement denials, conflicting stories by the stripper, negative DNA tests, and accumulating evidence of misconduct by District Attorney Mike Nifong, the university suspended two of the players. (The third player had already graduated.) This is a common procedure at Duke for students charged with felonies.[69] The suspension looked to be long-term, as it was expected that the trial might not commence for a year after the charges were filed.[70] Meanwhile, with such a tarnished reputation, the odds of another prestigious university allowing the suspended players to transfer were nearly zero. One of the players, David Evans, had a job offer rescinded from J. P. Morgan.[71] In January 2007, after Nifong dropped the rape charge and the North Carolina State Bar filed a complaint charging him with misconduct, the university allowed the players to re-enroll.[72] The salient point here is that universities, like companies, rush to divest themselves of disreputable students or employees even before their crimes have been proven in court.[73]

One does not have to be a rich stock broker or a student at a top-ranked university to suffer severe reputational penalties from conviction.

Krishan Taneja, a civil engineer convicted of trading on illegal stock tips, spent six months in federal prison in 1979. After his release, his wife divorced him and his former employer refused to re-hire him. Broke and unemployed, he applied unsuccessfully for licenses to become a stockbroker, a real estate agent, and then an insurance sales-man. Nine years later he was driving a yellow cab in New York City.[74] Likewise, S.G. "Rudy" Ruderman, who broadcast *Business Week*'s daily market report, was convicted in 1988 of trading on stock tips before the tips appeared in the magazine. For a year-and-a-half after he left prison, he held a part-time job reading the news on a small Westch-ester, New York radio station. After that stint ended, he lived off his wife's income.[75]

Aside from the loss of job and income, ex-convicts are likely to suf-fer from a variety of additional financial penalties that affect the wealthy more than the poor. These include being prevented from inher-iting property, the partial or total divestment of assets, loss of life and/or car insurance, and the loss of pension funds, including the dis-continuance of pension payments for ex-convicts who are already retired.[76] In fact, presidential task forces have emphasized the impor-tance of these collateral penalties and expressed concern that inatten-tion to them will create inequities in criminal penalties.[77] Of course, these penalties come on top of the loss of rights likely to be incurred by all ex-convicts regardless of their economic status, such as voting rights and parental rights, as well as the ability to serve as a juror, hold pub-lic office, and own firearms.[78]

Thus we see that once reputational penalties are considered, the wealthy tend to face significantly more punishment than the poor for committing the same crime. Since few people want to risk being per-ceived as sympathetic to white-collar criminals, however, reputational penalties are rarely mentioned in the public debate on the inequities of the judicial system.

# Reputations: Keeping Corporations Honest

> Consider the so-called corporate scandals of the early
> 2000s. The crimes committed by Enron included hidden
> partnerships, disguised debt, and manipulation of energy
> markets....The practitioners of such [criminal] acts [by
> firms], especially in the realm of high finance, inevitably
> offer this defense. "Everybody else was doing it." Which
> was largely true. One characteristic of information crimes
> is that very few of them are detected.
>
> —*Freakonomics*[79]

In the above quotation, Levitt and Dubner argue that corporate fraud
is rampant, but they say it's hardly ever detected. They might forgive a
reader for wondering how they can know that these misdeeds are so
prevalent if no one ever finds out about them. This claim is really just
an assertion of what they think might be happening; no evidence is
offered because—conveniently—no evidence is possible. It's a perfectly
unfalsifiable claim.

Popular belief in rampant corporate fraud has real consequences in
that it creates pressure for changes in government policy. Reflecting
popular opinion that penalties against corporate fraud were too low,
in 1991 the U.S. Sentencing Commission—the federal agency responsible for setting the penalty guidelines used by judges—raised median
corporate fraud penalties by over twenty-fold. I fought vehemently
against this move while I was chief economist at the Sentencing Commission during the late 1980s, but only succeeded in getting it temporarily delayed.

At the time, the penalties seemed small compared to the losses
imposed on customers due to corporate fraud. In the late 1980s, half the
corporate fraud convictions resulted in sanctions of less than fifteen cents

per dollar lost from the fraud, with the average fine amounting to only seventy-five cents per lost dollar. This was much lower than the relative penalties meted out for other corporate crimes such as environmental pollution, where half the fines were $3.71 or more per lost dollar.[80]

Yet, the research I did with Jonathan Karpoff, a professor at the University of Washington, convinced me that there is a solid economic reason for setting corporate fraud penalties lower than for other misdeeds such as environmental crimes. When convicted of fraud, companies face collateral penalties related to their loss of reputation. And these reputational penalties usually do not apply to other kinds of corporate crime. When firms defraud their customers or don't deliver what they promise, customers will stop buying their products or will insist on lower prices that factor in the extra risk. In contrast, aside from a small minority of activists, most customers will not reject a company's products because it was convicted of an environmental or similar crime that does not directly affect the customers' purchases.[81]

The reputational penalties suffered by a firm accused of fraud are substantial, even before the company is convicted. The market value of firms accused of fraud fell by $61 million during 1980s.[82] On average, only 6.5 percent of this decline reflects legal costs, and just 1.4 percent is accounted for by penalties and fines. The rest of the drop reflects expectations of reduced sales and earnings.[83] This contrasts sharply with the drop in stock prices when a firm is accused of an environmental crime, in which case virtually the entire decline reflects the firm's legal costs and penalties. In essence, reputational penalties, on average, are non-existent for environmental crime. People may not like hearing that a company pollutes, but overall they simply will not stop buying the firm's products based on environmental misdeeds.

Thus it is primarily the fear of legal penalties, not reputational ones, that deters environmental crimes. But this is not the case for corporate fraud. As previously noted, at the time when corporate fraud penalties were increased twenty-fold, government penalties for fraud averaged just seventy-five cents per lost dollar. When this is combined with the average reputational penalties in the form of declining sales, earnings, and stock prices, we find that the average total penalty due to a fraud accusation was already 11.5 times *greater* than the loss imposed on customers.

This is not mere academic curiosity; raising the criminal penalties for fraud too high can hurt customers and damage the economy. Large fraud penalties force companies to spend more money on guaranteeing product quality. While everyone values greater assurance that they are getting higher quality products, not everyone wants to pay more for this guarantee. Just as different people take different levels of risk in their everyday lives, different people are willing to pay different amounts for insuring quality. If a person wants the maximum guarantee that a car will perform as it should, he can shell out lots of money to buy a new Lexus. But for some people, price is more important than more quality assurance; they are willing to face a high risk of a car breaking down in return for paying a low price for it. As firms increase quality guarantees to avoid high fraud penalties, prices rise as well. Suppose that all firms were forced to make cars as dependable as a Lexus. We'd end up with very few accusations of fraud, but we'd also have many people who could no longer afford a car.

Aside from fraud cases, reputations factor unexpectedly into other aspects of business management. Let's look at just one everyday example—the franchising of gas stations. There are a lot of advantages to franchising. Franchises tend to be well-run because the owners, with a direct interest in profitability, are right there on the premises overseeing operations, as opposed to sitting in some remote corporate headquarters. Having well-managed franchises also burnishes the reputation of the franchisor corporation, whose logo, of course, is attached to the franchise.

So why aren't all gas stations franchised? The answer becomes apparent if we look at areas where corporations prefer not to franchise.

Corporate headquarters tend to operate directly the company's own gas stations in areas without many repeat customers, for example, next to a superhighway. The problem with a franchise in this situation is that the owner has less of an incentive than usual to operate the business because satisfied customers are unlikely to return to the station anyway. If customers get cheated or are subject to poor service, however, they may stop frequenting that chain in many other places, thus damaging other franchises carrying the same logo. The franchisee that actually provided the poor service will not suffer much of the consequences of its own poor service.[84]

Reputations play an important, though often unacknowledged, role in society. Notwithstanding the high-profile corporate and political scandals that will always occur from time to time, concern over reputations helps keep people honest; the loss of a good reputation can easily devastate the future prospects for a politician, corporation, or an individual, as we have seen. As long as this remains true, reputations will continue to function as a vital component of our free market democracy.

# 3 Government as Nirvana?

People frequently call for government intervention in the economy whenever the market is believed to be acting imperfectly.[1] Implicitly, the comparison is between the flawed way the market actually works on the one hand, and a nirvana-like state of government-run perfection on the other. Do distortions ever develop in the free market? Of course they do. Few people would argue that the market is flawless. But it's a long leap from showing that such imperfections exist to proving that they would be solved or even mitigated by government intervention. In fact, government intrusion in the economy tends to result in more inefficiency, unfairness, and even predation than we would find in a completely free market.

## C'mon and Take a Free Ride

One of the most common methods of government intervention is to encourage certain beneficial actions through subsidies. Recall our earlier discussion about LoJack, the car antitheft device. LoJack's social benefit—the overall drop in car thefts we would allegedly see due to the fear among thieves that any car might have a LoJack—was said to be ten times larger than the benefit for any individual LoJack users.[2] But the government would have to subsidize the device in order to get car manufacturers to install it in enough vehicles to capture the full social benefit.[3] Advocates of such a subsidy used this kind of argument to justify forcing insurance companies to give discounts to LoJack users.[4]

Remember the counter-argument, however. Porsche could solve this problem for its customers by putting LoJacks on its own vehicles, and thieves would consequently steal fewer Porsches and more of every other kind of car. But this would harm everyone who doesn't drive a Porsche. In that case, instead of being rewarded with a subsidy for installing LoJack, Porsche should instead have to pay a tax on it.

Here we see that having a subsidy when there really should be a tax—or visa-versa—is worse than doing nothing. If we subsidize a harmful activity, we end up encouraging it. If we tax a beneficial activity, we inadvertently discourage it. And if a subsidy or tax is too large or too small, we create market distortions. Smoking may be unhealthy, but excessively high cigarette taxes will create a black market in cigarettes. Similarly, growing wheat may be vital for feeding the country, but over-subsidizing it will induce farmers to stop growing other crops. In the case of LoJack, if the device has no significant impact on auto theft rates, as attested to by car manufacturers, insurance companies, and recent academic research, then the product should not have any special subsidies or taxes at all.

Even if the benefits of LoJack were confirmed and the proper subsidy could be precisely calculated, there is another problem: trusting the government to approve the right subsidy. Politicians representing districts where LoJacks are made would probably support a subsidy far in excess of the correct amount, while politicians representing competitors' districts would likely seek to reduce the funding.[5]

A similar example involves concealed handguns. Those who carry permitted concealed handguns deter criminals from attacking others in their localities because criminals fear that any potential victim may be carrying a gun. Despite this social benefit, it's not clear that the government should subsidize concealed handguns. As with most cases of government subsidies, the problem lies in the difficulty of calculating how much the subsidy should be. Even though a clear social benefit exists, figuring out the subsidy would require complex estimates of the number of crimes that would have taken place if concealed weapons weren't allowed, as well as calculations of the monetary and social cost of these crimes that never occurred. Keep in mind that the politicians and civil servants drafting these regulations are rarely experts in the areas they oversee. As for concealed handguns, all states in fact discourage permits by charging a mandatory licensing fee that is usually far above the administrative cost of issuing the permits. Far from being subsidized, concealed weapons permits are, in effect, taxed.

There is another similarity between LoJacks and right-to-carry laws. Some states allow residents to carry a gun openly. This certainly benefits the person carrying the gun—not many criminals would attack someone they knew to be armed. But open-carry doesn't produce the same social benefit as concealed handguns do. Although open-carry discourages crime around the person openly carrying a gun, criminals may simply go after other people without guns, just like installing LoJacks in Porsches would encourage criminals to steal other cars. So open-carry has a private benefit for gun carriers, but it also may increase the rate of attacks on people without weapons.[6]

The late economist Milton Friedman noted a further complication in subsidizing products or practices that create social benefits: subsidies may not even be necessary because people often have enough individual incentive to do the desired action without any government intervention. Take Friedman's example—education. Let's assume by the time a student enters high school, his education has instilled in him positive values such as support for democracy and the avoidance of criminality. Perhaps this indicates that education should be subsidized, since more overall schooling benefits society by strengthening the general commitment to democracy and reducing crime. Yet, education also offers the private, individual benefit of increasing a student's future job prospects. As Friedman pointed out, we can get the social benefit of education without subsidizing it because students will attend school to obtain this personal benefit.[7]

The debates over government subsidies are closely linked to the "free-rider problem" in economics. Suppose a person spends time or money on something that incidentally benefits others, but these beneficiaries pay little, if any, of the costs. Such free-riding situations tend to result in a dearth of the beneficial action, since many people will hope to get the benefit for free through others' actions. This situation often elicits demands for state subsidies to encourage the valuable activity. This applies to the use of crime prevention devices like LoJack as well as actions like charitable giving and volunteerism, which are sometimes effectively subsidized through tax deductions.

There are two questions involved in free-riding problems: Do others benefit from your action? And if so, is it possible to prevent them from getting this benefit? When it's impossible to exclude others from the benefit, a free-riding problem is likely to develop. For example, if LoJack were actually effective, a free-riding problem could easily appear, since those without LoJack would hope thieves will stay away from their own cars in fear that it might have the device. Enough free-riders might then stop buying LoJack that the social benefit—the overall drop in car thefts—would disappear.[8]

Another example of free-riding was seen during the early development of radio. Today, virtually everyone takes it for granted that advertising is a sensible way to finance radio broadcasting. Few people realize that free-riding problems initially seemed almost insurmountable in providing radio service. Because no one could figure out how to make listeners pay, radio hosts and entertainers usually had to work for free.[9] For over twenty years, broadcasting primarily involved hobbyists and a few public service transmissions by government stations.

Some people doubted there was any way to make listeners pay. In 1922, Herbert Hoover, then Secretary of Commerce, declared: "Nor do I believe there is any practical method of payment from the listeners."[10] Others assumed that radio transmissions would eventually be funded by paying subscribers, but no one could devise a method for limiting broadcasts to subscribers' receivers. Consequently, some believed the government would have to provide the service. In 1922, *Popular Radio* magazine claimed that radio was "essentially a public utility" and discussed using city telephone wires to sell broadcasts to subscribers—in other words, providing radio service over the phone.[11]

So what happened? Did private businessmen throw up their hands and invite the government to run the industry? Was society denied the benefit of radio because no one could solve the free-riding problem? Of course not. The problem was eventually resolved in 1922 when AT&T discovered it could make money by selling radio advertising airtime. In hindsight, it's hard to believe that private radio almost died in its infancy because people couldn't figure out how it could make money. And it's a good thing that the government decided not to turn radio into a subsidized enterprise, since it is highly unlikely that the state would have distributed payments as efficiently as advertisers do.

With enough at stake, companies find amazingly creative ways to solve free-riding problems. Government subsidies only deaden the incentive to discover these solutions. For example, many analysts used to regard beekeeping and apple farming as a classic free-riding problem.[12] Apple blossom nectar provides food for bees, which pollinate the blossoms as they gather the nectar. Economists feared that apple growers were free-riding from neighboring beekeepers, and that this would eventually result in too few apples as well as too little honey. But apple growers and beekeepers devised a number of solutions to this problem. The most obvious method was for apple farmers to set up their own bee-hives.[13] However, as Steven Cheung showed, the more common solution was for apple growers and beekeepers to create markets where they transacted regularly. The Yellow Pages in rural Washington State developed long listings of pollination services available to farmers. Yet, despite the evolution of free market solutions, beekeepers cited the existence of this potential free-riding situation as an excuse to lobby the government to implement a honey price support program. The program began modestly in the early 1980s, but quickly grew into a massive subsidy scheme costing U.S. taxpayers around $100 million annually by 1984.[14]

Government attempts to solve free-riding problems are typical examples of the state's economic inefficiency. In fact, we've grown so accustomed to the inadequacies of government that we typically use different standards for evaluating private and public spending. For example, economists deem private markets to be efficient when the cost of an additional unit of some product reflects how much buyers value it. But when is that ever a consideration in government spending? Just look at tax payments generally: the top 5 percent of income earners pay 57 percent of federal income taxes, while the bottom 50 percent pay just 3.3 percent.[15] In a democracy, those who provide little of the government's income have more of a say—in the form of their combined votes—over how to spend government funds than those who provide most of the money. Of course, this is not to suggest that the votes of big taxpayers should be weighted more than those of smaller ones. It's just to point out that government spending is inherently inefficient because those who actually pay for most government services are not the ones who determine how the money is spent.

This helps to explain why government intervention is so often inefficient.[16] In private markets, you can't get people to pay more for a product than they value it. If the asking price is too high, they simply say "no." But there is no similar limitation on the government, which pays for things by levying taxes. And taxes are coercive—you can't refuse to pay taxes just because the government is paying more for something than you value it.

Take government programs such as flood insurance. These aren't like traditional private insurance programs where people are charged according to the risk they represent. Private insurance companies closely match the premiums to the risk level or else they quickly go out of business. If they charge too much, their customers go elsewhere. If they charge too little, they lose money. While things have improved somewhat in recent years, for decades the government insurance programs charged everyone the same amount regardless of risk. The government charged the same flood insurance premiums for beachfront houses as it did for homes in the middle of the desert. As late as June 30, 2005, the Congressional Research Service was still reporting on the "repetitive loss problem," where people in high risk flood areas paid such low flood insurance premiums that they would keep on rebuilding only to have their homes repeatedly swept away.[17] As USA Today noted, "One Houston property valued at $114,480 has filed for losses 16 times and received $807,000 in total payments."[18]

Only the government can continually get away with this kind of wastefulness—a private insurance company that was this profligate would be driven out of business. Democratic Congressman Earl Blumenauer (Oregon) put it succinctly: "The federal government is aiding and abetting patterns of living that are unsustainable and draining significant resources."[19] By creating insurance programs with below-cost premiums, the government allowed its insurance clients to free-ride off the American taxpayers.

Many economists have pointed out severe problems caused by the government's inability to set prices correctly. Indeed, some blame the bankruptcies seen during the savings and loan crisis of the 1980s on the extremely low prices charged by the government for deposit insurance at risky banks. The bailout ultimately ended up costing taxpayers over $175 billion.[20]

If charging too low a price will create market distortions, then handing out services for free—which the government often does—will really create some perverse incentives. For example, government search-and-rescue teams frequently decline to charge anything for their services. These expeditions can be extremely expensive, with use of a helicopter costing $10,000 per day.[21] Even worse, free rescue services give hikers and mountain climbers an incentive to take more risks. In December 2006, a large-scale search and rescue operation was undertaken at Oregon's Mt. Hood to find three climbers stranded on the mountain. Tragically, one hiker was found dead, while the other two were never discovered. In light of the incident, Oregon lawmakers floated the idea of requiring high-altitude climbers to wear electronic locators. The proposal was opposed by climbers, who argued the devices would cut down on the "adventure" and the "beauty" of the sport's danger.[22] Perhaps after getting stuck with a $10,000 rescue tab, climbers might think twice about the kind of risks they take.

The government's difficulty in getting prices right is vividly illustrated in the application of eminent domain—laws that allow the government to confiscate homes in order to clear the land for other developments. The government—as well as private developers—face considerable economic problems when trying to clear out homes from a certain area. Suppose that a developer needs to tear down the houses on an entire block in order to build a skyscraper. The obvious approach would be to buy everyone's house, but this doesn't always work. Some homeowners with a sentimental attachment to their property will even refuse offers that far exceed the fair market value of their homes. In this case, developers who are unwilling to pay exorbitant amounts have little choice but to look elsewhere for their project.

Other homeowners might act strategically, hoping that by refusing early offers, they will entice much higher bids later. This presents a complex problem, for a single hold-out could stymie the project. Eminent domain seeks to solve this problem by forcing owners to accept the "fair market value" of their property. The government offers the fair market value—the price for which similar nearby houses have sold—and if the homeowner refuses, the government can pay this price anyway and seize the property. The recent U.S. Supreme Court decision *Kelo v. New London* decreed that eminent domain, until then usually invoked to allow for government projects such as highways and railroads, can also be enforced for private development projects if the local authorities determine that the projects will benefit the wider community.[23]

One of the main problems with eminent domain is that the fair market value is typically too low. If people only valued their homes at the market price, they would have already sold them before receiving the developer's offer. The fact that they haven't means that they value their abodes more than what is being offered on the free market. The real difficulty lies in figuring out how much more.

Fortunately, there is a solution that businesses used for years before they gained access to eminent domain. Whether they seek to build a pipeline, a road, or a building, companies almost always consider multiple possible locations. Koch Industries, the largest privately owned company in the United States, built 4,000 miles of natural gas and oil pipelines across the country without using eminent domain until relatively recently.[24] Instead, it typically offers a contract to property owners along different possible routs; the deal goes to whichever complete set of property owners signs the contract first. The owners might be offered, for example, 25 percent above the fair market value. If they value their property more than that, they don't have to sell. But this approach discourages people from indefinitely holding out for better offers. If homeowners don't really value their property much more than the market value, they risk losing this 25 percent profit. The government should consider this market-based approach as an alternative to forced sales at prices that, in reality, are anything but "fair."

Bill Dougan, former chairman of the Economics Department at Clemson University, devised a similar solution to a problem plaguing many academic departments.[25] When a department is hiring a new professor, there will often be several candidates who are roughly equally good. The risk is that when the job is offered to one candidate, he many take weeks to decide whether to accept, often using the offer simply to try to get a better deal from another school. If the candidate ultimately signs on with a different school, the department may be left with nobody, since the other candidates may have already taken jobs elsewhere. Dougan's solution? Offer the job simultaneously to all the top candidates, stipulating that the position goes to whomever accepts first. It's a good thing these kinds of free market solutions are developing before someone suggests imposing eminent domain on hiring practices.

University of Washington professor Jonathan Karpoff recently provided another striking example of how inefficient government enterprise can be. Karpoff studied the thirty-five government-sponsored expeditions, along with the fifty-seven privately funded voyages, that explored the Arctic, the Northwest Passage, and the North Pole from 1818 to 1909. Arctic exploration, like space missions, is an excellent example of a public benefit that many would assume could not be achieved privately. Much of the exploration is similar to pure scientific research that offers no immediate commercial benefit. Compared to their private counterparts, government expeditions to the Arctic enjoyed much better funding, bigger ships, and crews that were over four times larger (averaging seventy members versus seventeen for private voyages). Nevertheless, public expeditions were more likely to end in tragedy—an average of nearly six crewmen died on government voyages, compared to fewer than one on the average private trip. Furthermore, government expeditions lasting over a year suffered scurvy rates that were four times higher, while the chance of losing a ship was over double that of private expeditions.[26] Despite their smaller crews and lower funding levels, the private teams accomplished five of the six major Arctic discoveries.[27]

Karpoff elaborated some of the reasons behind these results. Government expeditions had to operate by committee and political factors played a role in dictating their crews' composition. Private expeditions, in contrast, were more efficient and much faster at learning from past experience. Perhaps most importantly, private voyages were more responsive to incentives for success—their decision makers directly bore the costs and reaped the benefits of their own actions.

These kinds of inefficiencies plague government efforts in realms ranging from welfare to education. Private charities ensure that 80 to 90 percent of donations get to those in need, while only 30 percent of government welfare spending actually reaches the intended recipients.[28] Likewise, non-teacher costs make up over 40 percent of the budgets in public schools compared to less than 20 percent in private ones.[29] Overall, the per pupil costs of public schooling are about twice as much as for private schools despite the fact that children typically learn much faster in private institutions.[30] These statistics indicate that private charities and schools can provide better service than public ones even if they receive just half the funding.

The market isn't perfect, of course. But the government is usually much further from perfection. Even when the state intervenes in the economy with the best intentions, it frequently only succeeds in making things worse.

## Diversified Stock Holding: A Free Market Approach to Keeping Corporate Peace

So what makes the free market superior to government planning? Part of the answer is that the market creates stronger incentives for people to consider the effects that their actions have on others. A clear example of this is seen in the growing practice of diversified stockholding. Some 5,000 stock mutual funds in the United States hold over $5.2 trillion in assets.[31] It has become common knowledge that investors should hold a well-diversified stock portfolio, but most people do not realize that this practice also encourages cooperation among competing companies.[32]

Consider a simple example I came across when I was teaching at the Wharton Business School. Albert J. Wilson, then vice president and secretary for TIAA-CREF, a huge teacher's retirement fund, gave an informal talk to some faculty in December 1992. Texaco and Pennzoil had previously been locked in a protracted, costly legal battle. Owning stock in both companies, TIAA-CREF was hurt by the litigation, which reduced the value of both firms. If one firm eventually won the dispute, it would not have benefited TIAA-CREF, since the result would just move a lot of money from one firm to the other. Lawyers were making a lot of money from the litigation, but unfortunately the retirement fund didn't own any stock in the lawyers. Wilson told us that the pension fund had used its influence as a large shareholder in both companies to get them to settle their lawsuit. He also revealed that the pension fund had similarly helped to convince Apple and Microsoft to settle some mutual legal disputes.

While investors care about the value of each stock they own, they care more about the value of their total portfolio. If some corporate decision causes the price of one stock in an investor's portfolio to rise but depresses the value of another of his stocks by an even greater amount, the investor will not be pleased. As stockholding in general and diversified stockholding in particular has risen over time, corporate decisions have increasingly come to affect other firms and their stockholders.

This phenomenon has been evident in Japan for decades. Japan's keiretsu are a group of companies that cross-own stock in each other in order to promote cooperation among the constituent firms. The practice represents a kind of halfway point between total independence and a complete merger. In 1989, the Texan tycoon T. Boone Pickens purchased a large stake in Koito, a Japanese automotive lighting and air conditioning company that belongs to the Toyota keiretsu. Toyota works closely with Koito and other suppliers in designing products to fit its cars.

Pickens became upset that Koito was charging Toyota low prices. But the other companies in the Toyota keiretsu did not share his concern. Unlike those companies, Pickens only owned shares in one of the keiretsu's firms. So he was only interested in maximizing Koito's share price, while the other shareholders cared about the overall value of all the keiretsu's companies. If Pickens had also owned Toyota stock, he wouldn't have had much of an incentive to try to charge Toyota higher prices. In fact, the income he hoped to gain from raising Koito's prices to Toyota would have been smaller than the loss imposed on Toyota.[33]

In the U.S., mutual funds and other financial institutions replicate some aspects of the keiretsu system. For example, a study I performed with Tuck Business School professor Bob Hansen found that 33 percent of IBM's stock and 50 percent of Intel's stock were owned by institutions that held stock in both companies. Likewise, 29 percent of Apple's stock and 20 percent of Microsoft's stock were possessed by institutions that were shareholders of both firms.[34] Additionally, some aspects of venture capital funds also resemble the keiretsu system. Typically, such funds specialize in investing in a small number of industries. Like the TIAA-CREF, the funds have an incentive to use their position as stakeholders to encourage cooperation among the companies in which they're invested and to discourage wasteful internecine disputes.

Hansen and I found that stock diversification also helps to explain other corporate behavior, such as the prices that firms bid in mergers. While merger announcements usually increase the stock price of the firm being acquired, there is substantial evidence that the stock price of the buyer actually falls. Furthermore, the size of this drop has been increasing over time. This can be explained by stock diversification: when shareholders own both the acquired and acquiring firm, they care much more about whether the merger will increase the total value of the two firms than they do about which firm's value increases and which decreases. If shareholders own both companies, a higher bid simply means more money going from one of their pockets to the other. If there are diversified shareholders and multiple suitors, then shareholders will care not about the size of the bid, but rather that the total value is maximized.[35]

During a merger, shareholders will only be indifferent to the buyer's stock price when they also hold shares in the target. When the target is a private, closely-held firm, you usually won't see this disinterest. In such acquisitions, a firm will only make a bid if the merger would increase its own value. Thus, in mergers involving a publicly-held company taking over a privately-held one, the buyer's stock price will usually rise upon the bid's announcement.[36]

The overall benefits we gain from stock diversification are another example of the market acting effectively when it's left alone. Sometimes these innovations take some time to evolve, but the inexorable direction of the market tends toward ever greater efficiency.

## State Predators and Private Lambs

What kind of company comes to mind when you think of a corporate predator? The textbook example is John D. Rockefeller's Standard Oil company, which ruthlessly gobbled up and closed down competitors in the late 1800s and early 1900s until the firm was ordered broken up by the Supreme Court.[37] More recently, American Airlines was the defendant in a high-profile predation case that was eventually tossed out by the courts. Inevitably, it is large, private companies that are associated with predation in the public mind. This is quite unjust, for it is government-run companies—not private firms—that have the biggest incentives to act like predators.

As noted in Chapter One, predation—the lowering of a company's prices below cost—usually proves too costly to be successful. After crushing a competitor, the threat of further predation has to be credible enough to keep new firms from entering the market. How is this threat issued? A typical predator has to convince potential competitors that it values something—perhaps overall sales or market share—more than it does profits, which can suffer dramatically while a firm is engaged in predation. This is usually a difficult threat to make convincingly—after all, the overall goal of any private company is to make money.

But government-owned companies are seldom geared primarily toward making profits. Because they are frequently motivated by extraneous factors such as maximizing employment, state-owned firms can make much more credible threats of predation. What's more, state-owned firms often don't need to drive their competitors out of business for predation to be successful; predation can work merely by allowing state-owned firms to expand their market share or create more jobs. Public firms also frequently enjoy state financing and tax advantages that give them the financial resources needed to sustain predation-related losses much longer than private companies can. Finally, because they often don't have freely trading stock, state-owned companies are typically immune to the stock-shorting strategy that makes it profitable for firms to enter a market dominated by a predator, as previously discussed.[38]

Airbus, the giant European aircraft maker, provides a telling example. Many European governments have an ownership stake in the firm, which lost billions in 2006 due to a two-year delay in the manufacture of its A380 super-jumbo. Nevertheless, the Germans worry that the French want to increase their stake in the company by up to 15 percent because "if France has the upper hand in [the company] boardroom, Germany fears it could be forced to bear the brunt of any [labor force] cut-backs." The UK has similar concerns.[39]

Looking at Airbus' production methods, we see how jobs are prioritized over profits:

> The contribution of the United Kingdom taxpayer alone
> towards the A380 program is 530 million [British

pounds]. In return for that, Broughton [in England]...got to make the wings. But it also means that each completed set of wings has to make a remarkable journey to the final assembly site in France by way of container ship, river barge and specially adapted road trailer. With the main fuselage having to travel from Germany and the tailfin from Spain, no wonder Christian Streiff, the man who was drafted in to head Airbus in July [2006], commented that there must be a simpler way.[40]

Because many state-run firms likewise refuse to prioritize profits, they make ideal predators. For example, weather forecasting offers a good case study in the effectiveness of public predators. During the 1980s, private meteorology services saw a chance to make money by providing television stations with specialized forecasts that the National Weather Service hadn't been offering. But soon after the private companies began providing this service, the National Weather Service started giving stations the same specialized forecasts for free, thus driving the private forecasting companies out of the business.[41] According to Jeffery Smith, executive director of the Association of Private Weather-Related Companies, "many commercial meteorologists have been reluctant to take an increased role in forecasting because of the constant threat of government provision of these specialized forecasting services. Private firms do not know what service the government will choose to offer next for 'free.' "[42]

Other cases of public predation are evident in higher education. Public universities can charge much lower tuition than private schools because public schools enjoy more state financing. My alma mater of UCLA, for example, spends almost $40,000 per student but charges only $6,522 tuition for in-state students.[43] Students generally pay a much smaller percentage of public university's costs than students at private universities.[44] Below-cost pricing sometimes also extends to the smaller operations run by public universities such as bookstores, food handling, and entertainment. These businesses may receive free building space or special tax privileges that allow them to charge artificially low prices with which private vendors simply can't compete.[45]

The comparatively low tuition for public universities undoubtedly has a big impact on a student's choice of school. Between 1965 and 2005, when average tuition at public universities and colleges fell from 22 to 18 percent of the average private tuition, the percentage of students enrolled in public schools rose from 67 to 79 percent.[46] This should come as no surprise—the ability to charge below-cost prices thanks to government subsidies gives public schools an enormous advantage over private universities.

In fact, state universities have acquired many formerly private universities after driving, or threatening to drive, the private schools into bankruptcy—examples include George Mason University School of Law, University of Buffalo, University of Houston, and University of Pittsburgh. In the case of the University of Buffalo, the State University of New York reportedly threatened to open up a public university across the street unless the University of Buffalo joined the state system.[47]

Private firms can't take over their rivals so easily due to antitrust regulations. These regulations create a real difficulty for private predation—a big company may drive a competitor out of business, but the latter's factory and other key assets are often left standing. Some new entrant can easily step in, purchase these assets at greatly discounted prices, and restart the competition. Then, the predator will face a new competitor with lower costs than its former rival had. State-owned firms, in contrast, are exempt from many antitrust rules, and this makes it easier for them to buy up a victim's assets and forestall the entrance of new competitors.

Post offices worldwide are notorious for adopting predatory tactics against private competitors. Post offices systematically use their profits from operations where they have a government-protected monopoly to subsidize money-losing operations in sectors where they face private competition.[48] In 2001, the European Commission found the German post office, Deutsche Post AG, to be illegally cross-subsidizing its parcel business with funds from its first class mail monopoly.[49] In 2005, the Danish, Spanish, and French post offices were fined for engaging in similar practices.[50]

The U.S. Postal Service engages in the same kind of chicanery. When the postal service raised first-class mail to thirty-three cents in January 1999, it simultaneously reduced the price of domestic overnight express mail from $15.00 to $13.70, even though it was already losing money at $15.00. The price, which was lowered in response to increasingly successful competition in overnight delivery from FedEx and UPS Overnight, remained below $15.00 for the next seven years.[51] Clearly the postal service was not seeking to drive its competitors out of business with this maneuver. But expanding its market share through below-cost pricing is still predation nonetheless.

There are almost endless examples of predatory practices by state-owned companies and services. One peculiar predator is the U.S. Forest Service, which requires lumber companies to bid on lumber that is profitable to cut as well as lumber that is unprofitable. Making companies bid on lumber that includes unprofitable trees reduces the amount the firms will pay and lowers the forest service's income. Why would the forest service do that? The key, once again, is that we're dealing with a state company that does not operate on the profit motive—the forest service's revenue must be turned over to the Treasury Department. But requiring that unprofitable lumber and profitable lumber be bid on together increases the total amount cut. This, in turn, increases the demand for the forest service to build more roads and provide other services—activities that justify the forest service's budget.[52]

Even a venerable government institution such as NASA is not above engaging in predation. For many years, one of the greatest obstacles to the private sector in space was the competition it faced from NASA's below-cost pricing of space-shuttle flights.[53] It may seem strange that NASA would charge private companies so little to launch their satellites into space. After all, a private company that enjoyed a near-monopoly like NASA does would typically charge high, monopoly prices for such a service. But, as a government-owned firm, NASA is not primarily interested in profits. To the contrary, it historically has charged below-cost prices in order to prevent private companies from competing in the market. NASA may not show a lot of concern for profits, but it likes to keep its near-monopoly on American shuttle launches, which sustains the agency's prestige.

Interestingly, the U.S. government has accused the Chinese government's space program of engaging in predation and even forced that program to change its pricing policies before it would allow U.S. firms to use Chinese satellite launch services.[54] Despite the propensity of U.S. government agencies to engage in predation themselves, these kinds of accusations against foreigners are not rare. In fact, the U.S. government accuses foreign government-run institutions of predatory practices even more frequently than it levels accusations against privately owned firms.

Predation often proves easy for government-owned companies because they benefit directly from the act of predation itself. A private predator suffers badly when it slashes prices below cost, even as sales rise. But this is not the case with a public firm that values sales and employment over profits. In fact, predation is so harmful to private companies that they don't actually want to do it; they are only really successful if they can scare away potential competitors through the *threat* of predation. If the threat is credible, then a firm doesn't actually have to follow through with it. But who is more likely to make a convincing bluff? A private company, which is geared toward maximizing profits and would lose a lot of money during a predation campaign? Or a public firm, which is not so concerned by lost profits, and which would actually benefit from predation by expanding output or market share? The evidence indicates that predation rarely occurs by private companies.[55] Government predation, however, is very easy to find.[56]

## The Modern Guild System

State intervention in the economy can take many forms other than direct government spending or the operation of state-owned companies. For example, the government establishes all kinds of regulations that govern private business. These rules are often presented as necessary measures to make the market more "fair." But a close look at one major type of regulation—state licensing of professionals—reveals how some of these laws not only hinder free competition, but are deliberately designed to do so.

Licensing of professionals is a practice that has existed for a very long time. For instance, Medieval European guilds made young apprentices work for years—sometimes over a decade—at low pay before they were allowed to practice their craft on their own.[57] If a skilled worker didn't go through the official training, he wasn't allowed to practice the craft. Looking at similar guild practices during his own day, Adam Smith, the father of economics, concluded that guilds existed largely to restrict the number of people entering a profession in order to keep wages high.[58]

This was already the case during the Middle Ages. Medieval guilds did not exist primarily to guarantee product quality, as guild leaders argued. Such guarantees were only really useful in cases where a product's quality was difficult to evaluate before purchasing it, such as medicine. But the longest apprenticeships were in professions in which it was easy to immediately judge the quality of the product. For example, in thirteenth-century Paris, apprenticeships lasted ten years for making iron buckles, tables, and buttons, while in Genoa it took eleven years to be certified as a chest maker. Rigidly enforced guild statutes dictated the length of Parisian apprenticeships, their pay (rarely any), and whether meals and lodging were included. These rules were partly designed to keep masters from enticing away each other's apprentices by offering better conditions—in other words, they aimed to hinder the creation of a free market in labor.[59]

The same dynamics are perpetuated today in many state-run programs for licensing professionals. To become a licensed professional, states typically require a person to fulfill various education requirements mandated by professional associations. But are these requirements really necessary? Why can't an aspiring professional get a license simply by passing a rigorous licensing test with practical components? If a student spends years educating himself and then aces his bar exam, is he really less qualified to be a lawyer than someone who studied in law school classes? He may not be, but a self-educated lawyer would be barred from the profession nonetheless—aspiring lawyers are required to spend two-and-a-half years in school. Oftentimes ambitious students are even prohibited from taking a heavier course load and finishing early.

Onerous education requirements exist for many other professions. For example, most states require optometry students to study at an accredited school for at least six terms of eight months each before they can take either the national or state certification exams.[60] Likewise, medical students must receive at least three-and-a-half years of schooling.[61] Medical schools, like law schools, lose their accreditation if they grant degrees faster than the rules allow.

Thirty-nine states exclude new barbers from the profession unless they attend a barbering school, usually for at least nine months.[62] Becoming a cosmetologist typically takes even longer.[63] Similar regulations exist for professions as diverse as addiction counselors, dental hygienists, electrologists, interior designers, morticians, nail technicians, nurses, and polygraph examiners.[64] Students who went to class may still be disqualified from practicing their trade if their class attendance was unsatisfactory; twenty-two states require 100 percent class attendance rates just to get a real estate license.[65]

Contrast these rules with those governing the acquisition of Ph.D.s. Here there are no state-imposed restrictions or minimum time limits for completing the course of study. A few amazing students finish their coursework and dissertations in just a few years, but most need a much longer time. In economics, students take an average of five-and-a-half years to complete a Ph.D., with 1 percent finishing in less than three years. On the other hand, the slowest 10 percent take eight years or longer, with some taking over twenty years.[66]

Thus, Ph.D. candidates are allowed to prove their energy and competency by completing their degrees quickly. This becomes a strong selling point to potential employers, who look favorably on such highly motivated job applicants. In academia, I frequently heard professors boasting among themselves as to who was able to complete their program fastest. It is a simple and obvious sign that a student is smart and dedicated.

This explains why universities don't require Ph.D. candidates to take some minimum amount of time to complete their degrees, as is the case with so many licensing professions. Such requirements would make it impossible for some of the best candidates to prove their worth by finishing their classes and dissertations quickly. The smartest students would be discouraged from working fast, while slower students would not be affected.

Let's take another look at the real estate profession. The real estate agent's exam centers on relatively straightforward questions involving basic mathematical calculations or real estate law. Many people could pass the test after briefly studying on their own, but this is prohibited by class requirements for aspiring real estate agents. What is the impact of these requirements? Some very smart people are discouraged from joining the profession. They could easily pass the licensing exam, but they won't do it if they first have to sit through nine months of classes, as required in Pennsylvania.

Here is a personal example. I have taught at major universities such as the University of Chicago Law School, the University of Pennsylvania's Wharton Business School, and Rice University. I have taught all levels of students from freshmen to Ph.D. candidates. But in my academic career, I discovered that there is one thing I cannot do: I can't teach public high school students. It's not that the students are incapable of following the lecture or that I wouldn't enjoy the work; for the last few years, I have occasionally guest lectured for a statistics class at my sons' high school. The problem is this: I am banned from getting a full-time job teaching in public high schools because I have not taken the required number of years of "teacher training" courses.

Most states require either an undergraduate degree in education or two to three years of training classes before a person can be certified as a public school teacher. These regulations discourage a lot of capable people from entering the profession. For this reason, some states such as Arkansas now allow public school teachers to work toward their teacher's certificate on the job. This is especially encouraged among science and math teachers, of whom there are real shortages. Misty Hern, a private school teacher with a degree in biological sciences, shows how the disincentive of class requirements discourages qualified teachers from working at public schools. Ms. Hern told the *Arkansas Democrat-Gazette* that she'd like to earn the higher salaries paid in public schools, but the class requirements kept her from entering the sector. However, she was willing to consider applying to a public school under Arkansas' new on-the-job teacher education program. "If I went back to school to get my teaching degree, it would take three years and a lot more money," she noted.[67]

I interviewed a group of administrators at professional schools, including law and medicine, as to why their students are required to take a certain amount of time to get through school.[68] Most respondents replied either that it is an arbitrary requirement, or that the American Bar Association or the American Medical Association mandates it. A few argued that a time requirement is needed because classes have to be taken in a certain order. One wonders, then, why such a rule is necessary for professionals ranging from lawyers to barbers, but not for Ph.D.-credentialed specialists like economists and scientists. Taking classes out of order may increase the difficulty of the coursework, but if a hardworking student taking extra classes each semester ends his schooling with a B average, shouldn't we assume he has mastered the material just as well as a student taking fewer classes each semester who earns the same grades?

Some administrators defended class requirements by insisting that certain skills are difficult to test, especially in medicine. Here's their argument: clinical, surgical, and laboratory skills are difficult to evaluate through written exams. True, practical skills are appraised during the licensing process through a range of tests that cover everything from diagnostic skills to bedside manners.[69] Still, these skills are better evaluated by observing the prospective physician over a long period of time in a classroom setting.

This argument, however, does not justify limits on how quickly a student can finish his course load; it only puts forward a plausible case for mandatory classes for aspiring healthcare professionals. But this is an exception that does not apply to most other professions that use time requirements to regulate entry into the field. What, for example, prevents licensing boards from adequately testing would-be barbers' hair cutting abilities or realtors' understanding of interest calculations and real estate law? The fact that these restrictions exist for a wide variety of licensed occupations suggests that difficulties in testing skills are not the primary explanation for minimum time requirements in occupational licensing regulations.

So why do professional associations adopt rules that effectively prevent some of the smartest and ablest people from entering a profession and thereby lower the average quality of new entrants? If Adam Smith is right and the point of making those entering a profession take a long time is to reduce their numbers and thereby maintain higher wages, why not just make the licensing exams more difficult? This course of action would eliminate the weakest qualified candidates, while eradicating the long schooling requirements that discourage bright, hard-working aspirants who can quickly learn professional skills.

The real justification for minimum time limits in school for aspiring professionals is that current professionals don't want too much new competition. Professionals need to admit enough new entrants to their field in order to secure the profession's interest. But allowing too many new entrants would create competition that could depress wages. By mandating minimum time limits in school, current professionals allow new entrants in a way that discourages many of the highest quality candidates who would provide the most competition for themselves.[70]

Unfortunately, state governments perpetuate this state of affairs by adopting licensing and accreditation processes that include mandatory minimum times in school. While these rules help prop up the salaries of current professionals, the professions overall would greatly benefit from a little more free competition.

## Smoking Bans–Light 'Em Up

All these contrasting examples of private market creativity and government inefficiency do not imply that government intervention in the economy is always undesirable. There are some areas in which businesses will impose unjust costs on others that can only be controlled by the government. One of the best examples of this is the regulation of pollution.

Environmental problems arise because the costs of polluters' actions are passed on to other people.[71] The classic case is the "common pool" or "overfishing" problem. Fishermen tend to overfish an area until the fishery is depleted. If one fisherman lets a fish go so that it can spawn, there is no guarantee that another fisherman won't catch that same fish. But this problem is eliminated in privately-owned fisheries like private lakes or fish farms. If a fishery is running low on fish, the owner can leave fish to spawn knowing that no one else will catch them.

Outdoor air pollution suffers a similar "common pool" problem; if too many individuals or companies emit too much pollution, the combined result can produce illness and even death. Everything from cars to power plants emit byproducts that could be classified as harmful, but no one would argue that we should eliminate cars and power plants because their pollution costs outweigh all their benefits. Similar to fishermen out at sea, individual car makers or factory owners are unlikely to take into account the cost that their pollution imposes upon others. Altruism only goes so far. This creates a legitimate space for government intervention—governments can regulate pollution levels by limiting, taxing, or otherwise restricting pollution emissions.

The problem here is that the government's inevitable tendency is to increase the scope of its authority. Allowing the government—whether federal, state, or local—to regulate pollution may be necessary, but we can only watch with dismay as the government uses this authority to steadily expand its coercive powers. In doing so, it inevitably begins mandating solutions to tangential "problems" that are best left to the market to solve.

This is most evident today in the restaurant industry, where local governments are becoming increasingly intrusive in ensuring clean air by banning smoking. A restaurant owner will face competitive pressures to decide whether his customers want to be allowed to smoke, just as he must figure out what food to serve, how big the portions will be, and what kind of décor to have. Restaurants that don't satisfy their customers on these issues will quickly go out of business.

That's why smoking in restaurants should not be considered a common pool problem subject to government intervention. Restaurants that allow smoking don't base their policy merely on their love of smokers; they are responding to competitive pressures and customer preferences. And of course, the choice doesn't have to be between perfectly pristine air and air so cloudy that you can't see more than a few feet; many restaurants simply create smoking and non-smoking sections. But this solution, too, is outlawed by government smoking bans.

If restaurants can go out of business when they don't get small things right, like whether to include an extra side dish with a meal or what kind of background music is played, why is there any less reason to believe their decision on smoking will likewise reflect customer demand? If anything, the fact that people feel so strongly about smoking—both for and against—implies that restaurants will very carefully tailor their smoking policies to their customers' wishes.

Restaurant smoking is more like a private fishery than a common pool. And the best thing the government can do to ensure people get the air quality they want is to let the market decide.

To conclude, the free market is remarkably inventive. Given enough time, all kinds of seemingly insurmountable problems can be overcome if someone stands to earn a profit by finding a solution. In contrast, government intervention, although often well-intentioned, faces inherent economic and political problems that make it costly and naturally inefficient. As Milton Friedman famously pointed out, "Nobody spends somebody else's money as carefully as he spends his own."[72] Looking at examples from Airbus to NASA to state licensing systems, it's hard to disagree.

# 4 Crime and Punishment

If something becomes more costly, people will do less of it. This is the fundamental principle of economics—a simple notion that also explains a lot of human behavior in realms seemingly far removed from trade, industry, and finance.

Take sports, for example. When college basketball's Atlantic Coast Conference increased the number of referees per game from two to three in 1978, the number of fouls dropped by 34 percent. Why? Basketball players fouled less often because they were more likely to get caught. In fact, the actual decline in fouling was probably even larger, since fouls that may have gone unnoticed by two referees were more likely to be caught when there were three.[1]

We find the same kind of incentives at work in baseball. The American League has more hit batsmen than the National League, but this difference only appeared after 1973, when the American League removed its pitchers from the batting lineup in favor of designated hitters. Since American League pitchers no longer worried that they themselves would be hit in retaliation if they threw at an opposing batter, they began throwing more beanballs.[2]

The reverse of this fundamental principle also holds true: when you make something less costly, people will do more of it. And if you offer a meaningful reward for some type of behavior, you can bet more people will do it, even if they shouldn't. This is borne out by a study of a specific type of fraud by air traffic controllers.[3] To receive disability benefits due to job-related stress, air traffic controllers must present a well-documented stressful incident—a collision or close call—that has caused a deterioration in their performance. Unsurprisingly, when it became easier to file for disability, flights suddenly started experiencing more "close calls." And these were not cases that the air traffic controllers could simply make up; they were reported by a sophisticated performance evaluation called the "Operation Error Severity Index."[4]

Analyzing incentives in this way is a particularly good method for studying crime. It helps reveal what factors increase criminality, and what methods work best to reduce crime rates. Studying incentives also leads us to some surprising conclusions about the effects of abortion, affirmative action, and the death penalty on crime, while showing how certain kinds of high penalties and other policies can inadvertently increase crime rates.

## Why did Crime Fall During the 1990s?

> "[It] remains one of the great mysteries of our time."
> —Wesley Skogan, a criminologist at Northwestern
> University, on the long and steady drop
> in crime during the 1990s.[5]

Violent crime in the United States shot up like a rocket after 1960. From 1960 to 1991, reported violent crime increased by an incredible 372 percent. The disturbing trend was seen across the country, with robbery

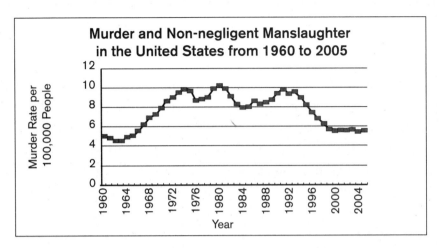

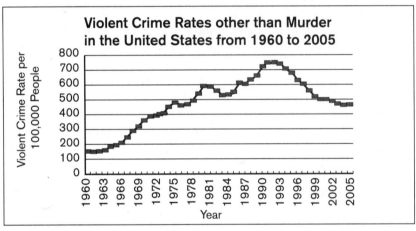

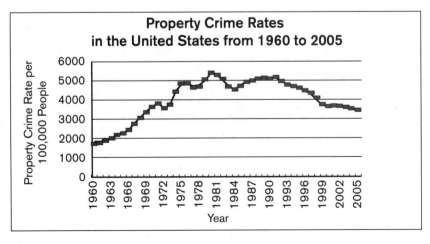

rates peaking in 1991 and rape and aggravated assault following in 1992. But then something unexpected happened—between 1991 and 2000, rates of violent crime and property crime fell sharply, dropping by 33 percent and 30 percent, respectively. Murder rates were more stable up to 1991, but then they also plunged by a steep 44 percent.[6]

This drop in crime was particularly surprising because it occurred after some academics had predicted that the advent of "super-predators"—a rising generation of conscienceless violent youth—would soon lead to an explosion of crime.[7] Also unexpectedly, the phenomenon was not confined to the U.S.—a remarkably similar pattern was evident in Canada, where violent crime rates peaked in 1992 and property crime

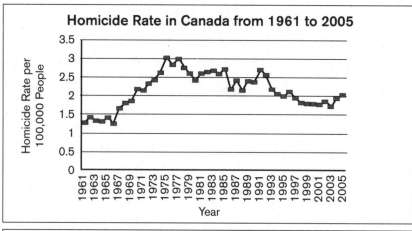

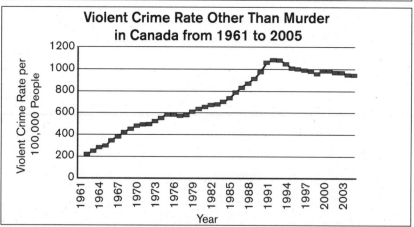

and murder rates topped out in 1991. While the declines in violent crime and murder rates during the 1990s were smaller in Canada than in the United States, the fall in Canadian property crimes was slightly larger.[8]

What's more, the drop in crime may be even larger than these statistics indicate due to one factor that is often overlooked: rising rates of crime reporting by victims. With the exception of the data on murder, the crime data cited above—supplied by the FBI—are based on crimes that victims reported to police departments. But, of course, not every victim reports when a crime occurs. Victims are most likely to report two kinds of crimes: the most serious crimes and the ones that they believe have the greatest chance of being solved. These trends reinforce each

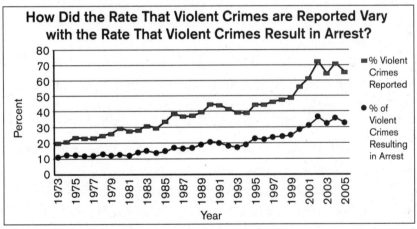

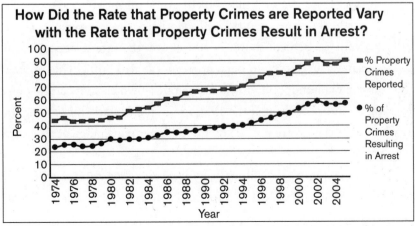

other: victims report the most serious crimes, which in turn receive the most attention from police. This makes serious crimes more likely to be solved and thus even more reporting is likely to occur. Two simple diagrams show how the rate of reporting of violent crimes and property crimes in the U.S. has increased alongside rising arrest rates, suggesting that the increased arrest rates have encouraged more reporting.[9]

Less serious crimes, receiving less police attention, are not as likely to be solved and are also less likely to be reported. During 2005, victims reported only about 20 percent of larcenies to police, compared to an estimated 63 percent of rapes and 68 percent of aggravated assaults. Since more than half of all larcenies involve items worth less than $100, this should come as no surprise.[10] Many people are deterred from reporting petty crimes by the inconvenience of dealing with the police and the slim chance of recovering the items.

So why is the rising rate of crime reporting important? Recall the example of the basketball referees: increasing the number of officials discouraged fouls, but it also made any given foul more likely to be noticed. The same effect is at play with the crime rate, which fell sharply in the 1990s even while the rate of reporting violent crime noticeably increased.

This trend indicates that anti-crime efforts in the 1990s were even more effective than is commonly believed. After accounting for the rise in crime reporting, we find that violent crime during the 1990s fell by about 10 percent more than the FBI's statistics show. Property crimes fell by about 30 percent more. Furthermore, the rate of reporting of violent crimes surged by 46 percent from 1999 to 2002. This implies that official data on recent violent crime rates—which show crime rates leveling off after the drop of the 1990s—are particularly misleading. In reality, fewer crimes are occurring, but a higher percentage of them are being reported.[11]

So what explains the fantastic plunge in crime rates during the 1990s? A lot of the individual pieces to this puzzle have been identified. Analysts have advanced a variety of plausible explanations, but it is not always clear how these fit together. Some stress law enforcement aspects such as increased arrest and conviction rates, longer prison sentences, "broken windows" police strategies, and the death penalty. Others emphasize different factors, including right-to-carry laws for concealed handguns, a strong economy, the waning of the crack cocaine epidemic, or affirmative action polices within police departments. It is even argued that legalized abortion has helped to stem crime. Many of these explanations may simultaneously be true, but there is lively debate about which factors are more important than others, and whether some policies actually did more harm than good.

So how do we evaluate the competing explanations? Before we identify the successful policies that reduced crime, let's look at a few factors that had the opposite result.

## What Increased Crime? Part I

### Legalized Abortion

> Out-of-wedlock births in the United States have climbed to an all-time high, accounting for nearly four in 10 babies born last year, government health officials said yesterday.
>
> —*Washington Post*, November 2006[12]

> Nearly everyone agrees that the breakdown of families— to take one indicator, one-third of all births in the country and two-thirds of black births are now out of wedlock— is feeding into a destructive cycle of poverty, educational and developmental deficits, and incarceration.
>
> —*New York Times*, July 2006[13]

Of all the explanations for the drop in crime rates during the 1990s, perhaps the most controversial is its attribution to *Roe v. Wade*, the Supreme Court's 1973 decision to mandate legalized abortion. The large number of women who began having abortions shortly after the *Roe v. Wade* decision were most likely unmarried, in their teens, or poor, the argument goes, and their children would have been "unwanted." This indicates a high probability that these children, if born, would have grown up to be criminals. But because they were aborted, these children, who would have been teenagers entering their "criminal prime" in the early 1990s, were not around to commit the crimes expected of them. According to *Freakonomics*, abortion thereby became "one of the greatest crime-lowering factors in American history."[14] An attention-grabbing theory, to be sure. But, as we shall see, a thorough analysis of abortion and crime statistics leads to a contrary conclusion—that abortion, in fact, *increases* crime.

Even before *Roe v. Wade*, supporters of abortion rights decried the crime and other social problems caused by "unwanted" children. Daniel Callahan summarized the argument in his 1970 book, *Abortion: Law, Choice, and Morality*: "To withhold the possibility of a safe and socially acceptable abortion for unmarried women is to start the chain of illegitimacy and despair that will continue to keep poverty, crime, and poor mental health high on the list of pressing social problems."[15]

The argument was reiterated in 1972 by the Rockefeller Commission on Population and the American Future. Established by Richard Nixon, the Commission cited research purporting that the children of women denied an abortion "turned out to have been registered more often with psychiatric services, engaged in more antisocial and criminal behavior, and have been more dependent on public assistance."[16]

The Commission appears to have been greatly influenced by a study published in 1966 by Hans Forssman and Inga Thuwe.[17] The two studied the children of 188 women who were denied abortions from 1939 to 1941 at the only hospital in Gothenburg, Sweden. They compared these "unwanted" children to another group—the next children born after each of the unwanted children at the hospital. The study found that the unwanted children were much more likely to grow up in adverse conditions, such as having divorced parents or being raised in foster homes. They were also more likely to become delinquents and have trouble in school. Unfortunately, the authors never investigated whether the children's unwantedness *caused* these problems, or were simply *correlated* with them. Perhaps a family's poverty was the real cause of these dysfunctions, and women who sought abortions were more likely to be poor.

Nevertheless, the argument became axiomatic among supporters of legalized abortion. During the 1960s and 1970s, before *Roe v. Wade*, abortion rights advocates attributed all sorts of social ills, including crime and mental illness, to unwanted children.[18] Furthermore, they found that "unwanted children are more likely to be abandoned, neglected and abused,"[19] and they tend to be "poorly fed, poorly housed and poorly clothed."[20] Weeding these poor, crime-prone people out of the population through abortion was therefore presented as a beneficial deed that would make society safer.

More recently, two economists—John Donohue and Steven Levitt—became the first analysts since Forssman and Thuwe to attempt to present systematic evidence that abortion reduces crime.[21] They argued that the drop in crime rates during the 1990s was primarily due to the increase in the availability of legal abortion in 1970—when abortion was deregulated in five states[22]—and especially in 1973—when *Roe v. Wade* deregulated abortion in the remaining states. The effect, they claimed, was staggeringly large—the pair attributed up to "one-half of the overall crime reduction" and up to 81 percent of the drop in murder rates from 1991 to 1997 to the rise in abortions in the early-to-mid 1970s.[23] If accurate, they had surely found the Holy Grail for reducing crime.

The theoretical link between "unwanted" children and crime is simple and powerful. Most people who oppose this thesis argue from a moral perspective instead of trying to rebut the evidence. But whatever weight people put on moral arguments, the claim that abortion can prevent some murders and save lives causes at least some people to rethink their position. Unfortunately, the original arguments never acknowledged the possible pernicious effects of abortion on crime. And when we look at the data, we find that the argument doesn't hold up empirically.

Let's begin by looking at the overall status of abortion in the United States in the early 1970s. This is when Donohue and Levitt find that the "legalization" of abortion laid the foundation for the future drop in crime. It should be noted that, contrary to popular belief, there was not a blanket ban on legal abortion before the early 1970s. While closely regulated, the procedure was legal in various circumstances, such as when the life or health of the mother was at risk. In some states, doctors interpreted this clause quite liberally. As a result, legal abortion was much more widespread before *Roe v. Wade* than is commonly acknowledged. In fact, in 1970-1973, when abortion was "legal" in five states but "banned" in the rest, some of the "banned" states had similar or even higher rates of legal abortion than in the "legal" states. For example, Kansas had 277 abortions per 1,000 live births in 1971, outstripping "legal" states such as Alaska (160), Hawaii (261), and Washington (265). High rates of abortion could be found in other "banned" states and districts, such as Washington, D.C. (703), New Mexico (219), and Oregon (206).[24] Donahue and Levitt, whose main results mistakenly assumed that no legal abortions occurred in any of the "banned" states before 1973, thus began their study with flawed statistics.[25]

A central problem with the "abortion reduces crime" thesis is that it conflates and blurs two different arguments. The first contention is that aborted children would have been more likely to cause crime specifically because they're unwanted—since their parents did not wish to have them, they would likely have grown up in an unloving household, and would have therefore been more prone to crime. A separate, less savory explanation is that abortion reduces crime by culling out certain demographic groups that commit disproportionate numbers of crime, for example, young African American males. If abortion really reduces crime, then this "eugenics" effect could be highly significant, since African Americans have an abortion rate that has consistently been about three times that of whites and a murder rate about 6.5 times that of whites.[26]

While their discussion emphasized the "unwanted child" theory, Donohue and Levitt never separated it from the eugenics approach, which was left without refutation in their work.[27] Indeed, Donahue and Levitt seem to have deliberately avoided the racial implications of their own theory, as their inquiry is one of the few academic studies on crime by economists that doesn't account for these demographics. Perhaps this was just too explosive to mention; after all, who would dare to state that abortion lowers crime rates by reducing the population of poor African Americans?[28]

The relationship between abortion and crime is complex. We must begin by considering the circumstances and expectations under which a woman becomes pregnant. Remember the fundamental principle of economics: if something becomes more costly, people do less of it. If abortion is illegal, the "cost" of sex is relatively high due to the possibility of pregnancy. No method of birth control is 100 percent effective, and without the option to have an abortion as a last-ditch safeguard, having sex carries a risk. When contemplating having pre-marital sex, women know that they might have to bear and raise a child, possibly on their own. Likewise, men know that they might end up having to support a child, and both know that having a baby could create pressures on them to marry even if they don't want to do so. Consequently, both men and women tend to be more reluctant to engage in casual sex, especially unprotected sex, when abortion is illegal.[29]

In contrast, if abortion is legal, the incentives are different. Knowing that the abortion option is there to save them from raising an unexpected child, women who are willing to have an abortion—as well as men in general—become less concerned with contraceptives and more likely to engage in premarital sex. As more women have premarital sex, social mores become more accommodating to the practice. This creates social pressure on other women to have premarital sex, including women who would never have an abortion. Increasing rates of premarital sex among these latter women leads to higher pregnancy rates. The result is rising numbers of women who are single, pregnant, and unwilling to have an abortion.

Indeed, multiple studies have shown that legalized abortion, by raising the rate of unprotected premarital sex, increases the number of unplanned births, even outweighing the reduction in unplanned births due to abortion.[30] From the early 1970s, when abortion was liberalized, through the late 1980s, there was a tremendous increase in the rate of out-of-wedlock births, rising from an average of 5 percent in 1965-69 to over 16 percent twenty years later (1985-1989). For African Americans, the numbers jumped from 35 percent to 62 percent. While not all of this rise can be attributed to liberalized abortion rules, it was nevertheless a key contributing factor.

Let's return to the personal level. In an environment of legal abortion, a man might well *expect* his partner to have an abortion if a sexual encounter results in an unplanned pregnancy. But what happens if the woman refuses? Maybe she is morally opposed to abortion, or perhaps she thought she could have an abortion, but upon becoming pregnant, she decides that she can't go through with it. What happens then?

Many men, feeling tricked into unwanted fatherhood, will likely wash their hands of the affair altogether, thinking "I never wanted a baby; it's her choice, so let her raise the baby herself." What is expected of men in this position has changed dramatically in the last four decades. The evidence shows that the greater availability of abortion largely ended "shot-gun" marriages, where men reacted to an unplanned pregnancy by doing the honorable thing—marrying their partner. But with abortion as a legal option, men became more reluctant to stay with a woman who refuses to have one.[31]

What happens to these babies of reluctant fathers? The mothers often end up raising the child on their own, as single mothers have become much less likely to give their children up for adoption. Even as out-of-wedlock births have surged, adoption rates have plummeted. In the two decades before *Roe*, 19.3 percent of babies born to unwed white mothers were placed for adoption and 1.5 percent for unwed black mothers. From 1973 to 1981, those percentages fell to 7.6 and 0.2 percent, respectively, and continued to decline thereafter. [32] How can we explain this? As stated above, after *Roe*, a rising number of out-of-wedlock children were born to women who opposed abortion, or at least would not have one themselves. These women have also proved less willing to give up their children for adoption.

With work and other demands on their time, single parents, no matter how "wanted" their child may be, tend to devote less attention to their children than do married couples; after all, it's difficult for one person to spend as much time with a child as two people can. Grandparents and other relatives may sometimes help out, but on average, the children of single parents still receive less care.

The children of unmarried, cohabiting couples also receive less care and attention than married couples' children. This is partly because cohabiting partners face much higher separation rates than married couples do.[33] Many cohabiting couples are not married because they are not yet ready to make a lifetime commitment to each other. And if partners believe their relationship may not be permanent, they are less likely to make career adjustments or other sacrifices for the sake of their family. Thus, single parents and unmarried couples are less likely than married parents to read to their children or take them on excursions, and more likely to feel angry at their children or feel that their children are burdensome. Children raised outside of wedlock experience a higher rate of social problems in nearly every area than children of married couples. Unsurprisingly, children from unmarried families are also more likely to grow up to commit crimes.[34]

### Percentage of Children with Different Types of Problems by Marital Status of Parents[35]

|  | Single Parents | Cohabitating Parents | Married Parents |
|---|---|---|---|
| Children who were poorly engaged in school (ages 6-17) | 30% | 31% | 20% |
| Children who were suspended or expelled from school in past 12 months (ages 12-17) | 23% | 23% | 10% |
| Children who skipped school two or more times in the past 12 months (ages 12-17) | 14% | 10% | 6% |
| Children in poor health | 8% | 8% | 3% |
| Children who are read to/told stories infrequently | 19% | 21% | 12% |
| Children who are taken on outings infrequently (ages 0 to 5) | 23% | 22% | 16% |
| Parents who reported "high" rates that their children were hard to care for, that they gave up more of their lives to meet their child's needs than they expected, that their children bothered them a lot, and that they were angry with their child | 17% | 11% | 8% |
| Children who have changed schools in the past year (ages 6-17) | 22% | 21% | 16% |

So the opposing arguments are clear—one stresses that abortion eliminates "unwanted" children, while the other emphasizes that abortion increases out-of-wedlock births. Both effects, conceivably, could be occurring at the same time. The question is: which one has the bigger impact on crime?

This must be answered empirically. Unfortunately for advocates of the "abortion decreases crime" theory, Donahue and Levitt's data were undermined by methodological flaws. As *The Economist* magazine noted in an article entitled "Oops-onomics," "Donohue and Levitt did not run the test that they thought they had."[36] Work by two economists at the Boston Federal Reserve, Christopher Foote and Christopher Goetz, found that when the tests were run correctly, they indicated that abortion actually *increases* violent crime.[37] I co-authored a study with John Whitley that found a similar connection between abortion and murder—namely, that legalizing abortion raised the murder rate, on average, by about 7 percent.[38]

We find particularly troublesome problems with the "abortion decreases crime" theory when we analyze the population according to age group. Suppose that liberalizing abortion in the early 1970s can indeed explain up to 80 percent of the drop in murder during the 1990s, as Donohue and Levitt claim. Then the impact of deregulating abortion, undoubtedly, would first reduce criminality among age groups born after

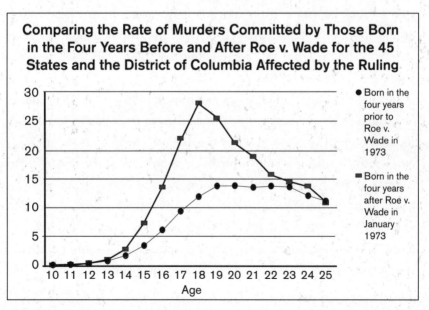

**Comparing the Rate of Murders Committed by Those Born in the Four Years Before and After Roe v. Wade for the 45 States and the District of Columbia Affected by the Ruling**

the abortion law was changed, when the "unwanted," crime-prone elements of these groups began to be weeded out through abortion. Yet, looking at the declining murder rate during the 1990s, Whitley and I found that this is not the case at all. Instead, the rate of committing murder began falling first among an older generation—those twenty-six and older—who were born *before* the *Roe v. Wade* decision.[39] It was only later that criminality among those born after *Roe* began to decline as well.

This pattern is more consistent with the theory that legalizing abortion led to a rise in crime. In fact, those born in the four years after *Roe* were much *more* likely to commit murder than those born in the four years prior to *Roe*. This was especially the case when they were in their teens—in other words, in their "criminal prime."

And that's not all. The "abortion decreases crime" argument encounters further inconsistencies when we compare U.S. crime and abortion trends to those in Canada. While crime rates in both the United States and Canada began declining at the same time, Canada liberalized its abortion laws much later than the U.S. did. Although the province of Quebec effectively legalized abortion in late 1976, it wasn't until 1988, in a case originating in Ontario, that the Canadian Supreme Court struck down limits on abortion nationwide.[40] If the legalization of abortion in the U.S. caused crime to begin dropping eighteen years later, why did the crime rate begin falling just three years after the comparable legal change in Canada?

In sum, even if one effect of abortion were to lower crime by culling out "unwanted" children—a conclusion derived from flawed statistics—the effect is greatly outweighed by the rise in crime that abortion causes by increasing out-of-wedlock births. It should be noted that African Americans are disproportionately harmed by the crime stemming from legalized abortion. That population has seen the biggest increases in abortion, premarital sex, and out-of-wedlock birth rates, resulting in more African Americans being raised by single parents and eventually committing crimes, mostly against other African Americans.[41]

Thus, "legalized" abortion actually served to increase crime since the 1970s. However this effect—both among African Americans and the population at large—was more than offset by other factors that caused the massive drop in crime of the 1990s. Before discussing these aspects, let's look at one other factor that proved counter-productive in fighting crime.

## What Increased Crime? Part II

### Affirmative Action Hiring in the Police Force

Many police departments implemented affirmative action policies in the 1990s, just as the crime rate was entering a steep decline. But a close study reveals that crime fell despite these programs, not because of them. Perhaps most unexpectedly, these policies not only resulted in the hiring of less qualified women and minorities, but also of less qualified white applicants as well.

We must specify at the outset that crime rates did not rise due to the hiring of more women and minorities per se. Rather, the fault lies with the particular affirmative action rules that were adopted. There is little doubt that adding women and minorities to an all-male, all-white police force carries substantial benefits. Minority police officers often function more effectively than whites in minority areas. Since minority residents tend to vest more trust in minority officers, they are often more forthcoming with information that leads to arrests and convictions of criminals. Especially if the minority police officers grew up in the community they are patrolling, they may also be better at predicting the behavior of criminals in those areas. Furthermore, minorities are essential for various kinds of undercover operations, such as infiltrating race-based gangs. Likewise, female officers tend to elicit more information and honest reports of rape and spousal abuse from female victims, and they are much more able than men to carry out certain operations such as prostitution stings.

But affirmative action programs are not simply focused on achiev-ing these benefits of a diverse police force. Instead, the trend has been toward boosting minority representation in a police department so that it reflects the demographic ratio of the surrounding community. The two goals are not necessarily the same, and the methods used to achieve the latter objective, unfortunately, have reduced the effectiveness of police in stopping crime.

Affirmative action policies have sought to transform traditional police hiring standards that rely on intelligence exams, strength tests, and criminal background checks. Because, on average, women are less likely to pass strength tests than are males, while African Americans have lower passing rates on intelligence exams and criminal background checks than whites, many police departments adopted new standards in an effort to increase minority hiring.

Police affirmative action programs have entailed two main approaches. The first is to lower testing standards across the board until they produce equal pass rates among minority and non-minority groups. This approach has become increasingly common over the last few decades. A leading method here has been to replace cognitive or intelligence exams with more nebulous psychological tests that aim to gauge a candidate's temperament. Asking questions such as what is an applicant's favorite color and whether he watches much television, the tests are designed to produce equal pass rates across different groups of applicants.[42] According to a 1993 survey of twenty-three large police and sheriff's departments, twenty departments had reduced their emphasis on cognitive skill testing due to the tests' "adverse impact" on minority hiring.[43] The other three departments had completely elim-inated cognitive testing in hopes of increasing minority recruitment. An example of the meager new hiring standards is that to pass the reading test, "applicants had to score only as well as the bottom 1 percent of current police officers."[44]

Louisiana provides a particularly instructive example. There, the Police Department discarded entrance exams in response to a lawsuit filed by the Department of Justice. The objections were that 66 percent of whites passed the test compared to just 25 percent of African Americans, and that the test did not relate to the abilities required for the job. The lawsuit was weak, failing even to explain what parts of the test were unrelated to the job. Moreover, a federal judge had previously ruled that the test did not discriminate against minority applicants to the police and fire departments in another city. Nevertheless, rather than incur the cost of litigation, the Louisiana State Police dropped the test and agreed to pay $1 million to African Americans who had failed the exam. The department even vowed to hire eighteen new officers from among this group [45]

In some cities, such changes have resulted in myriad problems caused by a less-educated police force. For example, between 1986 and 1990, 311 of the 938 murder cases that the Washington, D.C. police brought to the U.S. attorney's office were dismissed. One local prosecutor commented that "many D.C. cases were thrown out because prosecutors couldn't read or understand the arrest reports [written by the police]." The officers simply lacked the ability to write comprehensible English.

But lower standards do not guarantee the desired pass rates among all races. In Chicago, the city paid $5.1 million for consultants to develop "unbiased" exams, only to have unacceptable numbers of minorities once again fail the tests. The city then moved to a heavily weighted seniority system for promoting police officers and a lottery system for hiring firefighters in order to ensure the correct racial composition of new classes of recruits.[46]

The second method for implementing affirmative action programs in police departments is "norming." This assigns different standards to different groups of candidates in order to ensure similar pass rates. Norming is frequently used for female recruits, both to the police and to the military. For example, in the military, women are required to run two miles in eighteen minutes and fifty-four seconds, while men have sixteen minutes to run the same distance. Women have two minutes to do eighteen push-ups and two minutes for fifty sit-ups, while men must do forty-two push-ups and fifty-two sit-ups within the same time.[47]

Norming inevitably leads to the hiring of women who are, on average, physically weaker than men. Physical strength testing of public safety employees consistently finds large differences between men and women; women's upper body strength ranges from 44 to 68 percent of men's, while their lower body strength is typically 55 to 82 percent of men's.[48] Weaker officers face some obvious disadvantages: it is more difficult for them to chase and catch fleeing suspects or to control a resisting suspect without resorting to a weapon. Furthermore, an influx of weaker officers can affect police procedures. For example, police departments come under pressure to end patrols by single officers, as well as to reduce foot and bicycle patrols in favor of car patrols.

The risk inherent in hiring weaker officers is demonstrated by the case of Brian Nichols, a thirty-three-year-old, 196-pound rape defendant. In an Atlanta courthouse, Nichols overpowered his guard, seized her gun, and used it to kill a judge, a court reporter, a police officer, and a federal agent. Nichols' guard, a sheriff's deputy, was a five-foot-two, fifty-one-year-old woman. "Why was a tiny woman, or any woman, given such a job?" asked Mary Ellen Synon, a columnist for the *Mail on Sunday*. "Because the Atlanta police force, like many others in America, has been subjected for years to government demands for 'gender and minority' balance; changing hiring rules and lowering standards so more women and people from ethnic minorities can join up."[49]

Are such occurrences merely isolated instances, or do they speak to a larger problem created by affirmative action policies? To answer this question, I gathered statistics to analyze how changes in hiring rules and the demographic composition of police departments affect crime, arrest, and conviction rates.[50] I included detailed demographic, income, and socio-economic information to help explain changes in crime and arrest rates. I also considered related factors such as illegal drug prices, gun laws, and various policing policies.

The results were dramatic: crime rates jumped in cities using affirmative action policies that lowered testing standards. Interestingly, however, the use of norming had much less harmful results.

The implementation of consent decrees—agreements by local police departments to use affirmative action in hiring and promotions—increases the rate of murder, other violent crimes, and property crimes. Overall, using affirmative action to achieve a one percentage point increase in African American officers on the force is associated with an increase in murders of at least 2 percent, violent crime of almost 5 percent, and property crimes of 4 percent.[51]

But it is misleading simply to compare increases in African American officers with crime rates. When testing standards are lowered, the increase in the percentage of African American officers is *associated* with more crime, not the *cause* of it. The problem is not the presence of more African American officers per se, but rather the quality of all officers in departments that implement these methods. Most of the increased crime cannot even be attributed to more unqualified African American officers, but rather to the hiring of unqualified officers of all races. This is because the replacement of intelligence exams with psychological tests makes it more difficult to separate out high and low-quality white, Asian, and other recruits just as it does with African American ones.

The reduction in strength standards for female recruits, in contrast, has had only a small detrimental effect.[52] This is likely because these standards are typically lowered through norming; in other words, the standards are lowered for women but not for men. Strength standards for men can even be increased when the hiring of more women creates more competition among male recruits for the declining number of jobs available to them.

However, my study also found that lowered strength standards made female officers more vulnerable to assault and less able to control resisting suspects by themselves. This puts pressure on police departments to shift away from one-officer to two-officer patrol units as well as to reduce the number of walking and bicycle patrols.

To compensate for physical weakness, women may resort to other means of controlling criminals, in particular by using guns.[53] Guns are a "great equalizer," but they don't completely offset strength differences. Being less able to rely on physical strength to defend themselves from an attack, female officers have less time to decide whether to shoot a threatening suspect. This explains the sharp increase in accidental police shootings that typically follow the lowering of strength standards and the hiring of more female officers.[54]

Ironically, affirmative action consent decrees cause the biggest spikes in crime in poor African American neighborhoods—places already plagued by terrible crime. Lowering the effectiveness of the police force in such communities, as affirmative action policies do, clearly harms these struggling areas. If we want a more diverse police force, we should seek better ways of achieving it. Simply abandoning intelligence testing is not a beneficial approach.

## What Decreased Crime? Part I

### The Death Penalty

If abortion and affirmative action policies actually increased crime, then what caused the huge fall in crime in the 1990s? Although it would be nice and neat if we could identify a single element as *the* solution, the truth is that numerous factors combined to drive down crime. One of the most important of these was the Supreme Court's 1976 decision to rescind the ban on the death penalty. Three-quarters of the states soon re-imposed the death penalty, though it wasn't until the early 1990s that significant numbers of executions began occurring again.

Capital punishment clearly increases the risk to criminals of engaging in various crimes, especially murder. Does this increased risk affect criminals' behavior? Before trying to answer this question, let's first consider how another group that faces similar dangers reacts to the risk of death.

Academics classify being a police officer as an "extremely danger-ous" job.[55] In 2005, fifty-five police officers were murdered on the job, while another sixty-seven were accidentally killed.[56] With nearly 700,000 full-time, sworn law enforcement officers in the United States, the murder rate of police officers comes to one in 12,500,[57] a ratio that jumps to one in 5,600 when we include accidental deaths.

Although the risks of policing cannot be eliminated, police officers undertake a variety of measures to reduce the dangers: they wear bul-let-proof vests, develop special procedures for approaching stopped cars, and in some situations officers wait for backup even when this increases the probability that a suspect will escape.

Officers undertake all these measures as a natural human reaction to the risk of death—the riskier an activity, the more a person will usu-ally avoid it or take steps to make the activity safer. This rule applies to violent criminals just like anyone else. And the risk that a violent criminal faces from execution is much greater than the risk of a police officer being killed. In 2005, there were almost 16,700 murders in the United States and sixty executions.[58] That translates to one execution for every 278 murders. In other words, a murderer is twenty times more likely to be executed than a police officer is to be deliberately or accidentally killed on duty.[59]

Those who argue that the death penalty has no effect on violent crime assume that the risk of execution in no way deters criminals from com-mitting capital crimes. "It is hard to believe that fear of execution would be a driving force in a rational criminal's calculus in modern America," writes Steven Levitt.[60] While criminals, just like police officers, are nat-urally less adverse to danger than, say, school teachers or accountants, the notion that it is irrational for them to take into account such an enormous additional risk runs contrary to human nature.[61]

There is widespread public debate over the effectiveness of the death penalty. Sadly, this has included some misleading reporting in the popu-lar press. Take a widely publicized *New York Times* study that compared murder rates in 1998 in states with and without the death penalty.[62] The *Times* concluded that capital punishment was ineffective in reducing crime, noting that "10 of the 12 states without capital punishment have homicide rates below the national average...while half the states with the death penalty have homicide rates above the national average."

This simple comparison really doesn't prove anything. The twelve states without the death penalty have long enjoyed relatively low murder rates due to factors unrelated to capital punishment.[63] When the death penalty was suspended nationwide from 1968 to 1976, the murder rate in these twelve states was still lower than in most other states. What is much more important is that the states that reinstituted the death penalty had about a 38 percent larger drop in murder rates by 1998.[64]

There were no executions in the United States between 1968 and 1976, a time when murder rates skyrocketed.[65] Various theories were put forward in the 1970s to explain the jump in violent crime. Some claimed that the Supreme Court's Miranda decision—mandating that suspects be read their rights during arrest—reduced criminal confessions and otherwise hindered convictions. Others blamed softer criminal penalties or lower arrest rates.[66] Back in the 1970s these studies were generally inconclusive, however, due to the lack of data available at the time.[67]

Economists began to study the death penalty intently after its reimposition in 1976. Isaac Ehrlich, then a young assistant professor at the University of Chicago, conducted path-breaking research showing that each execution deterred as many as twenty to twenty-four murders.[68] His findings, however, were anathema in liberal academia. His conclusions were roundly condemned, and Ehrlich was denied tenure at the University of Chicago. He even became too controversial to find work at most universities. However, his contentious findings sparked a good deal of new research into the effectiveness of capital punishment, including a special panel convened by the National Academy of Sciences. The panel came to the curious conclusion that greater penalties generally fail to deter criminals.[69]

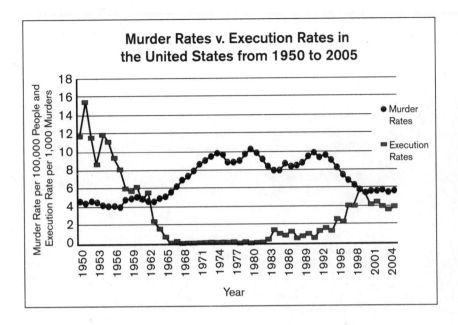

**Murder Rates v. Execution Rates in the United States from 1950 to 2005**

Murder Rate per 100,000 People and Execution Rate per 1,000 Murders

- ● Murder Rates
- ■ Execution Rates

Year

Although many states immediately re-approved the death penalty after the Supreme Court lifted the ban in 1976, executions were relatively rare until the 1990s, when execution rates spiked dramatically. This elicited a flood of new research on capital punishment. Moreover, the new studies drew upon much more extensive data than had previously been available, allowing researchers to study crime rates over many years and across every state.

This research was conducted as violent crime rates were plummeting while executions were rising sharply. Between 1991 and 2000, there were 9,114 fewer murders per year, while the number of executions per year rose by seventy-one. The fresh studies resurrected Ehrlich's earlier conclusions that the death penalty greatly deters murder. The vast majority of recent scholarly research confirms this deterrent effect.[70] Generally, the studies found that each execution saved the lives of roughly fifteen to eighteen potential murder victims.[71] Overall, the rise in executions during the 1990s accounts for about 12 to 14 percent of the overall drop in murders.

## Research by Economists since the
## Mid-1990s on the Death Penalty

|                              | Reduced Murder Rate | No Discernible Effect on Murder Rate | Increased Murder Rate |
|------------------------------|---------------------|--------------------------------------|-----------------------|
| Refereed Publications        | 1) Ehrlich and Liu, *Journal of Law and Economics*, 1999. | 1) Katz, Levitt, and Shustorovich, *American Law and Economics Review*, 2003 | None |
|                              | 2) Lott, *More Guns, Less Crime*, University of Chicago Press, 2000. | 2) Berk, *Journal of Empirical Legal Studies*, 2005 | |
|                              | 3) Cloninger and Marchesini, *Applied Economics*, 2001. | 3) Narayan and Smyth, *Applied Economics*, 2006 | |
|                              | 4) Dezhbakhsh, Rubin, and Shepherd, *American Law and Economics Review*, 2003. | | |
|                              | 5) Mocan and Gittings, *Journal of Law and Economics*, 2003. | | |
|                              | 6) Shepherd, *Journal of Legal Studies*, 2004. | | |
|                              | 7) Zimmerman, *Journal of Applied Economics*, 2004. | | |
|                              | 8) Zimmerman, *American Journal of Economics and Sociology*, 2006. | | |
|                              | 9) Liu, *Eastern Economic Journal*, forthcoming. | | |
| Non Refereed Publications    | 1) Lott and Landes, *Bias Against Guns*, 2003. | 1) Fagan, Zimring, and Geller, *Texas Law Review*, 2006. | None |
|                              | 2) Shephard, *Michigan Law Review*, 2005. | 2) Donohue and Wolfers, *Stanford Law Review*, 2005. | |

Despite the generally beneficial effect of capital punishment on crime, there are exceptions. One particular kind of crime where the death penalty shows no significant deterrent effect is multiple victim public shootings. This was the conclusion of a study I performed with Bill Landes at the University of Chicago.[72] This exception stems from the unique circumstances of these kinds of crimes: the vast majority of these killers either commit suicide or are killed at the scene of the crime. The threat of legal punishment, including the death penalty, doesn't really affect their actions since so many of these criminals expect to die in the course of their crime.

The death penalty has a beneficial effect even beyond deterring murders. Because capital punishment can be imposed if a victim dies in the commission of a rape, robbery, or aggravated assault, statistics show the death penalty also acts as a deterrent to these crimes as well.[73] This, however, doesn't mean that the death penalty should be applied directly to these crimes. There is such a thing as "too much" deterrence. For example, utilizing the death penalty too broadly can create some perverse incentives. Suppose the death penalty is used against robbers and rapists. These criminals would then become more determined to kill their victims and any potential witnesses since they would already be facing the death penalty. There would likely be fewer robberies and rapes, but those crimes would probably result in much higher numbers of dead victims.[74]

Polls consistently show that the vast majority of Americans support the death penalty. A 2006 ABC News/*Washington Post* poll found that 65 percent of Americans favor the death penalty for convicted murderers, with 32 percent opposed.[75] There is even majority support for the death penalty in such unlikely places as Brazil, Eastern Europe, Japan, and South Africa.[76] A plurality in Britain also supports it.[77] This should not be too surprising; as Supreme Court Justice Antonin Scalia noted, the death penalty was abolished in many countries by judicial fiat, despite widespread support for it among the general populations.[78]

A lot of people grasp intuitively an idea that economists only now are building a consensus toward: that the death penalty helps deter violent crimes and saves lives.

## What Decreased Crime? Part II

### Law Enforcement

> The nation's prison population grew 2.6 percent last year, the largest increase since 1999, according to a study by the Justice Department. The jump came *despite* a small decline in serious crime in 2002.... Alfred Blumstein, a leading criminologist at Carnegie Mellon University, said it was not illogical for the prison population to go up even when the crime rate goes down.... Professor Blumstein said... that it has become increasingly clear from statistical research that "there is no reason that the prison count and the crime rate have to be consistent." The crime rate measures the amount of crime people are suffering from, he said, while the prison count is a measure of how severely society chooses to deal with crime, which varies from time to time [emphasis added].
>
> —Fox Butterfield, *New York Times*[79]

Is it really surprising that the number of prisoners increased while crime rates fell?[80] Apparently it is to those who disregard incentives, a group that includes many criminologists as well as writers for the *New York Times*. Although these observers somehow doubt that locking up more criminals can deter crime, a large number of studies indicate that the more certain the punishment, the fewer the crimes committed.[81] Arrest rates of criminals are usually the single most important factor in reducing every type of crime. Sensational topics like the death penalty may get the most media attention, but it is everyday police work that really makes a neighborhood safer. Changes in the arrest rate account for around 16 to 18 percent of the drop in the murder rate.[82] Conviction rates explain another 12 percent. Arrest and conviction rates have an even larger effect on other types of violent crime. And their effect on property crimes is still greater, often two or three times larger than for violent crime overall.

While boosting arrest rates indisputably increases deterrence, the evidence on longer prison sentences is less clear. The reason is simple: methodologically, it's surprisingly difficult to measure how long criminals expect to be in prison. The actual time served is often much shorter than the official length of a criminal's sentence. Furthermore, the time that is served varies widely, even for a single type of crime, and depends on such factors as a suspect's criminal history and the severity of the offense. Unfortunately, this kind of data is not readily available to researchers.

Arrest and conviction rates and expected prison sentence lengths all deal with deterrence—the cost to the criminal of committing a crime. But some people commit crimes despite those threats. Obviously, locking up the most crime-prone individuals will further decrease crime by keeping habitual criminals off the streets. Indeed, putting more people in prison explains another 10 to 12 percent of the drop in crime rates.[83]

Simply being arrested or convicted, even without a prison sentence, carries its own substantial penalties. As we noted in Chapter Two, these reputational penalties are the worst penalties that many criminals face.

## What Decreased Crime? Part III

### Right-to-Carry Laws

Allowing citizens to defend themselves with guns may no longer be as controversial as the death penalty. There has been a remarkable change in attitude toward the benefits of concealed handguns over the last twenty years as thirty additional states have become right-to-carry states, bringing the total to forty by 2007. These states grant permits to people of a certain age (either eighteen or twenty-one) once they pass a criminal background check and, in some states, take a handgun training class. Of these states, Alaska, Vermont, and nearly all of Montana have no regulations at all. Eight additional states allow applicants to obtain concealed weapons permits if they can demonstrate a need for the weapon. Today, only Illinois and Wisconsin completely ban citizens from carrying concealed handguns.[84]

States have clearly found a societal benefit over the last few decades in expanding their citizens' rights to carry concealed handguns. It is revealing that no state that has relaxed its rules for obtaining concealed handgun permits has reversed course and instituted new restrictions.

The impact of these permits on crimes is no trivial matter; conservatively, there are over 4 million concealed handgun permits in the United States.[85] While relatively gun friendly states such as Pennsylvania and Florida have alone issued 1.1 million permits between them, even some places with strict gun regulations have a surprisingly large number of permit holders. This is certainly true for New York City (38,500) and Massachusetts (203,000).[86]

While concealed weapons allow people to protect themselves from criminals, there are obvious possible drawbacks to increasing the number of gun carriers. People can get hurt in accidents, or gun carriers may use their weapons irresponsibly. The main question is: do concealed handguns save more lives than they put at risk?

It is abundantly clear that legal gun owners themselves pose few risks.[87] The type of person who is willing to go through the permitting process tends to be law-abiding by nature. Most criminals, in contrast, aren't the type to go through the approval process, submit to a criminal background check, and pay their fees. For example, during the nineteen years between October 1, 1987 and December 31, 2006, Florida issued 1,228,284 concealed weapons permits but revoked just

158, or .01 percent, for any type of firearms violation. Even this figure exaggerates the risks, as almost all of these revocations were for non-threatening incidents such as unknowingly carrying a gun into a restricted area.[88] What's more, the rate of permit revocations in Florida has fallen over time, with zero to one revocations for firearms violations being recorded in each of the last five years.[89] Studying the issue, the *National Journal* found that permit holders "turn out to be unusually law-abiding, safer even than off-duty cops."[90]

It is also clear that legally owning a gun makes a person less likely to get hurt by a criminal. While police are, of course, extremely important in fighting crime, officers almost always arrive at the scene only after a crime has been committed. So what can individuals themselves do to deter criminals? Having a gun, in fact, is by far the most effective course of action. This is the finding of the U.S. Department of Justice's National Crime Victimization Survey, an annual survey conducted since 1973 of about 77,000 households comprising nearly 134,000 people.[91] This holds true whether the criminal is armed or unarmed and regardless of the location of the attack.

During the 1990s, for example, assault victims who used a gun for self-protection were injured 3.6 percent of the time. This contrasts with 5.4 percent of those who ran or drove away, 12.6 percent of those who screamed, and 13.6 percent of those who threatened the attacker without a weapon. Those who took no self-protective action at all fared the worst—55.2 percent of them were injured.[92] Gandhi's strategy of peaceful resistance may have worked against British imperialists who could be embarrassed by public attention, but criminals require other methods of persuasion.

Economist Stephen Bronars and I found significant evidence that criminals move out of areas where concealed handguns are legalized.[93] Our study analyzed counties that border each other on opposite sides of a state line. In such cases, counties in states that adopt right-to-carry laws see a drop in violent crime that is about four times larger than the simultaneous increase in violent crimes in the adjacent counties without such laws. Violent criminals may be brutal, but they're not necessarily stupid. At least they're smart enough to leave towns where they risk running into citizens carrying concealed handguns.

Concealed weapons clearly help to reduce crime. Overall, for the first eight to nine years that concealed-carry laws are in effect, murder rates fall by an average of 1 to 1.5 percent per year, while robbery and rape rates decline by about 2 percentage points.[94] The benefits of gun ownership also outweigh the drawbacks such as accidental deaths. These do happen, but they are relatively rare, with 649 cases reported among the nation's 100 million gun owners in 2004. What's more, academic research finds that accidental death rates do not increase with the passage of right-to-carry laws.[95]

Some analysts, however, continue to dispute the deterrent effect of concealed handguns. But even much of the research done by these supposed critics ends up showing substantial safety benefits associated with concealed weapons. For instance, in arguing that more guns create more crime, Mark Duggan provided thirty estimates of the impact of right-to-carry laws.[96] But after correcting for four typing mistakes, sixteen of his thirty estimates actually show statistically significant drops in crime, while only one shows a significant increase.[97] Some similar problems are found in the other major studies denying that right-to-carry laws reduce crime rates.[98]

### Academic Research by Economists on Right-to-Carry Laws:

|  | Reduced Violent Crime | No Discernable Effect on Violent Crime | Increased Violent Crime |
|---|---|---|---|
| Refereed Journal Publications | 1) Lott and Mustard, *Journal of Legal Studies*, 1997. | 1) Black and Nagin, *Journal of Legal Studies*, 1998. | None |
|  | 2) Bartley and Cohen, *Economic Inquiry*, 1998. | 2) Ludwig, *International Review of Law and Economics*, 1998. |  |

## Academic Research by Economists on Right-to-Carry Laws: (cont'd)

| | Reduced Violent Crime | No Discernable Effect on Violent Crime | Increased Violent Crime |
|---|---|---|---|
| Refereed Journal Publications | 3) Lott, *Journal of Legal Studies*, 1998. | 3) Donohue and Levitt, *Quarterly Journal of Economics*, 1999. | None |
| | 4) Bartley, *Economics Letters*, 1999. | 4) Hood and Neeley, *Social Science Quarterly*, 2000. | |
| | 5) Benson and Mast, *Journal of Law and Economics*, 2001. | 5) Duggan, *Journal of Political Economy*, 2001. | |
| | 6) Moody, *Journal of Law and Economics*, 2001. | 6) Duwe, Kovandzic, Moody, *Homicide Studies*, 2002. | |
| | 7) Mustard, *Journal of Law and Economics*, 2001. | 7) Kovandzic and Marvell, *Criminology and Public Policy*, 2003. | |
| | 8) Olsen and Maltz, *Journal of Law and Economics*, 2001. | 8) Dezhbakhsh and Rubin, *International Review of Law and Economics*, 2003. | |
| | 9) Plassmann and Tideman, *Journal of Law and Economics*, 2001. | 9) National Research Council, National Academies Press, 2005. | |
| | 10) Marvel, *Journal of Law and Economics*, 2001. | 10) Kovandzic, Marvell, and Vieraiis, *Homicide Studies*, 2005. | |
| | 11) Lott and Whitley, *Journal of Law and Economics*, 2001. | | |

## Academic Research by Economists on Right-to-Carry Laws: (cont'd)

|  | Reduced Violent Crime | No Discernable Effect on Violent Crime | Increased Violent Crime |
|---|---|---|---|
| Refereed Journal Publications | 12) Helland and Tabarrok, *Advances in Economic Analysis and Policy*, 2004.<br><br>13) Wilson, National Academies Press, 2005.<br><br>14) Lott and Whitley, *Economic Inquiry*, 2007.<br><br>15) Lott, University of Chicago Press, 1998 and 2000. |  | None |
| Non-Refereed Publications | 1) Bronars and Lott, *American Economic Review*, 1998.<br><br>2) Plassmann and Whitley, *Stanford Law Review*, 2003.<br><br>3) Lott and Landes, *The Bias Against Guns*, 2003. | 1) Ayres and Donohue, *American Law and Economics Review*, 1999.<br><br>2) Ayres and Donohue, *Stanford Law Review*, 2003. | None |

Overall, the three crime fighting techniques outlined above—increased use of the death penalty, rising arrest and conviction rates, and the passage of right-to-carry laws—account for between 50 and 60 percent of the drop in murder rates during the 1990s. While all these methods are the subject of much controversy, their effectiveness in reducing crime has been proven time and again.[99]

# What Didn't Really Matter? Part I

### Age and Race

As we saw in our discussion of abortion, different age groups commit crimes at different rates. Violent criminals are overwhelmingly male youths between the ages of seventeen and twenty-five. An offender's likelihood of committing murder rises until he is twenty years old, then falls after that. By the time a person is twenty-nine, his likelihood of committing murder has declined to about half of what it was at age twenty.[100] Although the relative rates that different age groups commit crime vary somewhat over time, in any year the odds of a person in his twenties committing murder are much higher than for those in their thirties. Presumably, if we could magically transform all the twenty-year-olds into thirty-five or forty-year-olds, there would be a huge decline in murder rates. Older people just don't commit as many violent crimes as the young.

Despite the sensitivity of the subject, it must be mentioned that race is also a very important factor in crime statistics.[101] African Americans are the most likely perpetrators of crime as well as the most common victims. In 2002, while the national murder rate was 5.6 per 100,000 people, the rate that African American males

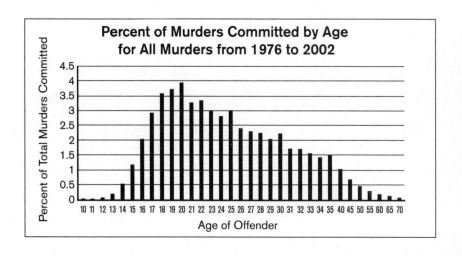

Percent of Murders Committed by Age for All Murders from 1976 to 2002

between seventeen and twenty-five committed murder was seventy-eight per 100,000, or about fourteen times the national rate. For white males of the same age group, the rate was fourteen per 100,000. It should also be noted that young African American males commit murder at a much higher rate than African Americans in general—in 2002, the overall African American murder rate was 24.1 per 100,000. This was well below its peak rate of 51.4 in 1991, although it is still much higher than the current rate of 3.6 for whites and 2.7 for all other ethnic groups. Murderers also overwhelmingly kill people of their own race. Ninety-one percent of African Americans are murdered by other African Americans, and 84 percent of whites are murdered by other whites.[102]

Although age and race are very important generally, these factors didn't play much of a role in pushing crime rates lower in the 1990s. The share of the population between sixteen and thirty slowly declined over most of the last thirty years. This slightly reduced crime, but is offset by the rise in the share of the African American population from 11.7 percent in 1976 to 13 percent in 2004. These and other demographic changes, however, are too minor and too slow to explain most of the year-to-year variations in crime rates. The impact of the changing age and demographic composition of America is simply swamped

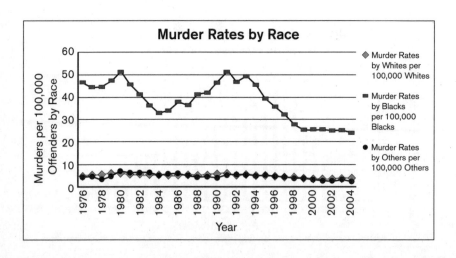

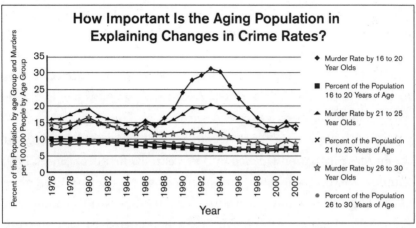

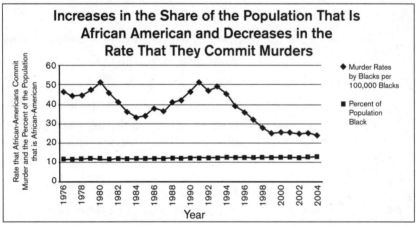

by the drastic fall in crime rates both among the young and among the
African American population at large.

## What Didn't Really Matter? Part II

### Gun Control

Gun control advocates seemed certain. They predicted that when the
federal assault-weapons ban expired on September 13, 2004—ten years
after taking effect—gun crimes would surge out of control. Sarah Brady,
a leading gun control advocate, warned that the ban's termination would

effectively "arm our kids with Uzis and AK-47s" and "fill" our streets with the weapons.[103] Senator Charles Schumer ratcheted up the rhetoric, labeling the banned guns "the weapons of choice for terrorists."[104] Firearm-related murders and robberies were expected to skyrocket. Only states with their own assault-weapon bans would escape the coming bloodshed, we were warned.

And what really happened? According to FBI statistics, during 2004 the murder rate nationwide fell by 3 percent, the first drop since 2000, with firearm deaths dropping by an impressive 4.4 percent. Even more remarkably, the monthly murder rate *fell* after the assault weapons ban expired. And not only did it fall, but it plummeted 14 percent from August through December.[105]

The murder rate in the seven states with their own assault-weapons bans declined by a smaller amount than in the forty-three states without such laws—an average 2 percent drop in states with bans compared to 3.4 percent in states without them. While it remains unclear how much of the drop in crime can be attributed to the expiration of the assault-weapons ban, it is readily apparent that the ban did nothing to reduce crime.

A study funded by the Justice Department during the Clinton Administration found that the effect of the assault weapons ban on gun violence "has been uncertain." The report's authors released updated findings in August 2004, analyzing crime data from 1982 through 2000 (which covered the first six years of the federal assault weapons ban). Their conclusion: "We cannot clearly credit the ban with any of the nation's recent drop in gun violence."[106]

The findings were unsurprising because there is nothing unique about the guns that had been banned. These weapons function the same as any semiautomatic hunting rifle does; they fire the same bullets with the same rapidity and produce the same damage. Although the phrase "assault weapon" conjures up images of military-style rapid-fire machine guns, machine guns were not covered by the ban—they were already illegal when the ban took effect, and remained so after the ban expired. The firing mechanisms in semiautomatic and machine guns are completely different. The entire firing mechanism of a semiautomatic gun has to be gutted and replaced in order to turn it into a machine gun.

The second most important piece of gun control legislation has been the 1994 Brady Act, which required criminal background checks for gun purchases and, until 1998, a five-day waiting period. But since its enactment, economists and criminologists have been unable to identify any impact on crime rates. The general problem with gun bans is that it's the law-abiding gun owners who obey them. Criminals find ways to get illegal guns, just like they find ways to get illegal drugs. If we want to further decrease gun crimes, banning citizens from owning guns has clearly shown itself to be an inefficient method.

## The Verdict Is Still Out

### Broken Windows and Community Policing

> Consider a building with a few broken windows. If the windows are not repaired, the tendency is for vandals to break a few more windows. Eventually, they may even break into the building, and if it's unoccupied, perhaps become squatters or light fires inside.
>
> Or consider a sidewalk. Some litter accumulates. Soon, more litter accumulates. Eventually, people even start leaving bags of trash from take-out restaurants there or breaking into cars.
>
> —James Q. Wilson and George L. Kelling[107]

In the early 1980s, James Q. Wilson and George L. Kelling articulated a persuasive new theory about crime. They argued that petty crime such as window breaking creates a vicious cycle whereby law-abiding citizens in a deteriorating neighborhood continually leave, to be replaced by criminals. If crime is rampant as evidenced by broken windows, criminals find it even easier to commit crimes with fewer law-abiding citizens around to witness them. So the key to fighting crime is to begin by cracking down on petty offenses. Some experts credit the huge drop in crime in New York City during the 1990s to a "broken windows" policy that strictly enforced laws against minor crimes like vandalism, public drunkenness, panhandling, and public urination.

There were 7,921 fewer murders in the United States in 2000 than in 1990.[108] New York City accounted for 1,572, or 20 percent, of that decline. The fall in New York City's murder rate in the 1990s was 2.4 times larger than the average drop for the thirty largest cities.[109] The declines in New York City's overall violent crime and property crime rates were not quite as large as the fall in murder rates, but they were still more than twice the national average.[110]

However, other factors in the city besides policing strategies were also changing in the 1990s. Probably the single most important factor was the increase in the number of full-time sworn police officers, which grew from 26,844 in 1990 to 39,779 by 2000.[111] The growth in the per capita number of officers in New York City was roughly two and a half times the rate in other large cities.[112] The city also greatly improved its hiring standards and increased officer pay.[113]

In fact, the entire nature of the city's police force was transformed in the 1990s. In the 1980s, the NYPD was undermanned, demoralized, and hamstrung by debilitating regulations. Michael Julian, a former NYPD chief of personnel, described how the department was hindered by the kinds of counterproductive affirmative action policies discussed earlier: "The department abandoned all physical screening of applicants in the '80s out of fear of lawsuits by minority applicants and women. Some officers hired under relaxed testing lack the strength to pull the trigger of a gun. There are hundreds, if not thousands of police officers on the streets today who, when a suspect runs from them, have no other option than to call another cop, because they do not have the physical ability to pursue them."[114] The NYPD, however, was one of the few departments during the 1990s that rejected the affirmative action trend. Starting in 1994, the police academy re-imposed strength standards that had been abandoned.[115] With more officers of higher quality, New York's arrest rates rose and criminals found it more difficult to commit crime.

Evidence for the overall effectiveness of the "broken windows" policy is mixed. On the one hand, there is strong evidence that when police step up enforcement efforts in an area through more frequent arrests or when private citizens become more able to defend themselves, criminals move on to more hospitable areas.[116] On the other hand, some analysts have found little relationship between young males' view of their neighborhoods as being crime-prone and the rate at which they themselves would commit crime.[117]

A more direct approach is to analyze crime rates across a range of cities that adopt the "broken-windows" approach or other similar policing strategies. Examining all U.S. cities with more than 10,000 people, I found that the effect of the different policing policies is decidedly mixed, with crime rates apparently going up and down in almost a random pattern. For cities with a "broken-windows" policy, murder and auto theft actually rose, while rapes and larceny fell.[118] Perhaps New York simply implemented this policy in a better way than other cities did. While "broken windows" may be one factor among many in reducing crime in the Big Apple, a city that implements the policy without taking additional measures should not expect positive results.

## A Few Odds and Ends about Crime

### How rent control killed the kitty cat: Enforcing the law when everyone involved wants to break it

Enforcing the law is difficult enough for violent crimes committed against innocent victims. But it's even more challenging in cases where both parties to an agreement want to break the law. A personal example will not only show how the law in such situations can be effectively enforced, but can even bring about self-enforcement by the parties involved. This is accomplished by creating an unusual disincentive— distrust between the two parties.

When I was a student at UCLA, a friend of mine who was moving away asked if he could leave with me an old stray cat that he had recently adopted. Because of its gray coat, he had named it Confederate. My wife and I felt sorry for the cat, so we asked the apartment manager about keeping him. She said that she had to check with the apartment's owners, but that we could keep the cat until she received an answer.

We didn't hear back for a few weeks. During that time I found out that Confederate had feline leukemia, a highly contagious disease among cats. Affected cats can still live long lives if given antibiotics, but without medication they can die from the most minor infection.

The manager eventually told us that we could only keep the cat if we paid a higher rent. Although I was willing to do this, she told us that this was not actually an option because it would violate rent control laws. I tried without any luck to find a new home for Confederate. His former owner said he couldn't keep pets in his new apartment, and other friends who I approached either already had a pet or simply didn't want to take in an old, sick cat. Workers at animal shelters told me they'd have to put the cat to sleep to keep him from infecting their other cats.

I called the rent control board, explained the situation, and asked if I could get a waiver from the rent control laws so that the owners would allow me to keep Confederate. The board's representative told me simply, "If they let you keep the cat, you can keep the cat. If they don't let you keep the cat, you can't keep the cat." I again related that I could only keep the cat if I paid a higher rent, but that this was illegal. Growing exasperated, the representative just repeated that I could keep the cat if the owners let me. The conversation went on like this for a good forty minutes.

Frustrated, I went to the legal aid clinic at the UCLA Law School to get advice from its young, aspiring lawyers. Their counsel was pretty straightforward: just break the law and pay the extra rent under the table. But the owners wouldn't consider it: if the city discovered that I was paying too much rent, the owners would have to repay me double the amount of the overpayment.

Perhaps, under some circumstances, a landlord might take the risk for a few months, but if someone were to overpay for several years, the penalty could be so huge that it would provide the tenant with an easy means to blackmail the landlord. Even if both the landlord and the tenant agreed to the overpayment, in such situations the landlord bears sole legal responsibility. The tenant is considered a victim.

This legal distinction is common in cities with rent control. Landlords who break rent-control laws in Los Angeles, for example, pay triple damages to the tenant. James Gordon of the Berkeley Rent Control board explained the law's rationale to me: "Depending on tenants to bring charges of overcharging works very well," he said.[119] He added that even though a complaint from a single tenant of illegal payments was not enough to ensure a landlord's conviction, "we do win most of these types of cases and the word of several different tenants is usually sufficient." Ultimately, illegal overpayments are rare, he explained, because landlords are so likely to be held accountable. They cannot even rest soundly after the tenants move out, since tenants can sue to recover payments even after leaving the apartment.

Sadly, left with no other choice, we had to put Confederate to sleep. What can the tale of my late kitty cat teach us about economics? It indicates that rent-control laws, by establishing clear legal categories of "perpetrators" and "victims" in deals agreed to by both parties, create distrust by landlords toward their tenants. Even when both sides would benefit from an under-the-table deal, the landlord knows the tenant will have a steadily growing incentive eventually to break their agreement and report the landlord to the authorities. And this distrust, in turn, creates an incredibly effective self-enforcement mechanism for the law.

The notion of creating self-enforcement through distrust may seem unusual, but we see the same mechanism at work in other realms, such as minimum wage regulations. Minimum wage laws naturally result in higher unemployment, since law-abiding firms will hire fewer workers if they have to pay more for them. Since some unemployed workers are willing to work for less than the minimum wage, and non-law-abiding firms want to hire them, it would seem that relying on workers themselves to enforce minimum wage laws would be doomed to failure. What can you do when both sides want to break the law?

Yet, self-enforcement of minimum wage laws is extremely effective. Only a fraction of 1 percent of U.S. citizens covered by the minimum wage are paid too little, and these rare violations primarily involve innocent mistakes by employers rather than outright lawbreaking. This law is successfully enforced by just a thousand federal agents who are additionally responsible for enforcing regulations on overtime pay, recordkeeping, and child labor standards. This result reflects the incentive that workers have to report the violations themselves. Although perhaps they first agree to the low salary because they badly need a job, the longer they work, the greater incentive they have to sue their employers, who are often forced to reimburse them double the amount of the underpayment. Thus we find that 75 to 80 percent of registered minimum wage violations are reported by the workers themselves.[120]

The self-enforcement mechanism, however, breaks down when it comes to illegal aliens. This group constitutes the overwhelming majority of workers who are paid less than the minimum wage. But why do companies prefer to hire illegals? Clearly, illegal aliens work for lower wages than U.S. citizens do. But firms have another, less widely-discussed incentive to hire them: they can count on illegals not to sue them at a later date for underpayment. Unlike U.S. citizens and legal residents, illegals risk being deported if they draw attention to themselves by filing lawsuits. The principle is similar to that of a street gang that requires someone to commit a violent crime before it will accept him as a full member. Like companies who hire illegals, the gang knows that it's safer to associate with others who would have something to lose by snitching to the police.

## Gunlocks and safe-storage laws

It seems indisputable that requiring gunlocks on handguns saves lives. President Bush clearly thinks so—although he may be perceived as a trigger-happy Texan cowboy, his administration distributed more than 32 million gunlocks by the end of 2005.[121] Furthermore, Bush approved the 2005 federal legislation helping to protect gun makers from reckless lawsuits, a bill that also required that all handguns be sold with locks.[122] State officials are increasingly adopting this view— eighteen states now impose criminal penalties on individuals whose guns are used improperly by juveniles.[123] Unfortunately, all these efforts are counter-productive because gunlocks and self-storage laws cause more deaths than they prevent.

Economists have found that other safety regulations have the same unintended effect of decreasing safety and increasing fatalities.[124] This is because some people offset the safety regulations by taking greater risks. One example is car safety regulations—some people drive faster and more recklessly when they feel safer inside their car. Car safety regulations reduce the number of injuries and deaths per accident, but they also lead to a greater total number of accidents. Overall, the number of deaths has stayed the same or actually increased with the adoption of car safety regulations.[125] A similar problem is evident with safety caps for medicine bottles. In the 1980s, child-resistant bottle caps actually resulted in "3,500 additional poisonings of children under age five annually from [aspirin-related drugs]...[as] consumers have been lulled into a less-safety-conscious mode of behavior by the existence of safety caps."[126] Some evidence even indicates that more children are being injured on playgrounds despite safety improvements because bored kids "are taking more risks in order to have fun."[127]

There is a similar trade-off for gunlocks. Locks may reduce accidental deaths, but they also make it more difficult for people to use guns defensively. And this encourages more criminal attacks, while simultaneously increasing the attackers' success rate. After these gunlock laws were adopted, there was about a 20 percent increase in the rate of both robberies and homicides inside people's homes. As previously noted, having a gun is by far the safest course of action when one is confronted by a criminal. But a locked gun is not nearly as accessible for defensive purposes.

Accidental gun deaths among children are, fortunately, much rarer than most people believe. Among America's 40 million children under the age of ten, there were just twenty accidental gun deaths in 2003.[128] While gun deaths receive a lot of attention, children in the same age range were forty-one times more likely to die from accidental suffocations, thirty-two times more likely to die from accidental drownings, and twenty times more likely to die as a result of accidental fires.[129] Among children under age fifteen, there were fifty-six accidental gun deaths in 2003—still a fraction of the deaths resulting from these other accidents for just the younger children.[130]

Given that there are over 90 million adults in the United States who own at least one gun, the overwhelming majority of gun owners must have been extremely careful, seeing as these figures were recorded before gunlocks were made mandatory.[131]

Even this relatively small number of tragic deaths is enough to convince many people that gunlocks are a good idea. If gunlocks can keep kids from accidentally killing themselves, their siblings, or their friends, then why not make them mandatory? But this logic is faulty, as the typical person who accidentally shoots and kills a child is not himself a child at all, but rather an adult male in his 20s.[132] In fact, very few children under age ten even have the strength to pull back the slide on a semi-automatic pistol. Most accidental shooters have a history of alcoholism and a criminal record.[133] They are also disproportionately involved in car crashes and are much more likely to have had their driver's license suspended or revoked. Even if gunlocks can stop children from using guns, they are simply not designed to stop adult males from firing their own weapons. Thus, it is hardly surprising that gunlocks show no significant impact on accidental gun deaths.

Gunlock laws, along with safe-storage regulations, are sometimes touted as a means to prevent suicides, but the great majority of academic studies have found this benefit to be small or non-existent.[134] There are a lot of ways to commit suicide, and people intent on doing so tend to find a way, with or without a gun. Economist John Whitley and I examined juvenile accidental gun deaths and suicides in all fifty states. We found that safe-storage laws had no impact on either type of death.[135] The laws were primarily followed by the kind of law-abiding families among whom hardly any accidental deaths were occurring. The laws did have an effect, however, in hindering the ability of these families to defend themselves against intruders. The states that adopted safe-storage laws from 1977 to 1998 faced over three hundred more murders and 4,000 more rapes per year. Burglaries also increased dramatically.[136]

Laws that force people to lock up their guns or discourage them from owning guns in the first place result in more deaths. Sometimes even the best-intentioned laws have unintended consequences that end up costing lives.

## Big Penalties for Small Environmental Crimes: A Surprisingly Good Policy

The United States Sentencing Commission sought to revamp the criminal penalties for corporations in the early 1990s. As mentioned earlier, one problem it addressed was an inconsistency in assessing penalties for environmental crimes. But there is another aspect of the problem. Traditionally, those who committed major environmental crimes—such as a massive oil spill from a tanker running aground—had to pay fines equivalent to the amount of the damages. In contrast, for minor environmental crimes—for example, dumping a barrelful of waste off the side of a ship—the fines were many times greater than the damage estimates. The commission reversed this relationship so that penalties for the more serious crimes became many times bigger than the damages.

While the new regulations seem logical, there was a sound reason for the earlier policy. A major oil spill is something that is nearly impossible to hide—we will know with near-certainty that the crime occurred and which ship was responsible. But it is much more difficult to identify the culprit—or even to detect the crime—for a smaller transgression like dumping just a barrelful of waste off the side of a boat. That's why the Sentencing Commission's policy change was actually counter-productive; if we want to create disincentives to environmental crime, we need to ensure that small-time offenders face relatively harsher penalties which act to offset the high probability that they'll get away with their crime.

# 5 Voting Rights and Voting Wrongs

Free markets and political freedom usually go hand in hand. While it's possible for an authoritarian government to preside over a free economy, such instances are very rare.[1] Regimes that don't trust their people enough to allow democratic elections usually like to keep close control over their subjects' economic activities and their access to information.

With so much at stake, it's worthwhile to subject our own electoral process and its history to some economic analysis. This kind of study leads to numerous unusual conclusions. First, we find that the growth of government, commonly attributed to President Roosevelt's New Deal, actually began earlier and was largely due to the enfranchisement of a single group of citizens. Second, measures meant to improve the voting system, such as the secret ballot, had some rather unintended consequences, particularly a large drop in the voting rate. Third, we can evaluate different types of fraud accusations in recent elections, distinguishing the legitimate problems from the partisan hype. And finally, we uncover some hidden agendas in the media and in public schools—the two mediums through which most people receive their information and form their world views.

## Women's Suffrage and the Growth of Government

Economists have long pondered why the government started growing precisely when it did. The U.S. federal government, aside from periods of wartime, consumed about 2 to 3 percent of GDP up until World War I. That was the first American war after which government spending did not return to pre-war levels. Then, in the 1920s, non-military federal spending began steadily climbing. President Roosevelt's New Deal in the 1930s—often viewed as the genesis of big government—really just continued an earlier trend. What changed before Roosevelt came to power that explains the growth of government? The answer is women's suffrage.

For decades, polls have shown that women as a group vote differently than men do. In presidential elections from 1980 to 2004, the "gender gap"—the difference between the way men and women vote—was in the double digits in six of the seven contests, reaching its peak of 22 percentage points in 2000.[2] This disparity—in which a higher percentage of women consistently vote Democratic—is very important politically. Excluding the women's vote, Republicans would have swept every presidential race but one between 1968 and 2004.[3]

Gender gaps exist on various issues. Perhaps the most significant one is the push for smaller government and lower taxes, which is a much higher priority for men than it is for women. This is seen in divergent attitudes held by men and women on many separate issues. Women were much more opposed to the 1996 federal welfare reforms, which mandated time limits for receiving welfare and imposed some work requirements on welfare recipients. Women are also more supportive of Medicare, Social Security, and education expenditures.[4]

Studies show that women are generally more risk averse than are men. Consequently, they are more supportive of government programs to insure against certain risks in life. Women's average incomes are also slightly lower and less likely to vary over time, which gives single women an incentive to prefer more progressive income taxes. Married women, however, bear a greater share of taxes through their husband's relatively higher income. Not surprisingly, married women are less supportive of higher taxes than are other women.[5]

But marriage also provides an economic basis for men and women to prefer different policies. Because women generally shoulder most of the child rearing responsibilities, married men are more likely to acquire marketable skills that help them earn money outside the household. If a man gets divorced, he still retains these skills. But if a woman gets divorced, she is unable to recoup her investment in running the household. Hence, single women who believe they will eventually get married, as well as married women who most fear divorce, look to the government for a form of protection against the risk of divorce—that is, a more progressive tax system and other government transfers of wealth from the rich to the poor. The more certain a woman is that she doesn't risk divorce, the more likely she is to oppose such transfers. This makes perfect sense—although every society has its altruists, most people don't want to share their household income with the government if they don't expect to benefit much from it.

So we see that certain kinds of women tend to support bigger government. Has it always been this way? Can women's suffrage in the late nineteenth and early twentieth century thus help to explain the growth of government?

A good way to analyze the direct effect of women's suffrage on the growth of government is to study how each of the forty-eight state governments expanded after women obtained the right to vote. Women's suffrage was first granted in western states with relatively few women—Wyoming (1869), Utah (1870), Colorado (1893), and Idaho (1896).[6] It was then extended to eight states between 1910 and 1914, and another seventeen states between 1917 and 1919. Thus, women could vote in twenty-nine states before women's suffrage was achieved nationwide in 1920 with the adoption of the Nineteenth Amendment to the Constitution.

If women's suffrage increased government, our analysis should show a few definite indicators. First, women's suffrage would have had a bigger impact on government spending and taxes in states with a greater percentage of women. And secondly, the size of government in western states should have steadily expanded as women comprised an increasing share of each state's voting populations.

Women's suffrage dramatically increased total voting turnout, as demonstrated in Figure 1. Voting participation as a percentage of the adult population[7] immediately rose from 25 to 37 percent after achieving suffrage, with a slower, continuing rise to 43 percent over the subsequent decade.[8] Figure 2 graphs the relationship between the granting of women's suffrage and per capita state government expenditures and revenue.[9] This chart shows that state governments grew significantly immediately after women were enfranchised.[10] State government spending had fallen for four of the five years before women began voting, reaching its lowest point just before the granting of suffrage. But within four years after women's suffrage, state government expenditures had risen above the previous peak. Within eleven years, real per capita spending had more than doubled—an amazing increase in the size of state governments.[11]

Yet, as suggestive as these graphs are, we must still consider whether women's suffrage itself caused the growth in government, or did the government expand due to some political or social change that accompanied women's suffrage?

Fortunately, there was a unique aspect of women's suffrage that allows us to answer this question: of the nineteen states that had not passed women's suffrage before the approval of the Nineteenth Amendment, nine approved the amendment, while the other ten states had suffrage imposed on them. If some unknown factor caused

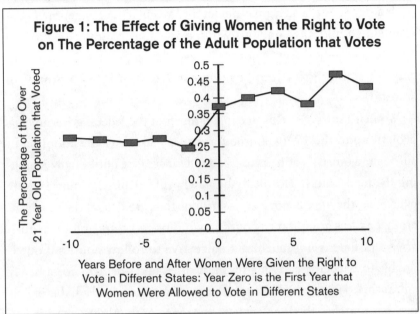

Figure 1: The Effect of Giving Women the Right to Vote on The Percentage of the Adult Population that Votes

The Percentage of the Over 21 Year Old Population that Voted

Years Before and After Women Were Given the Right to Vote in Different States: Year Zero is the First Year that Women Were Allowed to Vote in Different States

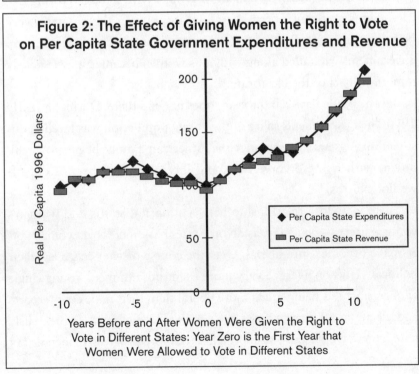

Figure 2: The Effect of Giving Women the Right to Vote on Per Capita State Government Expenditures and Revenue

Real Per Capita 1996 Dollars

◆ Per Capita State Expenditures
■ Per Capita State Revenue

Years Before and After Women Were Given the Right to Vote in Different States: Year Zero is the First Year that Women Were Allowed to Vote in Different States

both a desire for larger government and women's suffrage, then government should have only grown in states that voluntarily adopted suffrage. This, however, is not the case—after approving women's suffrage, a similar growth in government was seen in both groups of states.[12]

Women's suffrage helps to explain much of the federal government's growth up to the 1960s. In the forty-five years after the adoption of suffrage, women's voting rates gradually increased until finally matching the men's rates. This delay by newly enfranchised groups in fully exercising the vote is not rare, as groups that are denied the vote generally pay less attention to politics than those who are enfranchised—after all, there is not much of an incentive to follow politics if one is unable to participate.[13] As a result, it often takes decades for a newly enfranchised group to cultivate an interest in politics and a habit of voting that matches the involvement of groups with a longer voting history. The significance of this gradual increase in the women's vote between the 1920s and the 1960s is that the size of state and federal governments expanded along with it as women became an increasingly important part of the electorate.[14]

But the battle between the sexes does not end there. During the early 1970s, just as women's share of the voting population was leveling off, something else was changing: the American family began to break down, with rising divorce rates and increasing numbers of out-of-wedlock births.

There is a close relationship between marital status and women's voting patterns—generally, as divorce rates have increased, women voters have become more liberal. Over the course of women's lives, their political views on average vary more than those of men. Young single women start out being much more liberal than their male counterparts and are about 50 percent more likely to vote Democratic. As previously noted, these women also support a higher, more progressive income tax as well as more educational and welfare spending. But for married women this gap is only one-third as large, and married women with children become even more conservative. But divorced women with children suddenly become 75 percent more likely to vote for Democrats than single men.[15]

Perhaps not too surprisingly, government policies have helped to create more support for still more government. For example, no-fault divorce laws helped to drive up divorce rates, resulting in more divorcées who tend to support big government programs. Suppose, for example, that a man wants to leave his wife. With at-fault divorce, the husband must get his wife to agree to the divorce and essentially has to pay her for the right to leave the marriage. The more that the wife has invested in the relationship, the more she will demand in compensation before she will let the husband have the divorce. But no-fault divorce laws reverse this situation and greatly weaken the wife's bargaining position—if the husband wants to leave, the wife has to bargain to try to convince him to stay in the marriage. Thus, with no-fault divorce, women face a real risk if they invest heavily in family life; the more they invest in the family, the weaker their bargaining position becomes. Consequently, women are more likely to keep their careers in order to retain marketable skills in case their marriage fails. And the tendency to invest less in family life and more in preparation for a possible life after divorce makes relationships more fragile and divorce more likely.

Women's suffrage ushered in a sea change in American politics that affected policies aside from taxes and the size of government. For example, states that granted suffrage were much more likely to pass Prohibition, for the temperance movement was largely dominated by middle-class women.[16] Although the "gender gap" is commonly thought to have arisen only in the 1960s, female voting dramatically changed American politics from the very beginning.

## Suppressing Voter Turnout: The Poll Tax, Secret Ballots, and Literacy Tests

Most Americans today would agree that secret ballots were a great boon to democracy, while the poll tax and literacy tests—which were often designed to suppress the African American vote in certain states—were terrible injustices. These suppositions are doubtlessly true, but studies show a surprising effect of these measures on voter turnout: while the poll tax significantly reduced voting participation rates, secret ballots also lowered turnout. In contrast, literacy tests actually had little effect on voting rates during most of the years in which they were used.

The poll tax—a fee that must be paid before a citizen can either register or vote—was originally meant to ensure that those voting on government expenditures would also contribute something—even if just a symbolic amount—to the state coffers.[17] Yet, the poll tax became the clearest-cut example of a policy that discourages voting.[18] Sixteen states implemented a poll tax since 1870, although by 1963 only five still retained such fees, which were finally banned from federal elections in 1964 and from state elections in 1965.[19] While the poll tax was only used in a few northern and western states, including Massachusetts, Nevada, and Pennsylvania, it was implemented in all eleven southern states, primarily as a means to discourage African Americans from voting. Indeed, many southern whites viewed the practice as "the main solution to the suffrage problem of disenfranchising African Americans without disenfranchising too many whites."[20] Although poll taxes were relatively small (usually just a dollar or two) and changed little over time, they effectively reduced voter participation rates by around 10 percentage points.[21]

Poll taxes were in effect for so long that voting rates were still depressed long after their elimination. When the taxes were abolished, voter participation rates rose a mere 4 percentage points in the following election. It took over two decades before voting rates returned to their pre-poll tax levels. For Alabama, Arkansas, Mississippi, Texas, and Virginia, turnout rates were still reduced by around a percentage point even into the early 1980s.[22] Here we see the same delay in fully exercising voting rights that was evident after women gained the vote. Among African Americans, many would-be voters had lost interest in political issues while the poll tax prevented them from voting. After the tax was rescinded, it took African Americans a generation to recapture their previous level of political involvement.

One would not normally associate a manifestly discriminatory practice like the poll tax with a progressive reform like the introduction of secret ballots. But there are many aspects of secret ballots that defy conventional wisdom. Secret ballots were not a fixture of early American democracy. They were first introduced in Kentucky in 1882, with South Carolina representing the last state to adopt them in 1950. Secret ballots were implemented to encourage voting by making the system fairer. They certainly succeeded in this among many voters, who could finally vote without fear of offending or angering anyone by their choice.[23]

But overall, secret ballots had the opposite effect than intended—voting participation fell by an average of 4 to 5 percentage points when secret voting was introduced.[24] This can partly be explained by a more nefarious purpose for which secret ballots were used. As historians have noted, southern Democrats used the secret ballot "to depress the turnout of illiterate voters, and thus keep Republicans and Populists from power."[25] This was accomplished by switching the type of ballot simultaneously with the introduction of secret voting. Before the secret ballot, voting was as easy as selecting a colored card that represented a political party. But afterward, party names were written out on the ballots, thus making it more difficult for illiterate citizens to vote.[26] However, this only explains a small part of the drop in voting caused by the secret ballot—only a few percentage points of eligible voters were functionally illiterate, and many of them didn't vote even before the secret ballot's introduction.[27]

Much more significantly, secret ballots lowered voting rates in a beneficial way—they helped to reduce vote buying. With secret ballots, the practice of paying people to vote for a certain candidate became less useful, since it was difficult to verify for whom a person voted.[28] And when people stopped getting paid for voting, they voted less often.

Literacy tests arrived later than secret ballots. Nineteen states eventually instituted them, with nine of them adopting the requirement after 1900. Before casting a ballot, prospective voters were usually required to read some common document such as the U.S. Constitution.[29] Although literacy tests are commonly associated with the South, a majority of states with literacy tests—eleven of them—were in other regions: Arizona, California, Connecticut, Delaware, Maine, Massachusetts, New Hampshire, New York, Oregon, Washington, and Wyoming.

For decades, literacy tests had no discernable effect because illiterate voters and poor African Americans were already discouraged from voting by the poll tax.[30] From the 1930s to the early 1950s, however, southern states began phasing out the poll tax. In need of a new method to keep African Americans from the polls, southern state officials began subjectively administering literacy tests to achieve this goal. Literacy tests reduced voting in southern states that had them by an estimated 6 percentage points in 1948.[31] These tests helped to keep Southern Democrats in office until the tests were eliminated in all nineteen states by the 1965 Voting Rights Act. Despite the exploitation of literacy tests for these ends in the mid-twentieth century, however, it was the timeworn poll taxes and secret ballots—not literacy tests—that historically had the biggest effect on voting results in the south.

## Voter Fraud

Every honest person wants national elections to be fair and accurate. In the United States, we have adopted all sorts of regulations to encour-

age voting and to ensure the integrity of the electoral process, including ID requirements, absentee ballots, pre-election voting, voting by
mail, and registration procedures and deadlines. Some of these measures are controversial, with critics contending that they actually discourage voter turnout or increase voter fraud. These critics have a
point: from a basic economics perspective, if we make voting more
"costly" by wasting voters' time in fulfilling onerous regulations, we
can expect that fewer people will vote. However, a comprehensive
study of voting regulations leads to a different conclusion; while a few
regulations do indeed raise the likelihood of fraud, most of them
increase turnout by instilling confidence in the voting system.

Poll taxes indisputably lowered voter turnout—in many places, that
was their main purpose. But the effects of regulations meant to decrease
fraud are less clear. These are geared toward a legitimate purpose, for
electoral fraud remains a serious concern in the United States. Cities
such as Philadelphia, for example, have become so notorious for voting fraud that the old mantra "vote early and often" seems to have
become the city motto.[32] In one particularly egregious case in that city,
Democratic poll watcher Fani Papanikolau—who was actually a New
Jersey resident—voted over and over again by assuming the identity of
dead people. Papanikolau was ultimately indicted on over one hundred
counts of election fraud and forgery.[33] Similar cases have been found in
Atlanta,[34] while voter registration rolls in St. Louis are so out of date
that people's names were used to vote up to ten years after their
death.[35]

While Florida is best known for allegations of voter disenfranchisement in the 2000 presidential election, the state has long suffered from
serious electoral fraud. In the 1997 Miami mayoral election, thousands
of fraudulent absentee ballots changed the election's outcome.[36] The
following year, out of 8.1 million registered voters, Florida officials
found that 17,702 were deceased, 47,000 were registered to vote at
multiple locations, and 50,483 were convicted felons with no right to

vote.[37] These problems are also found in other states, some of which have jurisdictions that show more registered voters than there are people.[38] The *Wall Street Journal*'s John Fund, the author of a book on electoral fraud, has even speculated that the close 2006 Senate elections in both Montana and Virginia—and thus control of the Senate—were likely determined by voter fraud.[39]

This kind of fraud is enabled by certain voting regulations meant to increase turnout. For example, absentee ballots make voting more convenient for those outside of their voting district, but they are also "notorious" sources of voter fraud.[40] The Election Assistance Commission reported in 2006 that "there is virtually universal agreement that absentee ballot fraud is the biggest problem."[41] Consider one outrageous example: in 1998, former Pennsylvania Democratic congressman Austin Murphy was convicted of electoral fraud after forging the names of nursing home residents on absentee ballots. Nursing home administrators were even paid a bounty for access to their patients.[42]

In addition to enabling forgery, absentee voting makes it easier to buy votes because absentee ballots, like ballots before the advent of secret voting, can be shown to others before being submitted. With 25 percent of voters using absentee ballots in the 2006 general election, these drawbacks are hard to ignore.[43]

Similarly, while allowing prospective voters to register by mail makes it easier to vote, it also increases fraud. In October 2006 in Missouri, the left-wing Association of Community Organizations for Reform Now (ACORN) turned in at least 1,500 apparently fraudulent voter registration cards in St. Louis and another 3,000 more in Kansas City. Other problematic registrations appeared throughout the state, including forged signatures and the registration of ineligible teenagers and deceased individuals.[44]

As a result of these problems with voter fraud, bipartisan support has developed for stricter voter registration rules and for voter identification requirements.[45] Nevertheless, these requirements are opposed by some Democratic politicians who are concerned that anti-fraud rules will discourage legitimate voters from casting a ballot. Senator John Kerry (D-Mass) even denounced photo identification requirements as "a new Jim Crow era poll tax."[46] Republicans, for their part, tend to support stricter anti-fraud rules, claiming they will increase voting rates by instilling confidence in the voting system. The clash between the two sides has resulted in vigorous court battles in such states as Arizona, Georgia, Indiana, and Missouri.[47]

How can we ascertain whether stricter anti-fraud regulations increase or decrease voting turnout? One place to start is to study the impact such rules have had in other countries. A good example is Mexico, which implemented some unusually stringent anti-fraud regulations in 1991. To vote there, a person must present a voter ID card that includes a photograph as well as a thumbprint. The cards themselves are virtually counterfeit-proof, using holographic images, imbedded security codes, and a magnetic strip containing still more security information. As an extra precaution, voters' fingers are dipped in indelible ink to prevent people from voting multiple times.

Furthermore, Mexican voters cannot register by mail; they must go in person to a registration office to apply for a voter ID card, then return three months later to get it. Absentee ballots were banned due to their misuse during the 1988 presidential election. Although they were reintroduced for the 2006 election, their use is closely regulated, with voters required to request a ballot at least six months prior to the election.[48]

How have these measures affected voting rates? Voter turnout averaged 68 percent in the three presidential elections held since the reforms were adopted, compared to a 59 percent average rate in the three elections before the reforms.[49] Clearly, more citizens were encouraged to vote by the prospect of clean elections.[50]

We cannot expect to find this large of a change when American voting regulations are strengthened because there is nowhere near the same level of corruption as in Mexico. Additionally, in the United States, photo IDs have only been required in a few state general elections beginning in 2006, making it too early to evaluate their effectiveness. However, we do have data on the effect of other regulations. These include anti-fraud measures such as non-photo ID requirements and registration deadlines, as well as rules meant to increase voter turnout such as allowing provisional ballots, "no excuse" absentee ballots, registration by mail, and pre-election day voting.[51] Surprisingly, none of these regulations appear to have any effect on voter participation rates.[52]

Yet, these "non-results" may be misleading. Consider just the anti-fraud measures. On the one hand, these regulations may reduce the total number of votes cast either by usefully eliminating fraudulent votes or by detrimentally discouraging voters by complicating the voting process. On the other hand, anti-fraud regulations may increase voting rates by raising confidence in the voting system. A non-result may simply be the result of all these effects occurring at the same time.

How can we disentangle the different possibilities? One solution is to study the effect of the two kinds of regulations—those that make voting more "costly" by making regulations more strict, and "easy" regulations that make voting less costly by simplifying voting procedures—on voting rates in counties with low rates of fraud. We can then compare these results with the regulations' effect on voting rates in high-fraud counties known as "hot spots."

The American Center for Voting Rights provides the only comprehensive national list of voter fraud hot spots.[53] Its 2005 report listed six major hot spots: Cuyahoga County, Ohio; St. Clair County, Illinois; St. Louis County, Missouri; Philadelphia, Pennsylvania; King County, Washington; and Milwaukee County, Wisconsin. Analyzing the effect of voting regulations in these counties, we find that "costly" regulations increased voting rates, while "easy" regulations reduced them. The changes were small, never exceeding a few percentage points, but neither type of regulation had any discernable effect outside the fraud hot spots. This result strongly indicates that "costly" regulations encourage voting by instilling confidence in the voting system, while "easy" regulations lower turnout by increasing the perception of a high likelihood of fraud.[54]

There is only one regulation that impacts turnout outside of fraud hot spots: pre-election day voting. Allowing voting before election day results in a 1.5 to 5 percentage point drop in voter participation. This would surprise some analysts who would expect pre-election day voting to increase voting rates either by making voting easier or by allowing the casting of more fraudulent votes.[55] Yet, the result is quite consistent with the general connection between voting turnout and fraud outlined above: by loosening voting regulations, pre-election day voting increases fraud and thereby discourages voters from participating in an election.

## Voting Machines

> 1 million black votes didn't count in the 2000 presidential election. It's not too hard to get your vote lost—if some politicians want it to be lost.
>
> —*San Francisco Chronicle*, June 20, 2004

Ballot fraud by individuals is clearly a problem in the American electoral system. But many people believe there is a far more extensive crisis in American voting. There is a corrosive perception that the voting system selectively prevents certain people, especially African Americans, from voting through the widespread manipulation of voting machines. Democratic operatives repeatedly asserted that punch card machines disenfranchised large numbers of Florida voters in the 2000 presidential election. Since then, litigants with complaints about punch card voting

machines tried unsuccessfully to derail California's 2003 special gubernatorial election, which was eventually won by Arnold Schwarzeneg-
ger. Other states, such as Ohio, faced similar litigation from the
American Civil Liberties Union during the 2004 election.[56]

Polls show that a high percentage of Americans believe that systematic disenfranchisement is occurring. A 2006 poll found that only 30
percent of African Americans and 45 percent of Democrats feel confi-
dent that their votes will be counted. Among all voters, the number is
still low at 60 percent.[57] The question of disenfranchisement, it seems,
has become an increasingly pressing political issue.

Concerns over punch card ballots have led to billions of dollars
being spent to develop new voting methods, reversing a decades-long
increase in the prevalence of punch cards. The number of voters using
punch cards plummeted from 34 million in 2000 to just over 4 million
in 2006. Optical scan ballots, used by 69.5 million people, are now the
most frequent method for voting. Electronic machines are a close second, with 66.6 million users.[58] All these efforts to eliminate punch
cards, however, were counter-productive because punch cards perform
better in many ways than the machines that are replacing them.

Some legitimate problems with voting machines do exist. Perhaps
the most famous of these is the occurrence of "non-voted" ballots—
punch cards on which a vote is recorded either for more than one candidate in a single race or for none at all. During the 2000 presidential
election in Florida, representatives from both parties—as well as their
lawyers—spent hours discussing ballots that lacked a recorded vote for
the presidential race. Some argued that non-voted ballots stemmed
from problems in using punch card machines, while others maintained
that they largely reflected a voter's choice simply not to vote for the top
race on the ballot.

Nationally, the non-voted ballot rate for typical presidential elections
is about 3 percent for punch cards, 2.9 percent for electronic voting
machines (DREs), 2.1 percent for optical scans, and 1.9 percent for

paper ballots and lever machines.[59] In a study of the 2004 presidential elections in Ohio, I arrived at a similar finding. Votomatic punch cards, used in 69 of Ohio's 88 counties, averaged a 2.4 percent rate of non-voted ballots, compared to 2 percent for optical scans, 1.5 percent for levers, and 1.1 percent for electronic machines.[60]

These findings, however, do not tell the entire story. The debate has overwhelmingly focused on the presidential race, which is understandable in light of the worldwide publicity generated by the 2000 Florida vote. But if we look at races lower down the ballot than the presidential race, such as those for Congress and state legislatures, we find that Votomatic punch card machines actually perform much better than electronic or lever machines and are about as reliable as optical scans.

People naturally cast fewer votes for races lower down the ballot because they don't know or care as much about those positions as they do about the presidency. But the drop-off rate varies systematically according to the type of voting machine. And, most interestingly, this drop-off is much less evident for punch cards than for other types of machines. The rate of non-voted ballots for Ohio Senate races on Votomatic punch card machines was just under 10 percent, compared to 18 percent for electronic and lever machines. Looking across all of Ohio's races, switching from Votomatic punch cards to electronic or lever machines—as so many precincts have done nationwide—would have resulted in about 200 more non-voted ballots in the average Ohio ward of 1,696 voters.[61]

Why do punch cards do so well at the bottom of the ballot? The answer lies in what I call "voter fatigue." People will vote in fewer races when it takes them more time or effort to vote. Recent research indicates that electronic machines encounter problems with "the willingness of voters to navigate through multiple ballot screens before casting a vote (and) delays caused by the use of the review feature when coupled with extended ballots."[62] These extra screens and reviews mean it takes up to 20 percent longer to use electronic voting machines than punch cards. Consequently, voters on electronic machines get tired faster, and some don't make it to the end of the ballot. The ability of elderly voters to master the technology of electronic voting has also been questioned, as "older adults consistently perform more poorly than younger adults in performing computer-based tasks."[63] Whatever their other faults, punch cards are relatively quick and simple to use.

Contrary to popular belief, Votomatic punch card machines were also the only voting method for which African Americans had consistently lower rates of non-voted ballots than whites had.[64]

With all the debate over voting machines and non-voted ballots, one would think that the machines must be too complicated for many people to figure out. But education is not systematically related to the rate of non-voted ballots. The pattern appears completely random, with the rate high for those with less than a ninth grade education, low for those with some high school, high for high school graduates, low for college graduates, and high again for those with post-graduate degrees. Nor does income level consistently correspond to the rate of non-voted ballots although, quite interestingly, the richest voters are fifteen times more likely to cast a non-voted ballot than the poorest ones.[65]

Ironically, the switch to electronic machines not only failed to rectify the problems they were supposed to solve, but they have sparked new concerns over potential vote fraud. These range from the lack of a "paper trail" on most machines to the possibility of manipulating their programming.[66] Similar to the concerns over punch cards, these new objections are largely misguided—paper records are not necessarily superior to electronic voting machines, which keep three separate "read only" memories that are unchangeable. Likewise, tampering would be near-impossible, since electronic voting machines are stand-alone units that are not connected to the Internet or any other network.[67] Tampering with them would be akin to someone trying to hack into your own personal computer while it isn't online.

Most electronic voting machines transfer election results to a compact disk or some other "read only" format. These CDs are then taken to a central location where they are read into a computer. In the twenty-plus years that these machines have been used in counties across the nation, there has never been a verified case of tampering.[68]

When computer scientists warn of possible tampering with voting machines, they are not referring to hacking attempts, but to someone physically breaking open the lock on each individual machine and reprogramming each computer. Even if someone could break into a machine and overcome the supposedly tamper-proof seals without being noticed, going through one computer at a time hardly seems like a realistic way to steal an election. Besides, accuracy checks conducted on the machines before, during, and after the votes would detect any reprogramming to transfer votes from one candidate to another.

Contrary to the various conspiracy theories, many people who registered non-votes for some races were most likely conflicted over whom to vote for and simply decided not to support anyone. Undoubtedly, the promotion of these unfounded accusations of selective disenfranchisement offer a short-term political benefit for certain groups. But such claims risk poisoning the political debate for years to come.

## The 2000 Florida Vote

Florida's 2000 presidential election was a battleground for not just punch card voting, but for explosive charges of systematic discrimination against African American voters. Reverend Jesse Jackson was not alone in charging "a clear pattern of suppressing the votes of African Americans."[69] Mary Francis Berry, then chairwoman of the U.S. Civil Rights Commission, called for a criminal investigation of the vote. But how does one determine empirically whether there was systematic discrimination against African Americans during the Florida election and whether such discrimination cost Al Gore the election?

Data are available for every Florida precinct on vote totals for each candidate, the number of non-voted ballots, and on voters' race and party affiliation. At first glance, the numbers seem to confirm the disturbing claims that African American had higher rates of non-voted ballots than other groups. But critics are wrong in charging that this aberration cost Gore the election, for the group most "victimized" by non-voted ballots, in fact, was African American *Republicans*.

African American Republicans who voted in Florida were an incredible fifty-four to sixty-six times more likely than the average African American to have had a ballot declared invalid. Another way of phrasing this is that for every two additional African American Republicans in the average precinct, there was one additional ballot that did not register a vote for president.[70]

In 2000, there were 22,270 registered African American Republicans voters in Florida—or about one for every twenty registered African American Democrats. In a state where the 2000 presidential race was decided by fewer than 1,000 votes, this is no trivial number. Since we can assume that these voters, as Republicans, would vote mostly for the Republican candidate, the overall numbers show that George W. Bush was hurt more by the loss of African American votes than was Al Gore.

These results are indeed disturbing. They indicate that, if there was a conspiracy to disenfranchise some group of Florida voters, that effort was directed at Republicans, not at African Americans as a race. This conclusion conforms with another fact that the data reveal: among white voters, Republicans were much more likely than Democrats to cast non-voted ballots. Additionally, I found that the overall rate of non-voted ballots was 14 percent higher when the county election supervisor was a Democrat, and 31 percent higher when the supervisor was an African American Democrat.[71]

So where does all this leave us? It's hard to believe that there was some nefarious plot to disenfranchise Republicans overall or African

American Republicans in particular. More likely, a significant propor-
tion of these Republicans, particular those living in heavily Democratic areas, simply did not like the choices for president and therefore
declined to vote for that race. Although tampering cannot be definitely
ruled out, we can dismiss claims that the poor and African Americans
overall were disenfranchised, since figures show that income and race
were only one-third as important in explaining spoiled ballots as were
the methods and machines used in voting.[72]

## Early Media Calls

What happens when exit polls leak out on election day? Would you still
vote if you knew the election was already decided and your candidate
had lost?

As noted earlier, people are usually most interested in voting for the
top races on the ballot—for president, governor, or U.S. Senate. Close
contests in these top races typically increase voter turnout, while an
expected blowout keeps more voters at home. It is widely assumed that
an expected landslide primarily discourages those who support the losing candidate, since no one wants to be on the losing side. This is borne
out by post-election surveys in which greater proportions of respondents claim to have voted for the winning candidate than is indicated
by the actual vote count. [73]

The media has made three early calls in presidential elections: 1980,
1996, and 2000. During the landslide Republican victory in 1980,
NBC named Reagan the winner at 8:15 p.m., well before voting ended
on the West Coast. President Jimmy Carter "dispirited" many fellow
Democrats when he conceded the election at 9:45 p.m., an hour and
fifteen minutes before voting had ended in California.[74] Many Democratic candidates on the West Coast blamed their own losses on
Carter's early concession, which allegedly discouraged Democrats from
going to the polls.[75]

Carter's defenders countered that Reagan's landslide ensured that these Democratic candidates would have lost anyway. His supporters also cast doubt on surveys showing that Democratic voters were discouraged by the early concession, arguing that fellow Democrats wanted to blame the party's losses on a tactical mistake by Carter.

When Bob Dole challenged Bill Clinton for the presidency in 1996, it was the Republicans' turn to suffer from an early election call. Citing exit polls, the networks called the election for Clinton before the polls on the West Coast had closed. Republicans blamed the media for discouraging their West Coast supporters from voting, while Democrats insisted that Republican candidates would have lost anyway.

What impact do early media calls actually have on voting? It is hard to estimate their impact in the 1980 and 1996 elections because they affected all the races in the Western states—it is difficult to determine whether it was the early election call or something unique to those states that caused the drop off in voting. Fortunately, the 2000 election was different: polling had ended in most of Florida, but was still ongoing in the state's ten western Panhandle counties, when the media declared that the Democrats had won the presidential race as well as the Florida Senate races.[76]

Florida's polls were open until 8:00 p.m. on election day. But Florida's heavily Republican Panhandle counties are on central, not eastern, time, so they stayed open for an additional hour. Yet, beginning at 8:00 p.m. EST, all the major networks (ABC, CBS, CNN, FOX, MSNBC, and NBC) incorrectly and repeatedly announced that the polls were closed in the entire state. CBS national news alone made eighteen statements indicating that the polls had closed.

Even for the western Panhandle voters who knew that their polls were actually still open, they still had to consider the media claims that the races' outcomes had already been determined. The Florida Senate race was called for the Democrats fifty-eight minutes before the polls closed in the western Panhandle, while the presidential race was called for Al Gore twelve minutes before the polls closed. Even before the presidential race was called, the media offered numerous reports indicating that Gore appeared likely to win.[77]

After the election, surveys showed that the early media call and the perception of Democratic victories had discouraged voters in the western Panhandle. Two-thirds of voters in that region voted Republican, so even if the early call discouraged voters from both parties at the same rate, more Republicans ended up not voting. According to Democratic strategist Bob Beckel, George W. Bush suffered a net loss of up to 8,000 votes due to the early media call. Another survey of western Panhandle voters by John McLaughlin & Associates, a Republican polling company, estimated 10,000 lost votes for Bush. But both surveys suffer from the same problem afflicting the polls done after Carter's defeat: respondents may have let their political interests color their answers. In this case, disgruntled Republicans may have been more likely to exaggerate the effect of the early call.[78]

That voting dropped, at least to some degree, after the early call is confirmed in the sworn statements from many election clerks and poll workers. According to a Clerk for Elections in Okaloosa County, for example, "We had over 1300 people turn out with an average of about one hundred voters per hour until the last hour. When the doors were open, there were quite a number of people waiting in line to vote. There was a heavy flow throughout the day....Soon after 7:00 p.m., I noticed that the volume dropped to almost zero."[79]

Statistical evidence supports this, too. During the 2000 election, the western Panhandle counties suffered a drop in turnout not only relative to their past turnout rates, but also compared to the rest of Florida. Comparing how each county's turnout changed during the day, the western Panhandle counties also suffered a drop relative to the rest of the states.[80] The evidence indicates that the early call cost Bush a net loss of at least 7,500 votes.[81]

The early call in Florida probably also affected other races across the country because it made it appear as if Gore had won the election before the polls closed in many other states. But it is much more difficult to estimate the effect outside of Florida, since only that state has data to allow for a comparison between polling stations that remained open after the early call and polling stations that were closed. However, a simple look indicates that if the results for Florida are correct, the early call most likely affected some other races. For example, Democrat Maria Cantwell won a Senate seat in Washington state by just 2,200 votes. If the early call's effect in Washington was 1/24th of the smallest estimated effect of the early call in Florida, then Cantwell would have lost to Republican Slade Gordon. This outcome alone may have significantly changed U.S. political history, as Gordon's victory would have meant that the Republicans would not have lost control of the Senate when Vermont's Jim Jeffords left the Republican Party in 2001.

The presidential race was ultimately decided by Bush's victory in Florida by just 537 votes. The turmoil that engulfed the nation after the vote would probably have been avoided had there not been the early media call, as Republicans would likely have won Florida by a larger, indisputable margin.

Incentives matter in voting, just as they do in determining so many other kinds of behavior. And early media calls can reduce the incentive to vote. In the 2000 election, this caused Americans a lot of sleepless nights.

## Felon Voting

Michael Milken, Martha Stewart, and Leona Helmsley share something in common besides being convicted felons—they are all Democrats.[82] While their wealth sets them apart from the typical felon, their party registration is the same as most former convicts. Ever since the razor-thin outcome of the 2000 presidential election, some Democrats have led an effort to restore voting rights to former prisoners. If felon voting had been allowed in 2000, it could easily have tipped the election to Gore who, as previously mentioned, lost Florida by a mere 537 votes. Since that election, twenty states have made it easier for felons to vote,[83] leaving only ten states with lifetime voting bans for felons.[84] Senators Hillary Rodham Clinton and John Kerry introduced the Count Every Vote Act in 2005, which Clinton claimed was "critical to restoring America's faith in our voting system."[85] The bill, which never became law, included a measure to restore voting rights to "felons who have repaid their debt to society" by completing their prison terms, parole, or probation.

As discussed in Chapter Two, many convicted criminals face severe penalties in addition to a prison sentence. Many jobs are forbidden to felons, often making it hard for them simply to earn a living. Yet, since the 2000 election, the loss of voting rights has suddenly emerged as the most pressing problem that former convicts supposedly face. Restoring voting rights, we are told, is indicative "in so many ways of citizenship that it is more important than owning a gun or being able to hold [a particular job]."[86]

Felons themselves, however, have other priorities. In addition to finding a job, felons, who frequently live in poor, high-crime neighborhoods, want to be able to defend themselves. In Virginia, the number one reason felons cite for asking for clemency is the desire to regain their right to own a gun.[87] The Assistant for Clemency for the Governor of Virginia for 1994 and 1995 reported that restoring "voting rights was never on the application for clemency."[88]

According to academic studies, from 1972 to 1996, on average 80 percent of felons would have voted Democratic. An overwhelming 93 percent ostensibly would have voted for Bill Clinton in 1996. In addition to giving the Democrats the White House in 2000, this "felon vote" would have given Democrats control of the Senate from 1986 to 2004.[89]

But these studies are problematic. Felons' voting patterns are assumed to be the same as those of non-felons of the same race, gender, age, and educational status. The estimates do not account for the possibility that there is something fundamentally different about felons that could cause them to vote differently. If two people are of the same race, gender, age, and educational status but one person commits murders or rapes, there might be something quite different between these two people that could affect how they vote.

Public Opinion Strategies surveyed 602 adults in Washington State in May 2005. Of the respondents, 102 were felons who had their voting rights restored, while 500 were non-felons. They were asked about their political preferences, as well as background information about their race, gender, education level, religious habits, employment, age, and county of residence. This survey makes it possible to test the assumption that felons and non-felons are essentially the same.[90]

The survey's results indicate that felons vote even more frequently for Democrats than one would estimate based solely on their personal characteristics. After accounting for all these factors, I found that felons were 36 percent more likely than non-felons with the same characteristics to have voted for Kerry over Bush and 37 percent more likely to be registered Democratic. While African-American and Asians in Washington tend to vote for "a few more Democrats than Republicans," felons among those groups vote for "mostly Democrats." In fact, felons in both groups voted exclusively for Democratic Presidential candidate John Kerry.[91]

While not all felons may be as Democratic as those in Washington State, the survey indicates that the previous estimates understated how frequently felons vote Democratic. Remarkably, it looks as if virtually all felons are Democrats. Felons are not just like everyone else. And the fact that felons are even more likely to vote Democratic than previously believed surely guarantees that some Democratic operatives will continue their efforts to get them to the polls.

## Is the Media Biased?

Voting is widely viewed as a civic obligation. People who don't vote are embarrassed to admit it—post-election surveys routinely show a 20 percent higher turnout than the actual number. Yet, a large portion of eligible voters don't even bother to vote in presidential elections: 39.3 percent of eligible voters didn't vote for president in 2004. Even more—45.7 percent—did not vote in 2000,[92] while nearly 60 percent did not vote in the 2006 midterm elections.[93]

Do people abstain from voting because they don't follow the debate? Fortunately, one does not have to be an expert on every issue in order to cast a well-informed ballot. For information and recommendations, voters can rely on groups that specialize in particular issues. Gun owners can look for advice to the NRA, union members to their unions, and environmentalists to the Sierra Club.[94] Furthermore, one can ask friends, neighbors, or family members for further insights.

But most voters, to a greater or lesser extent, depend on the media for much of their information on contemporary issues. This raises a commonly-asked question: Is the media biased? Conservatives such as Ann Coulter, moderates like Bernie Goldberg, and liberals such as Eric Alterman may disagree on virtually everything, but they all concur that media bias exists, and that it significantly alters people's views. Liberals and conservatives alike keep their own lists of the most biased news sources. They may dispute which outlets are biased toward which side, but these days there seems to be near-unanimous agreement that bias is a common feature of today's media establishment.

So does media bias matter? To answer this question, we must first determine whether media bias in fact exists.

For many conservatives, the fact that most members of the media classify themselves as liberal Democrats is proof enough of bias. Surveys of journalists by the Pew Research Center found that between 1995 and 2004, the number of journalists who consider themselves conservatives rose slightly from 4 to 7 percent, while the number of self-identified liberals jumped from 22 to 34 percent.

Campaign finance records are even more lopsided. Television network employees give overwhelmingly to Democratic candidates, with

98 percent of CBS's employee donations going to Democrats in 2004. The equivalent figure for NBC is an incredible 100 percent. Even employees of FOX News, which is widely regarded as a conservative channel, donate 81 percent of their contributions to Democrats.[95] Journalists vigorously deny that such figures indicate bias, insisting that their reporting is based on their professionalism, not their personal political values.

It is interesting, then, to see that surveys of reporters indicate that they also believe the media is biased—against Democrats.[96] What does all this mean? Are journalists biased or aren't they? Is it possible that reporters are so biased that they don't even realize it? This last possibility is reminiscent of an e-mail I recently received from a history professor at the State University of New York at Binghamton, who told me, "As you are well aware, the social sciences tilt strongly to the left. I've seen so many Far Left presentations that a mere left-leaning presentation strikes me as moderate and objective."

Like this e-mail, most studies of media bias are anecdotal. It is difficult to determine what purely "unbiased" coverage would even look like. The problem is that bias is often in the eye of the beholder. Media watchdogs such as the Media Research Center regularly report examples of reporters slanting stories in some way. But viewers tend to filter the reports through the prism of their own political views. Democrats might regard a critical story about President Bush as justified and true, while Republicans would view it as biased.

In order to assess media bias, we must first find some objective news item and then analyze how it's covered in the media. But what kind of news can be identified as "objective?" Economist Kevin Hassett and I studied media bias between 1985 and 2004 by analyzing how the media presented economic data such as the unemployment rate, gross domestic product (GDP), retail sales, and durable goods. Here, there is little ambiguity over what the "objective" news is: it's the economic number itself and how it has changed over time. We confined our study to the headlines. This was done because headlines not only create the strongest image in readers' minds, but more importantly, they are easier than is a long text to classify objectively—by conveying that things are getting "better," "worse," or that the news is "mixed."[97]

Our study found pervasive media bias. Even after accounting for whether the economy was in an upswing or downswing at any given time, the headlines were more positive during Clinton's presidency than during any of the Republican administrations. This bias—the difference in positive headlines during Democratic and Republican presidencies for the same underlying economic news—meant that headlines were between 10 and 20 percentage points more positive during a Democratic presidency. Headlines about economic news also became relatively more positive when Democrats controlled Congress, but reached their most negative when Republicans controlled both the presidency and the legislature.

Among the top ten individual newspapers, we found strong evidence that the *Chicago Tribune*, the *New York Times*, and the *Washington Post* were much more likely to portray economic news positively during a Democratic presidency. The same was true for the Associated Press. However, there was a bit of a "hometown effect" for Republicans. The *Houston Chronicle* treated both Bushes about the same as Clinton, while the *Los Angeles Times* covered Reagan slightly more positively than it did Clinton.

Perhaps most importantly, we found that media coverage does indeed affect public opinion. Media coverage better explained whether people thought that the economy was getting better or worse than did the underlying economic data. Comparing our results with public opinion data from the Gallup Poll, we found that media bias resulted in people being 4 percentage points more likely to view the economy positively under President Clinton than they would have been under the same conditions during a Republican presidency.[98] This translates into a comparable percentage difference in presidential approval ratings, an important finding in light of the close presidential races of 2000 and 2004.[99]

## Government Control of Information: From Public Schools to Television

The topic of media bias has recently drawn much attention, but public schools may be even more influential in molding the worldview of future voters. A majority of Americans probably assume this is a good thing, as they hold education, as well as the teachers who provide it, in high regard. Anyone who has witnessed school board battles over curriculum or even individual textbooks knows how much is at stake in determining what future generations will be taught. But what most people don't realize is that public education was actually designed to spread government-approved values.

Before delving into the history of American education, let's first look at education systems in totalitarian countries. In order to instill the proper adherence to the ruling ideology, totalitarian leaders must attack the most common locus for spreading oppositional values—the family.[100] To weaken parental influence, the Soviet Union during the 1920s and again in the 1950s experimented with raising children in "communal children's houses, dining halls, and other institutions that would decrease the importance of the individual household." These efforts were rekindled decades later during the Soviet war in Afghanistan, when the Soviet government forcibly transferred tens of thousands of three- and four-year-old Afghanis to the USSR. By educating the children away from their families, the Soviets hoped to instill Communist ideals and then return their subjects to Afghanistan years later as part of a loyal government administration.[101]

The danger of the family in passing on the "wrong" values to their children was summed up by a Soviet refugee shortly after World War II: "In many respects, the family is most immune to the pressures of the regime. It thus constitutes the single most significant seedbed for the generation, preservation, and transmission of antiregime attitudes and information which the regime would like to suppress."[102]

Government attempts to supplant parents as the primary source of social values are not even limited to totalitarian countries. A particularly disturbing example is evident in the justification given for the creation of Sweden's extensive nursery school system. Declaring that "School is the spearhead of Socialism," Ingvar Carlsson, Sweden's education minister from 1969 to 1973 (and later prime minister), insisted that removing children from the home through "pre-school training is essential 'to eliminate the social heritage'" of undesirable, reactionary parental views.[103] Swedish educational theorists even advocated tax and government employment policies that would "get both parents out of the home, so that children are forced out as well."[104]

By abolishing the very concept of the family, totalitarian governments hope to create a government monopoly on the transmission of social values. Once this is achieved, the main avenue through which this monopoly spreads the regime's values is through the education system. By instilling in young students the idea that the regime is legitimate and acts fairly, totalitarian governments seek to reduce potential opposition to their rule. They invest enormous resources in these endeavors for a very rational reason—evidence shows that government-provided schooling reduces political opposition and predisposes students to support the government when they get older.[105]

In totalitarian countries, the hiring and firing of educators is often based explicitly on political grounds. Reporting on the Soviet Union, one observer noted that, "promotions based on non-academic criteria tend to dilute the quality of senior academics, and such promotions are common. Many educational administrators are essentially Party bureaucrats moved into this line of work."[106] In Communist Czechoslovakia, school administrators were "instructed to gather information from selected Communist students in the Pioneer and

Youth Union organizations to present 'a view from below'" regarding the political reliability of teachers.[107] Soviet teachers also had to
deal with the presence of "informers in the class."[108]

Apartheid-era South Africa placed a similar value on ideological
education. Four separate school systems were established for whites,
blacks, Asians, and coloreds. Segregated racially, teachers taught to students of their own race. Being a black teacher in a government school
was a dangerous job. Perceived as complicit in perpetuating apartheid,
black teachers were pariahs in their own communities and were sometimes killed by other blacks. Ironically, despite the prevailing ideology
of white-supremacy, the government was forced to pay black teachers
the highest premiums over what they would normally earn to compensate for the risks they faced and to try to ensure their political reliability.

Today, this kind of state indoctrination is commonly found in radical Muslim states. In Saudi Arabia and other fundamentalist Muslim
countries, "Arab children are being taught that Jews are inherently not
humans, that they are born from monkeys and pigs, that it is perfectly
alright to kill them."[109] Routinely portraying the United States as a
manifestation of Satan, the Saudi and Iranian regimes teach that Islam
will inevitably rule the world and that all non-Muslims will perish.[110]

One would assume that even if state education is used for these
malign purposes in totalitarian or highly authoritarian countries, surely
this isn't the case in the United States. However, while the degree of
indoctrination in American schools never reached totalitarian levels, a
brief history of the evolution of American public schooling reveals that
public schools, in fact, did develop specifically as a method to inculcate
values supported by the government.

As in many other countries, public education in the United States
began at the instigation of churches. For a long time, schooling was
openly religious. In the 1820s, in New York and in other states, legislators became concerned that many students were receiving the wrong

type of education. It was not that children were going uneducated—in 1821, about 93 percent of New York's school age youths were already attending private schools.[111] As expressed in legislative debates, the fear was that students educated in private Catholic schools would learn the wrong values and end up becoming criminals. If Protestant schools could be made less expensive through government subsidies, the legislators reasoned, some Catholics would transfer their children there, thus saving them from a life of crime.[112]

The subsidies began as a kind of voucher system in which approved Protestant schools received a per pupil payment. However, this had an unintended consequence: the subsidized Protestant schools started competing against each other to attract Catholic students. To compete, they began teaching more of what Catholic parents and students wanted— reading, writing, and math—and less of what they didn't want—Protestant religious training. Advocates of the subsidies found that the subsidized schools were no longer providing the religious training that justified the funding program in the first place.

In response, subsidies were limited to the approved Protestant school nearest to a student's home. This reduced the incentive for the schools to compete against each other, and thus to limit their Protestant religious instruction. As government programs tend to do, over time the subsidy scheme grew until it began eliciting complaints that the subsidized schools were getting most of their money from the government while being protected from competition. With the Free Schools Act of 1867, the state simply took over the subsidized schools, which then became public institutions.[113] This is the surprising, true origin of America's public school system.

So what are these government values that are spread in the education system? In short, the government has a vested interest in teaching the young to believe that government policies can effectively solve problems. Public school teachers have a natural incentive to teach this axiom as well. Recall my personal story form this book's introduction, in which I related how public university professors abhorred the prospect of tax cuts, which could result in reductions of their own university budgets. Public high school teachers face the same incentives. They have an abiding, personal interest in perpetuating the growth of government, which is the source of their own livelihood.[114]

Government spending on education is widely viewed as an indisputably positive endeavor. Rival political candidates regularly compete by trying to top each other's promises to spend more on schools. But our discussion raises a few doubts about this precept, as public schooling has always been aimed, at least partially, at instilling government values. Thus it should not be too surprising to learn that totalitarian states on average spend twice as much on education per student as do free countries with the same total income.

This isn't because totalitarian countries generally care more about their children. In fact, on average, totalitarian states have spent less money on health care than freer countries have,[115] and they have lower immunization rates of children against tuberculosis, DPT, polio, and tetanus. Thus, when Communism collapsed in Eastern Europe and the Soviet Union, education spending fell sharply in the newly free countries while health care spending soared.[116]

Governments have always used public education as a form of indoctrination, and the more authoritarian a regime is, the more constraints we find against private education. It's interesting to note that countries with socialized medical care usually allow much more competition between government hospitals or doctors than they allow between schools.[117] If patients can pay to travel a long distance to see a certain doctor, they're typically allowed to do so. Students, however, can't so easily choose which public school to attend. The reason for this is clear in light of the above discussion: while competition between hospitals or doctors produces better health care, competition between government schools reduces the effectiveness of government indoctrination efforts.

# Parting Thoughts

Altruism is a noble quality—but in a large economy, it only goes so far. Adam Smith had it right: individuals, by pursuing their own self-interest, enrich society. Smith understood the fundamental principle of economics: when you make something more costly, people will do less of it. In other words, incentives matter. Studying the incentives that underlie our everyday decisions shows us that economic, criminal, and political policies work best when they direct individuals' natural motivations toward a common good. These are policies that allow people the freedom to profit from their own work, that create meaningful and fair disincentives to committing crimes, and that carefully consider what factors encourage people to participate in our democracy by voting.

In a free market, those who only see the incentives of professionals and corporations to rip off their consumers are only considering one type of incentive. They miss the complex and fascinating process of how markets tend to evolve to solve cheating problems without government intervention. They fail to see not only that reputations matter, but that there are great incentives for the continual evolution of new mechanisms to guarantee the quality of products and services. As technology improves, these mechanisms become ever more efficient and creative.

It is easy to point to some area of economic dissatisfaction, claim that the market is failing, and demand that the government step in. Whether forcing insurers to give discounts for LoJacks, lobbying for government subsidies for honey producers, or mandating professional licenses to ensure the quality of professionals, advocates of government intervention fail to understand that consumers and producers tend to find solutions themselves when their own money is at stake. Solutions to free-riding problems that seem so simple and obvious today, such as advertising on radio, almost didn't come along in time before the government stepped in. Because a modern economy is so complex, the wise men tasked with devising regulations frequently create more problems than they solve.[1]

There will always be some duplicity in the free market. But there is also an ever-present incentive ingrained in the system for individuals and companies to behave honestly. If someone can make a buck by treating his customers better than someone else, eventually someone will try it. Political markets also have their own mechanisms to limit cheating, resulting in the election of politicians who, by and large, accurately represent their constituents.

The free market isn't perfect, but that isn't the right standard by which to judge it. The government is hardly perfect either.

Markets not only increase our wealth, they also increase our freedom. And so long as people have the freedom to act on their own incentives, the U.S. economy will continue to embody the best, most creative, and—I would dare say—the most honest aspects of our society.

# Acknowledgments

This book has more than the usual share of people to thank because it is based on my academic research, much of which I coauthored with other scholars. The coauthors whose work is touched on here include: Bruce Bender, Stephen Bronars, Michael Davis, Andrew Dick, Gertrud Fremling, Robert Hansen, Kevin Hassett, Gi-Ryong Jung, Jonathan Karpoff, Larry Kenny, William Landes, Richard Manning, Tim Opler, Robert Reed, Russell Roberts, Eric Wehrly, and John Whitley. Bronars, Hansen, Karpoff, Kenny, and Roberts have worked with me on up to five papers each, and I am especially indebted to them. I also must express my gratitude for the useful comments I received from numerous faculty members at hundreds of academic seminars, presentations, and conferences held around the world.

Jack Langer, my editor at Regnery, has been extremely helpful, dedicating a large amount of time to this project and offering consistently excellent advice. I would also like to thank Bob Hansen, Peter Hartley, and Jon Karpoff for allowing me to bounce ideas off them, and Gertrud Fremling, Craig Newmark, and Maxim Lott for reading and commenting on the manuscript.

The list of hardworking research assistants who helped in the production of all my academic papers is too long to fully elaborate here, but from the last five years, I'd like to thank Brian Blasé, James Knowles, Maarten Burggraaf, Ilyse Fishman, Michael Roth, Jack Soltysik, Drew Johnson, Jill Yablonski, Jill Farias (formerly Jill Mitchell), Soojin Kim, Refael Lav, Benjamin Berthomieu, Gregory D'Angelo, Alykhan Velshi, and Lydia Regopoulos. My three oldest sons, Maxim, Ryan, and Roger, also provided me with many hours of valuable research assistance.

This book is largely a statement of my personal views on economics, but I could not have written it without the influence of others. The thinking and writing of my teachers have had a major impact on me, and I'd like to acknowledge in particular Armen Alchian, Gary Becker, Harold Demsetz, David Friedman, Ben Klein, Ed Leamer, Earl Thompson, Thomas Sowell, and Finis Welch. Among the many others who influenced my work are Bill Landes, Sam Peltzman, Richard Posner, George Stigler, and James Q. Wilson. Finally, I would like to thank the late M. Bruce Johnson. I became an economist only through a series of unlikely events that all began with my conversations with Bruce after he moved next door to me in Florida when I was sixteen years old.

# Notes

## Introduction

1.  Adam Smith, *The Wealth of Nations*, edited by Edwin Cannan, (Chicago: University of Chicago Press, 1976), 18.
2.  From the official *Freakonomics* website: http://www.freakonomics.com/the-book.php.
3.  Steven Levitt and Stephen Dubner, *Freakonomics* (New York: William Morrow, 2006), 63.
4.  Regarding corporate crime in the early 2000s, Levitt and Dubner argue that the feeble justification given by corporate criminals that "everybody else was doing it," in fact, "may be largely true." See *Freakonomics*, 69. In addition to attacking corporate America in books like *Downsize This!*, Michael Moore introduced viewers to the character "Crackers," a corporate crime-fighting chicken, in his series *TV Nation*.
5.  Paul Resnick, Richard Zeckhauser, John Swanson, and Kate Lockwood, "The Value of Reputation on eBay: A Controlled Experiment," *Experimental Economics*, June 2006, 79-101.
6.  In a Gallup Poll, only 14 percent of respondents rated the honesty and ethical standards of congressmen as "high" or "very high." Senators received

a 15 percent rating, while business executives registered at 18 percent. The Gallup Poll, "Honesty/Ethics in Professions," December 8 to 11, 2006. Http://www.galluppoll.com/content/?ci=1654&pg=1.

7. One example involved a famous paper by Orley Ashenfelter and Robert Smith that was published in the *Journal of Political Economy*. The study drew attention to a puzzle: that minimum wage laws only punished violators for a fraction of the underpayment to the workers, but at the same time few people seemed to violate the law. Their paper generated many attempts by economists to explain this conundrum. It was only in talking to some people involved in enforcing minimum wage laws while I was at the Sentencing Commission that I learned the authors' claim that the penalties were small, in fact, wasn't true. Ashenfelter and Smith had simply misread the law, which provided for much bigger penalties than they assumed. All the succeeding economists who addressed the issue took it for granted that Ashenfelter and Smith's figures were correct. See Orley Ashenfelter and Robert Smith, "Compliance with the Minimum Wage Law," *Journal of Political Economy*, April 1979, 333-350. Among the many papers that attempted to explain this puzzle were Gilles Grenier, "on Compliance with the Minimum Wage Law," *Journal of Political Economy*, February 1982, 184-187. See also John R. Lott, Jr. and Russell D. Roberts, "The Expected Penalty for Committing Crime: An Analysis of Minimum Wage Violation," *Journal of Human Resources*, Spring 1995, 397-408 and John R. Lott, Jr. and Russell D. Roberts, "Why Comply: One-sided enforcement of Price Controls and Victimless Crime Laws," *Journal of Legal Studies*, June 1989, 403-414.

8. Milton and Rose Friedman, *Free to Choose*, (New York: Harcourt Brace Jovanovich, 1979) 214.

9. Jac C. Heckelman, "Economic Freedom and Economic Growth: A Short-run Causal Investigation," *Journal of Applied Economics*, May 2000, 71-91.

## Chapter One: Are You Getting Ripped Off?

1. Jad Mouawad, "2 Senate Committees Interrogate Wary Oil Company Executives," *New York Times*, November 10, 2005.

2. The concern among politicians is bipartisan. For example, after Katrina in August 2005, Republican governors such as Missouri's Matt Blunt, Georgia's Sonny Perdue, and Kentucky's Ernie Fletcher, as well as Democratic governors like Illinois' Rod Blagojevich, Pennsylvania's Ed Rendell, and

Michigan's Jennifer Granholm all advocated prosecuting gas companies who profited from the price increases. The Bush administration got into the act by ordering the Justice Department and the Federal Trade Commission to investigate allegations of price-gouging and expressing concern that retail and wholesale gasoline prices were "too high." See "In Praise of 'Gouging,'" editorial, *Wall Street Journal*, September 7, 2005, and John R. Lott, Jr. and Sonya D. Jones, "A Look at the Positive Side of Price-Gouging and Greed," *Houston Chronicle*, August 31, 2005.

3.  Armen A. Alchian and William R. Allen, *Exchange and Production: Competition, Coordination, and Control*, Belmont: Wadsworth Publishing Co. (3rd edition), 1983. See also John R. Lott, Jr. and Gertrud Fremling, "Time Dependent Information Costs, Price Controls, and Successive Government Intervention," *Journal of Law, Economics, and Organization*, vol. 5, no. 2, Fall 1989: 293-306, and John R. Lott, Jr. and Russell D. Roberts, "A Guide to the Pitfalls of Identifying Price Discrimination," *Economic Inquiry*, vol. 29, no. 1, January 1991: 21.

4.  The prices may not be exactly equal due to storage and interest costs, but the current price plus storage and interest rate costs should equal what the price is expected to go up to.

5.  "As Prices Rise, Car-Pooling Begins to Win Out Over Privacy," *New York Times*, September 8, 2005.

6.  Jad Mouawad, "2 Senate Committees Interrogate Wary Oil Company Executives," *New York Times*, November 10, 2005.

7.  Alchian Allen, *Exchange and Production*. See also John R. Lott, Jr. and Gertrud Fremling, "Time Dependent Information Costs, Price Controls, and Successive Government Intervention," *Journal of Law, Economics, and Organization*, vol. 5, no. 2, Fall 1989: 293-306.

8.  Leonard Theberge, "Coverage of the Oil Crisis: How Well was the Public Served?," vol. 1, Washington, D.C.: Media Institute, 1982, 24.

9.  U.S. drug companies just can't say that they won't sell drugs to these companies. If they don't, they risk losing their drug patent and foreign companies in those countries will be able to sell generic versions of the drugs. The American companies will not receive any compensation for this loss. In their view a small profit is better than no profit. James Glassman and John R. Lott, Jr., "Cheaper Drugs Are No Cure-All," *The Globe and Mail* (Canada), Monday, November 17, 2003. See also John R. Lott, Jr. and James Glassman, "The Drug World's Easy Riders," *Wall Street Journal Europe*, Wednesday, July 23, 2003.

10.  Ibid.

11.  Price controls, even when intended as a short-term remedy, often prove difficult to abolish for political reasons. For example, the gasoline and oil price controls discussed here, first imposed on August 15, 1971, were not removed until almost ten years later, on January 28, 1981 See National Public Radio, "Fuel Prices Chronology," NPR Online (http://www.npr.org/news/specials/oil/gasprices.chronology.html). An even longer example is found in New York City, where older apartments are still subject to price controls dating back to World War II. See Robert Bartley, "New York's Self-Destruction," *Wall Street Journal*, May 19, 2003.

12.  Ben Stein, "Don't Beat Up Big Oil. It's Just Doing Its Job," *New York Times*, November 20, 2005.

13.  The actual statement by Menken was "There is always an easy solution to every human problem—neat, plausible, and wrong." H. L. Menken, "The Divine Afflatus," *New York Evening Mail*, November 15, 1917

14.  Some of the discussion in this section is based upon John R. Lott, Jr. and Russell D. Roberts, "A Guide to the Pitfalls of Identifying Price Discrimination," *Economic Inquiry*, vol. 29, no. 1, January 1991: 14-23

15.  David Asman, "Why We See Less and Less Life-Saving Breakthrough Drugs," Foxnews.com, January 5, 2007 (http://www.foxnews.com/story/0,2933,242098,00.html), and John R. Lott, Jr. and James Glassman, "The Drug World's Easy Riders," *Wall Street Journal Europe*, Wednesday, July 23, 2003.

16.  Meghan Daum, "$4k Cat Is Nothing to Sneeze At," *Los Angeles Times*, October 7, 2006, and "Hypoallergenic Cats for Sale," ABC News, October 6, 2006 (http://abcnews.go.com/Nightline/story?id=2537618).

17.  Http://www.amazon.com/Seagrams-Seltzer-Pack-oz-Cans/dp/B0005YW4HS/sr=85/qid=1162946960/ref=sr_1_5/102-2738756-5711361?ie=UTF8&s=gourmet-food and http://www.amazon.com/Canada-Dry-Seltzer-Water-Cans/dp/B00061EXQK/sr=81/qid=1162946860/ref=pd_bbs_sr_1/102-2738756-5711361?ie=UTF8&s=gourmet-food.

18.  Http://www.amazon.com/Coca-Cola-Diet-Coke-Pack-Cans/dp/B0005ZXEB2/sr=8-4/qid=1162946960/ref=sr_1_4/102-2738756-5711361?ie=UTF8&s=gourmet-food. These purchases were made on November 7, 2006 in Springfield, Pennsylvania.

19.  I checked the prices at the supermarket near my home, Genuardi's, which is owned by Safeway. The situation there was similar: cola costs less than carbonated water across the board. For two-liter bottles, the cheapest seltzer

was a Safeway brand costing $1.49, while Coca-Cola Classic sold for ten cents less. Safeway's own cola brand, Go2 Cola, normally sold for $1.49—the same price as their Seltzer—but was temporarily discounted for Genuardi's members to just eighty-eight cents. Another brand of seltzer, Vintage, also normally went for $1.49, but was on sale for $1.09.

20.     John R. Lott, Jr. and Russell D. Roberts, "A Guide to the Pitfalls of Identifying Price Discrimination," *Economic Inquiry*, vol. 29, no. 1, January 1991, 14.

21.     After all, New York City had 24,600 restaurants as of September 2006. (David B. Caruso, "NYC weighs ban on artificial trans fats," *Chicago Tribune*, September 27, 2006).

22.     John R. Lott, Jr. and Russell D. Roberts, "A Guide to the Pitfalls of Identifying Price Discrimination," *Economic Inquiry*, vol. 29, no. 1, January 1991,18-19. I would also like to thank my cousin Jim Lyden, who has managed two different Outback Steakhouses, for helpful discussions on these topics.

23.     Ibid.

24.     Http://www.southwest.com.

25.     Another puzzle is the requirement that consumers have to spend a Saturday night at their destination in order to receive the discount. This is typically explained as an example of price discrimination against business travelers, but it may only be a form of peak load pricing if those who stay over Saturday night travel on Sunday, the quietest day of the week. The puzzle remains as to why there is not an explicit discount for returning on Sunday, but this is also a problem for the price discrimination explanation.

26.     John R. Lott, Jr. and Russell D. Roberts, "A Guide to the Pitfalls of Identifying Price Discrimination," *Economic Inquiry*, vol. 29, no. 1, January 1991.

27.     Rhode Island Gas Prices (http://riroads.com/everyday/gas.htm).

28.     National Petroleum News Factbook, Des Plaines, Illinois: Hunter Publishing Co., (1987). An Associated Press story in July 1986 showed a similar pattern: "Regular unleaded gasoline at self-service stations costs about 80.13 cents a gallon, compared with 1.0994 at full-service stations, and premium unleaded costs about 95.01 cents a gallon, compared with $1.1965 at full-service stations." Associated Press, "Gasoline Prices at 7-Year Low," *New York Times*, July 28, 1986.

29.     People would undoubtedly claim monopoly power if the price spread between full-and self-serve regular and premium unleaded were reversed. The explanation provided here would ask one to look at the number of gallons sold on average per customer.

30.   John R. Lott, Jr. and Russell D. Roberts, "A Guide to the Pitfalls of Identi-
      fying Price Discrimination," *Economic Inquiry*, vol. 29, no. 1, January
      1991: 14-23.

31.   This section is based upon Robert G. Hansen and John R. Lott, Jr., "Prof-
      iting from Induced Changes in Competitors' Market Values: The Case of
      Entry and Entry Deterrence," *Journal of Industrial Economics*, vol. 43, no.
      3, September 1995, 261-276.

32.   *Brooke Group Ltd.* v. *Brown & Williamson Tobacco Corp.*, 113 S. Ct.
      2578 (1993).

      For a discussion of the American Airlines case and the Federal jury's deci-
      sion to acquit, see Neuborne, Ellen, "Lawsuit could curb price wars," *USA
      Today*, August 25, 1993. Continental and Northwest Airlines sought more
      than $3 billion in damages from American Airlines. They alleged that a
      price war that American instigated in 1992, where they reduced coach fares
      by an average of 38 percent and eliminated most discounts, was an attempt
      to drive them out of business.

      Not everyone was satisfied with this decision. Alfred Kahn has argued
      that "The way big airlines respond to competition from start-ups could
      objectively be described as predation." Richard Tomkins, "When Fares
      Aren't Fair," *Financial Times* (London), February 10, 1998.

      Two papers that provide empirical evidence of predation are Malcolm R.
      Burns's paper about American Tobacco ("Predatory Pricing and the Acqui-
      sition Cost of Competitors," *Journal of Political Economy*, 1986) and
      Granitz and Klein on Standard Oil ("Monopolization by 'Raising Rivals'
      cost': the Standard Oil Case," *Journal of Law and Economics*, 1996. 1–47).
      See also my book, *Are Predatory Commitments Credible*, (Chicago: Uni-
      versity of Chicago Press, 1999).

33.   It should be noted that predation is not a factor in the phenomenon of large
      chains like Wal-Mart, Target, or Home Depot driving small mom-and-pop
      stores out of business. The success of these companies in eliminating smaller
      competitors stems from their huge selection and especially their low costs,
      which enable them to charge lower prices than small, independent stores.
      These low prices are permanent; the chains do not lower prices to drive out
      competitors, and then subsequently raise them once they no longer face
      competition. Therefore, these are not examples of predation.

34.   Ibid., Chapter 1. See also Robert H. Bork, *The Anti-trust Paradox: A Pol-
      icy at War with Itself*, (New York: The Free Press, 1978) 39-40.

35. Matthew Josephson, *The Robber Barons* (New York: Harcourt, Brace, 1934), 205. For a longer discussion of this and other examples, see my book, *Are Predatory Commitments Credible?: Who Should the Courts Believe?*, (Chicago: University of Chicago Press) 1999.

36. The predator must be a publicly trade firm for this tactic to be successful. Additionally, the maneuver is most successful when the predator is a non-diversified company.

37. Levitt and Dubner, *Freakonomics* (2005 ed.), 67.

38. The Lemons argument has actually been around for decades, though the person who first brought up the concern realized that there could be strong forces to solve the problem. See George Ackerlof, "The Market of Lemons," *Quarterly Journal of Economics*, August, 1970, 488–500. There are other papers that have found evidence that the market solves this lemons problem (Eric W. Bond, "A Direct Test of the 'Lemons' Model: The Market for Used Pickup Trucks," *AER*, 72(4), September 1982, 836–840, and Wimmer and Chezum, "An Empirical Examination of Quality Certification in a 'Lemons Market,'" *Economic Inquiry*, 41(2), April 2003, 279–91).

39. Http://www.carsense.com/about.asp.

40. The study was conducted on September 27, 2006.

41. http://www.kbb.com/kbb/CompanyInfo/FAQ.aspx#nc_1.

42. This assumes that the car is in "excellent" condition.

43. Steven Levitt and Chad Syverson, "Market Distortions when Agents are Better Informed: The Value of Information in Real Estate Transactions," University of Chicago working paper, January 2005.

44. Stephen Dubner, "The Probability That a Real-Estate Agent Is Cheating You (and Other Riddles of Modern Life)," *New York Times*, August 3, 2003.

45. Levitt and Dubner, *Freakonomics*, revised edition, 49, 64. The authors claim that "The fear created by commercial experts may not quite rival the fear created by terrorists like the Ku Klux Klan, but the principle is the same." The chapter is entitled, "How is the Ku Klux Klan like a group of Real-Estate Agents?"

46. Levitt and Dubner, revised edition, 66.

47. The amount of the difference cited by Levitt has changed over time. The original paper by Levitt and Syverson ("Market Distortions when Agents are Better Informed: The Value of Information in Real Estate Transactions") put the difference at 3.7 percent, but in *Freakonomics* Levitt and Dubner quoted it at 3 percent, and the book's revised edition pegged it at 2 percent.

48.  There were a few very important measures that were missing from Levitt and Syverson's estimates. For example, their empirical work and discussion looks at only the final sale price that property receives and ignores the impact that being an expert has on the original purchase price. Additionally, they did not have a measure of square footage for the house. If realtors happen to own slightly larger houses, this alone could explain the difference in prices. It might also explain the length of time on the market, because their results indicate that larger houses in terms of more bedrooms, other rooms, and bathrooms tend to be on the market longer.

49.  Melody Jameson, "Changes in Real Estate Arena Prompt Focused Approaches," *The Observer News* (Florida), November 9, 2006.

50.  Ian Ayres and Steven Levitt write that "The car owner who installs LoJack internalizes only 10 percent of the total social benefit, however, implying that LoJack will be undersupplied by the free market." See "Measuring Positive Externalities from Unobservable Victim Precautions: An Empirical Analysis of LoJack," *Quarterly Journal of Economics*, February 1998, 43-77.

51.  Unfortunately, Ayres and Levitt were unable to provide to others their primary data on the number of LoJack devices installed in cars. An attempt to test whether there was a drop in auto thefts did not confirm these original claims. John R. Lott, Jr., "Does a Helping Hand Put Others at Risk?: Affirmative Action, Police Departments, and Crime," *Economic Inquiry*, April 2000, 257.

52.  A check with State Farm, Allstate, and GEICO insurance indicates that this pattern is still true as of November 2006. For example, here are some statistics by state for Allstate, the nation's second largest auto insurance company—Connecticut: no state mandate, no Allstate discount for LoJack (Carol A. Sarabia, Associate Examiner, Connecticut Insurance Department); Florida: state mandated discount of 10 percent, Allstate discount of 10 percent (Valerie, Consumer Service Agent, Florida Office of Insurance Regulations, 11/6/06); New York: state mandated discount of 15 percent, Allstate discount of 15 percent (Car Alarms and Car Insurance in New York, Transportation Alternatives. Campaign Memo. April 28, 2004); New Jersey: state mandated discount of 20 percent, Allstate discount of 20 percent (New Jersey Administrative Code, 11:3-39, obtained via Michie's Legal Resources, http://www.michie.lexisnexis.com/newjersey); Pennsylvania: state mandated discount of 10 percent, Allstate discount of 10 percent (Chuck Romberger, Director, Property and Casualty Bureau, Pennsylvania Insurance Department); and Oregon: no state mandated discount, no Allstate discount (Greg

Ledbetter, Senior Consumer Advocate, Oregon State Insurance). This pattern is also true for State Farm Mutual and Progressive Casualty Groups. State Farm, Allstate, and Progressive were the three largest insurance companies in 2005. (http://www.iii.org/media/facts/statsbyissue/auto/).

The quote is from Ian Ayres and Barry Nalebuff, "Stop, Thief!" *Forbes*, January 10, 2005 (http://www.forbes.com/forbes/2005/0110/088_print.html). The authors point to one insurance company, Liberty Mutual, that gives "large discounts" to those with LoJacks: "A study by Ian Ayres and Steven Levitt showed that each dollar spent on LoJack resulted in $10 of reduced car theft. Alas, this doesn't make the device a winner for insurers with less than 10% of the market, because most of the benefit will accrue to their rivals. Even so, Liberty Mutual gives a large insurance discount to LoJack users, even where it isn't required by law." This would imply that if LoJack was effective, then the largest insurance companies would be the ones most likely to give a discount. However, the opposite is true. (Liberty Mutual is only the ninth largest insurance company.)

53.  Telephone interview with Amy Kelly, GEICO Sales Agent, October 16, 2006 (1-800-861-8380). See also a publication from Transportation Alternatives on Car Alarms and Car Insurance in New York that quotes GEICO as claiming that they do not support LoJack discounts because "it does not prevent the initial theft."

54.  Unfortunately, Ayres and Levitt were unable to provide the primary data used in their paper to others on the number of LoJack devices installed in cars. An attempt to test whether there was a drop in auto thefts did not confirm these original claims. John R. Lott Jr., "Does a Helping Hand Put Others at Risk?"

55.  Williams v. Walker-Thomas Furniture Co., 350 F.2d 445 (D.C. Cir. 1965) (http://www.scu.edu/law/FacWebPage/Neustadter/e-books/abridged/main/cases/Williams.html).

56.  *Reyes* v. *Wyeth Laboratories*, 498 F.2d 1264 (5th Cir. 07/31/1974) (http://biotech.law.lsu.edu/cases/vaccines/reyes_v_wyeth_laboratories.htm).

57.  The award was for $200,000 in 1970.

58.  For example, take something as simple as football helmets, where helmet makers are now held liable for neck injuries even though manufacturers warn customers that helmets will only protect the skull, not the neck. (*Bell Sports* v. *Brian j. Yarusso*, Supreme Court of the State of Delaware, C.A. No. 93C-10-132, September 7, 2000) In hopes of avoiding liability, helmet manufacturers are placed in the absurd situation of having to warn their customers not to play

sports. Some helmets now carry the following warning: "NO HELMET SYS-TEM CAN PROTECT YOU FROM SERIOUS BRAIN AND/OR NECK INJURIES INCLUDING PARALYSIS OR DEATH. TO AVOID THESE RISKS, DO NOT ENGAGE IN THE SPORT OF FOOTBALL" (emphasis in the original). See http://www.amazon.com/Schutt-Air-Jr-Football-Helmet/dp/B0000AQKCS). The columnist George Will also ridiculed the climate of corporate fear created by excessive litigation, citing the example of a baby stroller carrying the warning, "Remove baby before folding." See "The Law vs. Good Sense," http://www.jewishworldreview.com/cols/will060302.asp.

59. Richard L Manning, "Changing Rules in Tort Law and the Market for Childhood Vaccines," *Journal of Law and Economics*, vol. 37, 1994.

60. Richard L. Manning, "Is the Insurance Aspect of Producer Liability Valued by Consumers?: Liability Changes and Childhood Vaccine Consumption," *Journal of Risk and Uncertainty*, 37-51.

61. John R. Lott, Jr. And Richard L Manning, "Have Changing Liability Rules Compensated Workers Twice for Occupational Hazards?: Earnings Premium and Cancer Risks," *Journal of Legal Studies*, January 2000.

62. This assumes a real interest rate of 3 percent.

63. Lott and Manning, "Have Changing Liability Rules Compensated Workers Twice for Occupational Hazards?"

64. The premiums fell by 43 to 108 percent. A drop of 108 percent indicates that workers were being overcompensated by the ability to sue and now took on low wages to get this right.

65. Lott and Manning, "Have Changing Liability Rules Compensated Workers Twice for Occupational Hazards?"

## Chapter Two: Reputations

1. This according to Michael Moore's official website, http://www.michael-moore.com/books-films/index.php.

2. Benjamin Klein and Keith Leffler, "The Role of Market Forces in Assuring Contractual Performance," *Journal of Political Economy*, 1981, 265-267. See also John R. Lott, Jr. "Brand names, Ignorance, and Quality Guaranteeing Premiums," *Applied Economics*, 1988, 165-176 and Benjamin Klein, "Hold-ups Occur: The Self-Enforcing Range of Contractual Relationships," *Economic Inquiry*, July 1996, 444-463.

3. Ibid.

4.  John R. Lott, Jr., "Political Cheating," *Public Choice*, vol. 52, no. 2, 1987: 169-186.

5.  About a quarter of this 40 percent announced that the upcoming term would be their last. See John R. Lott, Jr., "Political Cheating," 169-186. See also Stephen G. Bronars and John R. Lott, Jr., "Do Campaign Donations Alter How Politicians Vote?" *Journal of Law and Economics*, 1997.

6.  Ibid.

7.  David Laband and Bernard Lentz, *The Roots of Success: Why Children Follow in Their Parent's Career Footsteps*, Praeger Publishers: New York, New York, 1985, 64. This refers to the numbers where the father's occupation is known. See also John R. Lott, Jr., "Political Cheating," 169–186.

8.  Children of parents who are self-employed, licensed professionals will become self-employed, licensed professionals themselves at a rate of nearly 15 percent. This example, however, includes children choosing other self-employed, licenses careers than their parents, such as a doctor's child becoming a lawyer, accountant, or even a plumber. Laband and Lentz, *The Roots of Success*, 23.

9.  See, for example, Jeremy Rabkin's "The Sorry Tale of David Souter, Stealth Justice," *The Weekly Standard*, vol. 1, no. 8, 1996, 30.

10. This is not to say that the tenure system functions perfectly in this respect, or that unproductive professors never gain tenure. Studies have found relatively small drops in productivity among professors after receiving tenure. These, however, are most pronounced among those professors who were least productive to begin with. See Sharon M. Oster and Daniel S. Hamermesh, "Aging and Productivity Among Economists," *Review of Economics and Statistics*, vol. 80, no. 1, (1998): 154-157. See also Flora F. Tien and Robert T. Blackburn, "Faculty Rank System, Research Motivation, and Faculty Research Productivity," *Journal of Higher Education*, vol. 67 (January/February, 1996): 13 and 14.

11. Daniel B. Klein and Charlotta Stern, "Professors and Their Politics: The Policy Views of Social Scientists," *Critical Review*, vol. 17 (2005): 257-303.

12. Including the hard sciences at other schools such as the University of California at Berkeley and Stanford, professors who are registered as Democrats out number Republicans by a 9 to 1 ratio. Daniel B. Klein and Andrew Western, "How Many Democrats per Republican at UC Berkeley and Stanford: Voter Registration Data Across 23 Academic Departments," Department of Economics, Santa Clara University Working Paper, 2004.

See also Christopher Cardiff and Daniel B. Klein, "Faculty Partisan Affiliations in all Disciplines: A Voter-Registration Study," *Critical Review*, vol. 17 (2005): 237-256.

13.  Cass Sunstein, David Schkade, and Lisa Ellman of the University of Chicago Law School examined 4,488 published circuit court panel decisions from 1982 to 2002 on the most ideologically controversial issues—abortion, capital punishment, affirmative action, the Americans with Disabilities Act, campaign-finance laws, criminal procedure, federalism, race and sex discrimination, and takings (the rules under which the government can seize private property). They argue that for many of these decisions the way judges vote "can be predicted by the party of the appointing president." Sunstein, Schkade, and Ellman, "Ideological Voting on Federal Courts of Appeals: A Preliminary Investigation," working paper no. 03-9, University of Chicago Law School, September 2003. I think that they exaggerate this finding some, but their work is the most comprehensive on the topic to date.

14.  See for example, John R. Lott, Jr. and Stephen G. Bronars, "Time Series Evidence on Shirking by Members of the U.S. House of Representatives," *Public Choice*, invited conference volume, vol. 76, no. 1-2, June 1993: 125-14 and Bruce Bender and John R. Lott, Jr., "Legislator Voting and Shirking: A Critical Review of the Literature," *Public Choice*, vol. 87, nos. 1 and 2, April 1996: 67-100.

15.  Stephen G. Bronars and John R. Lott, Jr., "Do Campaign Donations Alter How Politicians Vote?" *Journal of Law and Economics*, 1997.

16.  The proof commonly cited to support the notion that donations are systematically used to buy politicians' votes does not withstand scrutiny. For example, one study found that "contributors who attempt to influence the voting behavior of members of Congress give the most money to legislators whose constituency interest suggests that they are likely to be undecided on how to vote." (See Thomas Stratmann, "Are Contributors Rational?: Untangling Strategies of Political Action Committees," *Journal of Political Economy*, 1992, 647.)

The study, which examined farm issues, discovered that pro-farmer donors tend not to give to candidates in areas where all the constituents are farmers, nor in districts where none of the constituents are farmers, but in districts that are evenly split. In the view of this study's author, the results show that donors are buying candidates' future votes by making their election dependent on the donors' support.

But the study's results, while consistent with vote-buying, really just demonstrate that donors don't want to waste their money on candidates who are highly likely to either win or lose their race. If you care about farmers, why waste your money donating to candidates in districts where all the voters are farmers and candidates from both parties support them. These findings are perfectly consistent with the alternative explanation that donors try to elect candidates who already support their positions.

The same author ostensibly also found pervasive vote buying the timing of political donations. According to this analysis, although a candidate benefits most from donations received early in an election cycle, many donors, when uncertain about a candidate's beliefs, refrain from donating to him until after he's elected and casts the desired vote on some key issue. The author interprets this donation as a quid pro quo—a kind of pay-off for voting the right way. This study, however, suffers from the same problem as previously mentioned; donors would behave the same way if they were donating to politicians who already agree with their views. When donors are faced with a candidate without a well-established reputation, they simply wait to learn what he believes before they donate to him. See Thomas Stratmann, "The Market for Congressional Votes: Is Timing of Contributions Everything," *Journal of Law and Economics*, vol. 61 (April 1998), and also Randall S. Kroszner and Thomas Stratmann, "Interest-Group Competition and the Organization of Congress: Theory and Evidence from Financial Services' Political Action Committees," *American Economic Review*, vol. 88 (December 1998): 1163–87.

Thomas Stratmann, "The Market for Congressional Votes: Is timing of Contributions everything," *Journal of Law and Economics*, vol. 61 (April 1998). See also Randall S. Kroszner and Thomas Stratmann, "Interest-Group Competition and the Organization of Congress: Theory and Evidence from Financial Services' Political Action Committees," *American Economic Review*, vol. 88 (December 1998): 1163-1187.

17.    Anderson Cooper, "Louisiana Congressman Facing Bribery Investigation," Cnn.com, May 22, 2006 (http://transcripts.cnn.com/TRANSCRIPTS/0605/22/acd.01.html); Associated Press, "Rep. Ney's Plea Deal Tests Corruption as Election-Year Issue," Foxnews.com, Friday, September 15, 2006. (http://www.foxnews.com/story/0,2933,214146,00.html); and Associated Press, "Ohio Rep. Bob Ney Admits Guilt in Corruption Probe,"

Foxnews.com, Friday, September 15, 2006. (http://www.foxnews.com/story/ 0,2933,213927,00.html).

18.   Stephen Bronars and John R. Lott, Jr., "Do Campaign Donations Alter How a Politician Votes?," *Journal of Law and Economics*, vol. 40, no. 2, October 1997: 342-343.

19.   Bruce Bender and John R. Lott, Jr., "Legislator Voting and Shirking: A Critical Review of the Literature," *Public Choice*, vol. 87, nos. 1 and 2, April 1996: 67-100. See also John R. Lott, Jr and Stephen Bronars., "Time Series Evidence on Shirking by Members of the U.S. House of Representatives," *Public Choice*, invited conference volume, vol. 76, no. 1-2, June 1993: 125-149.

20.   Press Release, "Biden Praises Passage of McCain-Feingold Legislation", Sen. Joseph Biden's website, April 2, 2001. Http://biden.senate.gov/newsroom/details.cfm?id=229522&&.

21.   In the Supreme Court decision in *Nixon v. Shrink Missouri Government PAC*, Justice David Souter cites the argument from the *Buckley v. Valeo* decision that contribution limits have "served the important governmental interests in preventing the corruption or appearance of corruption of the political process that might result if such contributions were not restrained."

22.   See Justice Bryer's concurrence in *Nixon v. Shrink Missouri Government PAC* (98-963) 528 U.S. 377 (2000) 161 F.3d 519.

23.   John R. Lott, Jr., "The Effect of Nontransferable Property Rights on the Efficiency of Political Markets: Some Evidence," *Journal of Public Economics*, vol. 32, no. 2, March 1987, 231–246. Jeffrey Milyo and Timothy Groseclose, "The Electoral Effects of Incumbent Wealth," *Journal of Law and Economics*, 1999, 699–722. Jeffrey Milyo, "The Economics of Political Campaign Finance: FECA and the Puzzle of the Not Very Greedy Grandfathers," *Public Choice*, December 1997, 245–70.

24.   Much of the discussion in this section is based on John R. Lott, Jr. "Campaign Finance Reform and Electoral Competition," *Public Choice*, 2006.

25.   Given that many state senate races will involve candidates who have held previous elected office, the arguments discussed here can apply even when there are no incumbents in a race. Similarly, the advantage possessed by incumbents will be mitigated to some extent when challengers have held other offices such as the state assembly or city council.

26.   This discussion is based on John R. Lott, Jr., "The Effect of Nontransferable Property Rights on the Efficiency of Political Markets: Some Evidence,"

*Journal of Public Economics*, vol. 32, no. 2, March 1987: 231-246; John R. Lott, Jr., "Brand Names and Barriers to Entry in Political Markets," *Public Choice*, vol. 51, no. 1, 1986: 87-92; and John R. Lott, Jr., "Explaining Challengers' Campaign Expenditures: The Importance of Sunk Nontransferable Brand Name," *Public Finance Quarterly*, vol. 17, no. 1, January 1989: 108-118.

27.  Norman J. Ornstein, Thomas Mann, and M.J. Malbin, *Vital Statistics on Congress: 2001-2002*, (Washington, D.C.: The American Enterprise Institute, 2002). Reed and Schansberg found that the U.S. House of Representatives experienced a large, sudden increase in tenure during the mid-1970s. After examining alternative explanations such as increased gerrymandering or increased congressional compensation, they concluded that the increase in tenure length arose from suddenly "greater incumbent advantages as the source," (198). W.R. Reed and D.E. Schansberg, "The Behavior of congressional Tenure Over Time: 1953-1991," *Public Choice*, 1992, 183-203.

28.  John R. Lott, Jr., "Campaign finance reform and electoral competition," *Public Choice*, 2006, 263.

29.  McCarthy raised a total of $11 million in 1968, an amount that was equivalent to almost $55 million in 2000. By contrast, George Bush had raised $67 million by the first primary in 2000. George Thayer claims that "The bulk of McCarthy's campaign funds came from a wealthy few." See George Thayer, *Who Shakes the Money Tree*, (New York: Simon and Schuster, 1974) 92. Among those making these donations were Stewart Mott, Jack Dreyfus and his wife, Marin Peretz, Ellsworth Carrington, and Alan Miller. "David Hoeh, the organizer of McCarthy's New Hampshire campaign, recalled later that a single 'financial angel' saved their media effort at a crucial point" (CATO, A Free Speech Kind of Thing, http://www.cato.org/pub_display.php?pub_id=5331). For information on the number of donors giving to Bush see Michael Isikoff, "The Money Machine," *Newsweek*, January 24, 2000, 46.

30.  Four years later, George McGovern was able to continue his 1972 presidential primary campaign against four other senators, several congressmen, and a governor solely thanks to extremely large donations from a single person, Stuart Mott. Mott provided McGovern with a total of almost $600,000 ($212,361 in donations and $377,500 in loans that were likely forgiven). See "Who's Who Among the Big Givers," *Time*, October 23, 1972.

31.  If regulations reduce the amount raised and spent on campaigns, the benefit for incumbents will decline the longer the rules are in effect, though the initial impact will never be offset. While equal reductions in spending during the election benefits the incumbent because of his relatively large stock of reputation, over time as restrictions affect the amount raised and spent in more and more of an incumbent's past elections, the stock of reputation that the incumbent has in future elections will decline, thus somewhat reducing the gap between the incumbent's and the challenger's total reputation.

32.  The case was *Victoria Jackson Gray Adams, et. al. v the Federal Election Commission, et. al.* The brief was largely based on an article Stratmann had co-authored with Francisco Aparicio-Castillo, "Competition Policy for Elections: Do Campaign Contribution Limits Matter?" *Public Choice* (2006).

33.  Given his assumptions, Stratmann's theory holds true for cases in which a well-qualified candidate competes against a lesser qualified one. But in races between two candidates of equal quality, reducing the amount of available information about the candidates would increase win margins and lower competitiveness.

34.  "Bowen wants changes to initiative system," *Sacramento Bee*, September 6, 2006.

35.  John R. Lott, Jr., "Campaign finance reform and electoral competition," *Public Choice*, 2006, 263-300. The information on expenditure limits is available in an earlier working paper version of that paper.

36.  Ibid. States with such regulations for state offices during at least part of the period examined by that study included: California, Colorado, Hawaii, Maine, Massachusetts, Minnesota, Nebraska, New Hampshire, Oregon, Rhode Island, Vermont, West Virginia, and Wisconsin.

37.  Levitt and Dubner, *Freakonomics* (2005 Ed.), 11-12.

38.  *Congressional Quarterly*'s CQPolitics.com offers an analysis of the 60 races determined by less than 10 percentage points (http://public.cq.com/public-content/2007Jan3-Chart.pdf). There are some uncontested races where fund-raising levels will generally not affect the races' outcome. In these races, however, incumbents will often raise money to assist other candidates from their party. Thus even in uncontested races fund-raising can still be productive.

39.  Http://www.nydailynews.com/front/story/485008p-408347c.html.

40.  "Clinton Enters '08 Field, Fueling Race for Money," *New York Times*, January 21, 2007.

41.  For a small selection of this research see: Gary C. Jacobson, *Money in Congressional Elections*, (New Haven: Yale University Press, 1980); Kevin Grier, "Campaign Spending and Senate Elections, 1978 - 1984," *Public Choice*, December 1989,201-19; Gary C. Jacobson, *The Politics of Congressional Elections*, 2nd ed. (New York: Little, Brown, 1987); John R. Lott, Jr., "The Effect of Nontransferable Property Rights on the Efficiency of Political Markets: Some Evidence," *Journal of Public Economics*, vol. 32, no. 2, (March 1987): 231-246; and John R. Lott, Jr., "Explaining Challengers' Campaign Expenditures: The Importance of Sunk Nontransferable Brand Name," *Public Finance Quarterly*, vol. 17, no. 1, January 1989: 108-118.

42.  John Carlson and Kirby Wilbur are the two Seattle areas radio talk show hosts who are being sued. Ralph Thomas and Andrew Garber, "Talk-radio case heard by state high court," *Seattle Times*, June 9, 2006, and George F. Will, "Speechless in Seattle," *Newsweek*, October 9, 2005, 72.

43.  In 1976, federal House races spent $71.5 million, Senate races spent $44 million, and presidential races spent $160 million. By 2004, federal House races spent $660.3 million, Senate races spent $496.4 million, and presidential races spent $1,016.5 million. Adjustments for inflation and population growth were obtained from the consumer price index and the U.S. Census. Joseph E. Cantor, Congressional Campaign Spending: 1976-1996; CRS Report for Congress, August 19, 1997. Herb Alexander, *Financing the 1976 Election*, 1979, 166.

44.  Much of the discussion in this section is based on John R. Lott, Jr., "A Simple Explanation for Why Campaign Donations are Increasing: The Government is Getting Bigger," *Journal of Law and Economics*, vol. 42, no. 2, October 2000, 359-393.

45.  The Bureau of Economic Analysis at the U.S. Department of Commerce, https://bea.gov/bea/newsrel/gdpnewsrelease.htm.

46.  John R. Lott, Jr., "A Simple Explanation for Why Campaign Donations are Increasing: The Government is Getting Bigger," *Journal of Law and Economics.*, vol. 42, no. 2, October 2000: 359-393. These numbers hold true even after accounting for factors such as personal income, term limits, population, the closeness of races, the number of candidates running for office, and how closely divided party control of the state government is.

47.  "Soros's Deep Pockets vs. Bush," *Washington Post*, February 1, 2005.

48.  Ibid.

49.  Ibid.

50.  Byron York, "America Coming Together Comes Apart," *National Review Online*, August 3, 2005.

51.  "Turned-off voters shouldn't be a big surprise," Editorial, *The Pantagraph*, Bloomington, Ill., November 1, 2006.

52.  Lee Covan, "Negative Campaign Ads," *The Early Show*, CBS News, October 24, 2006.

53.  Supreme Court Justice Anthony Scalia notes: "A report prepared for Congress concluded that the total amount, in hard and soft money, spent on the 2000 federal elections was between $2.4 and $2.5 billion. J. Cantor, CRS Report for Congress, Campaign Finance in the 2000 Federal Elections: Overview and Estimates of the Flow of Money (2001)" McConnell v. Federal Election Comm'n (02-1674) 540 U.S. 93 (2003) 251 F.Supp. 2d 176, 251 F.Supp. 2d 948. Data on the Federal government's expenditures is available from the Office of Management and Budget (http://www.whitehouse.gov/omb/budget/fy2004/hist.html).

54.  "Procter becomes nation's largest ad spender," *The Business Courier* (Cincinnati), June 26, 2006. The Proctor & Gamble Company Annual Income Statement (http://www.hoovers.com/procter-&-gamble/—ID__ 11211,period__A—/free-co-fin-income.xhtml). This comparison was first made by the political scientist Herb Alexander.

55.  "No need to choose sides, some donors give to both gubernatorial candidates," Associated Press, August 4, 2006.

56.  Gabriel Kahn, "PACs Hedge Bets, Contribute Twice: Even Robb, North," *Roll Call*, October 24, 1994. The same article notes that "AT&T's political director, Donald Goff, insisted that it was against his company's policy to give to both candidates in a race. However, he said, 'in a contested primary, you might see money going to both candidates.'"

57.  Press release, "Double-giving in the Presidential Campaign," Public Campaign, March 3, 2000 (http://www.publicampaign.org/pressroom/2000/03/03/whoever-wins-they-win).

58.  Much of the discussion in this section is based on Stephen Bronars and John R. Lott, Jr., "Do Campaign Donations Alter How a Politician Votes?," *Journal of Law and Economics*, vol. 40, no. 2, October 1997: 317-350.

59.  John R. Lott, Jr., "Campaign finance reform and electoral competition," *Public Choice*, 2006, 272-273.

60.  This quote, and the succeeding ones from Murry, Farrell, Karpinsky, and Tobin, were made in interviews with the author.

61. These included Americans for Democratic Action, the American Dental Association, the National Rifle Association, the Realtor's PAC, the National Association of Home Builders, United Auto Workers PAC, the National Association of Automobile Dealers PAC, United Food & Commercial Workers International Union, and Lockheed Employees PAC.

62. "Ex-Tyco Officers Sentenced," *Washington Post*, September 20, 2005.

63. Much of the discussion here is based on John R. Lott, Jr., "The Effect of Conviction on the Legitimate Income of Criminals," *Economics Letters*, vol. 34, no. 12, December 1990: 381-385; John R. Lott, Jr., "Do We Punish High Income Criminals too Heavily?" *Economic Inquiry*, vol. 30, no. 4, October 1992: 583-608 and John R. Lott, Jr., "An Attempt at Measuring the Total Monetary Penalty from Drug Convictions: The Importance of an Individual's Reputation," *Journal of Legal Studies*, vol. 21, no. 1, January 1992: 159-187.

64. Ibid.

65. McCries is a professor at the John Jay College for Criminal Justice. See David Henry, "Junk-bond wheeler-dealers face dishonor of life after prison," *Chicago Sun-Times*, February 18, 1992.

66. A federal appeals court later overturned his conviction. See "Justice Reaches into Allenwood," *Wall Street Journal*, May 4, 1990.

67. Devlin Barrett, "Merrill Lynch Assistant Pleads Guilty to being Paid for Keeping Secret Information on ImClone," Associated Press, October 1, 2002. "Facts about Peter Bacanovic," Associated Press, July 16, 2004. "Soap Opera," *New York Post*, September 20, 2006, 12. Case Digest, "Stewart Conviction Upheld," *New York Law Journal*, January 12, 2006, 22.

68. "Martha Stewart and Peter Bacanovic Agree to Settle SEC Insider Trading Charges," SEC News Digest, August 7, 2006. Administrative Proceedings of the SEC, 34-50284. In the matter of Peter Bacanovic. File No. 3-11615. Securities and Exchange Commission. Http://www.sec.gov/litigation/admin/34-50284.htm.

69. "Two Arrested in LAX Rape Case," *Duke Chronicle*, http://www.dukechronicle.com/media/storage/paper884/news/2006/04/19/News/2.Arrested.In.Lax.Rape.Case.Players.Maintain.Innocence-1861119.shtml?norewrite200701041334&sourcedomain=www.dukechronicle.com

70. Ed Bradley, "Duke Rape Suspects Speak Out," *60 Minutes*, CBS News, October 15, 2006 (http://www.cbsnews.com/stories/2006/10/11/60minutes/main2082140.shtml).

71.  "Living a Nightmare: LAX Players Speak Out," *Duke Chronicle*, http://media. www.dukechronicle.com/media/storage/paper884/news/2006/07/19/MLacross e/Living.A.Nightmare.Lax.Players.Speak.Out-2132857.shtml?sourcedomain=www.dukechronicle.com&MIIHost=media.collegepublisher.com.

72.  "Duke Offers to Reinstate Finnerty, Seligmann for Spring Semester," *Duke Chronicle* (http://media.www.dukechronicle.com/media/storage/paper884/ news/2006/12/11/News/Duke-Offers.To.Reinstate.Finnerty.Seligmann.For. Spring.Semester-2600229.shtml?sourcedomain=www.dukechronicle.com& MIIHost=media.collegepublisher.com). At the time of this writing, Nifong has been removed from the case, but the three players are still awaiting trial for charges of kidnapping.

73.  Data show that a person's income drops dramatically upon arrest, even before a conviction. For example, those charged with anti-trust offenses face an average drop in income of about 60 percent at the time of arrest. Walter M. Grant, John LeCornu, John A. Pickens, Dean H. Rivkin, and C. Roger Vinson. "Special Project—the Collateral Consequences of a Criminal Conviction," *Vanderbilt Law Review*, vol. 23, October 1970, 929–1241.

74.  Bryan Burrough, "After the Fall: Fates are Disparate for those charged with insider trading," *Wall Street Journal*, November 18, 1987.

75.  David Henry, "Stubborn taint of Wall Street scandals clings to the innocent and guilty alike," *Newsday*, February 9, 1992.

76.  Grant, et. al, "Special Project," 929-1241.

77.  President's Commission on Law Enforcement and Administration of Justice. Task Force Report: Corrections. U.S. Government Printing Office, Washington (1967), 88.

78.  Velmer S. Burton, Jr., Francis T. Cullen, and Lawrence F. Travis III, "The Collateral Consequences of a Felony Conviction: A National Study of State Statutes." *Federal Probation Quarterly* 33 (September 1987): 52-60., 55. See also Benson, Michael L. "The Fall from Grace: Loss of Occupational Status as A Consequence of Conviction for a White-Collar Crime." *Criminology* 22 (November 1984): 573-594.

79.  Levitt and Dubner, *Freakonomics*, 69.

80.  Jonathan Karpoff and John R. Lott, Jr., "The Reputational Penalty Firms Bear for Committing Fraud," *Journal of Law and Economics*, vol. 36, no. 2, October 1993: 757-758. The money lost to environmental crimes is typically borne by those directly affected by the pollution.

81. Jonathan Karpoff, John R. Lott, Jr.,and Eric Wehrly, "The Reputational Penalties for Environmental Violations: Empirical Evidence," *Journal of Law and Economics*, vol., no. 2 (October 2005): 653-675.

82. This is over $100 million in 2005 dollars. See Karpoff and Lott, "The Reputational Penalty."

83. Karpoff, Lott, and Wehrly, 2005.

84. I owe this example to Benjamin Klein who taught me industrial organization when I was a graduate student at UCLA in the early 1980s.

## Chapter Three: Government as Nirvana?

1. Harold Demsetz, "Information and Efficiency: Another Viewpoint," *Journal of Law and Economics*, April 1969, 1-22, and Joseph P. Kalt, "Public Goods and the Theory of Government," *Cato Journal*, Fall 1981, 565-584. The title of this chapter is taken from Demsetz's paper.

2. Ian Ayres and Barry Nalebuff, "Stop, Thief!" *Forbes*, January 10, 2005. Http://www.forbes.com/forbes/2005/0110/088_print.html.

3. Ayres and Levitt, "Measuring Positive Externalities from Unobservable Victim Precautions: An Empirical Analysis of Lojack," *Quarterly Journal of Economics*, February 1998, 43-77.

4. Steve Levitt made this claim when he presented his paper on this topic at the University of Chicago.

5. This does not imply that the politicians would be bought off by LoJack or its competitors. Rather, it reflects politicians' natural desire to pass legislation that benefits the people and companies in their communities.

6. The comparison between open carry and LoJack is not exact because open carry may benefit people without guns if those with the guns can protect them.

7. Milton Friedman, "The Role of Government in Education," *Economics and the Public Interest*, 123-153, Edited by Robert Solow, New Brunswick, NJ: Rutgers University Press, 1955.

8. Note, however, that if only certain cars like Porsche were to use LoJack, there would be no free-riding problem because there'd be no benefit for anyone except Porsche owners. Additionally, one might assume that putting a "protected by LoJack" sticker on cars that have LoJacks would solve the free-riding problem, However, this would most likely spur a black market in such stickers for use by free-riders who don't actually have the device.

9.   Thomas H. White, Financing Radio Broadcasting (1989-1927), in United States Early Radio History (http://earlyradiohistory.us/sec020.htm).

10.  Ibid.

11.  Waldemar Kaempffert, "Who will pay for broadcasting?: A frank and searching outline of Radio's most pressing problem and the possible ways to solve it," *Popular Radio*, December, 1922, 236-245.

12.  Steven N.S. Cheung, "The Fable of the Bees: An Economic Investigation," *Journal of Law and Economics*, 1973.

13.  Harold Demsetz, "The Exchange and Enforcement of Property Rights," *Journal of Law and Economics*, October 1964, 15.

14.  Mary Muth, Randall Rucker, Walter Thurman, and Ching-Ta Chuang, "The Fable of the Bees Revisited: Causes and Consequences of the U.S. Honey Program," *Journal of Law and Economics*, October 2003, 479-516.

15.  National Taxpayers Union, "Who Pays Income Taxes? See Who Pays What: For Tax Year 2004," National Taxpayers Union Foundation, (http://www.ntu.org/main/page.php?PageID=6).

16.  See also Joseph P. Kalt, "Public Goods and the Theory of Government," *Cato Journal*, Fall 1981, 565-584.

17.  Rawle O. King, "Federal Flood Insurance: The Repetitive Loss Problem," Congressional Research Service, June 30, 2005.

18.  Owen Ullman, "High Risk Life, High Expense to Taxpayers: Federal Disaster Aid Makes It Feasible to Build In Harm's Way," *USA Today*, July 24, 2000, 6A.

19.  Ibid.

20.  Bert Ely, "Savings and Loan Crisis," *The Concise Encyclopedia of Economics* (http://www.econlib.org/library/enc/SavingsandLoanCrisis.html), and Edward J. Kane, "The Gathering Crisis in Federal Deposit Insurance," *The MIT Press*; New edition (August 9, 1985).

21.  Bill Redeker, "Mount Hood Climbers: What Price Glory?" ABCnews.com, December 12, 2006 (http://abcnews.go.com/US/story?id=2720158&page=1).

22.  "After Mount Hood tragedy, Ore. lawmaker wants mountain locators," *Seattle Post Intelligencer* website, http://seattlepi.nwsource.com/local/6600ap_wst_climber_safety.html.

23.  Prior to *Kelo*, eminent domain had also been used to develop blighted neighborhoods. For a related discussion, see Sonya D. Jones, "That Land Is Your Land, This Land Is My Land . . . Until the Local Government Can Turn It for

a Profit: Analysis of Kelo v. City of New London," *BYU Journal of Public Law*, Fall 2005, 139-165.

24. Http://www.kochind.com/industry/pipelines.asp.

25. Based on a personal conversation with Bill Dougan on January 6, 2007.

26. Jonathan Karpoff, "Private versus Private Initiative in Arctic Exploration: The Effects of Incentives and Organizational Structure," *Journal of Political Economy*, January 2001, 38-78.

27. Government expeditions seemed to make up a larger share of the lesser know accomplishments. We can speculate that perhaps government-funded explorers, like their private counterparts, were motivated partly by the desire to acquire fame. Robert Peary, a government-funded explorer who was the first man to make it to the North Pole, wrote his mother that the fame of Christopher Columbus "can be equaled only by him who shall one day stand with 360 degrees of longitude beneath his motionless feet and for whom East and West shall have vanished—the discoverer of the North Pole." Even more directly, he told her, "Remember, mother, I must have fame." Bruce Henderson, *True North: Peary, Cook, and the Race to the Pole*, (New York: W. W. Norton & Company, April 18, 2005).

28. Michael Tanner, Congressional Testimony before the Finance Committee, U.S. Senate, March 9, 1995 (http://www.cato.org/testimony/ct-ta3-9.html). Here are some examples of private charity administration and fundraising expenditures as a percent of total expenditures: Habitat for Humanity, Washington D.C.—13.8%; The Salvation Army – 16.8%; YMCA of Metropolitan Washington – 19.4%; and American Red Cross of the National Capital Area – 11.6%. Source: charitablechoices.com, Charity Descriptions, All Charities A to Z (http://www.charitablechoices.org/categories/all.asp).

29. Kelly Bedard and William Brown, "The Allocation of Public School Expenditures," Claremont Colleges Working Paper, August, 2000, 19 (http://econ.claremontmckenna.edu/papers/2000-16.pdf).

30. The relative costs of private schools assumes that religious teachers in parochial schools are paid at the same rate as lay teachers. For further discussion, see John R. Lott, Jr., "Why is Education Publicly Provided?: A Critical Survey," *Cato Journal*, Fall, 1987: 476-77.

31. Jay Hancock, "Traded Funds May be Trend T. Rowe Price Can't Let Pass," *Baltimore Sun*, September 17, 2006, D1. Congressman Michael Oxley, "Mutual Fund Industry Practices and their Effect on Individual Investors,"

hearing before the Subcommittee on Capital Markets, Insurance, and Government Sponsored Enterprises Committee on Financial Services, March 12, 2003 (http://commdocs.house.gov/committees/bank/hba87798.000/hba87798_0.HTM).

32.   71 percent of Americans understood that a "well-diversified portfolio will experience less volatility." American Century Investments, On Plan I.Q. Quiz, KANSAS CITY, Mo., April 7, 2005 (http://www.americancentury.com/welcome/news_release2_2005.jsp?press_release=20050407a).

33.   Robert Hansen and John Lott, "Externalities and Corporate Objectives in a World with Diversified Shareholders/Consumers," *Journal of Financial and Quantitative Analysis*, (March 1996).

34.   Ibid.

35.   Ibid.

36.   Ibid.

37.   For a discussion of the role of a private predator acquiring the assets of firms that were driven out of business see John McGee, "Pedatory Price Cutting: The Standard Oil (NJ) Case," *Journal of Law and Economics*, 1958–69. He also provides strong evidence that even if such actions were in fact behind Standard Oil's acquisitions, it could not have been a successful strategy.

38.   This discussion is connected to questions on the general growth of government. Related studies include Bennett and Johnson's survey of the theories explaining why government has grown over time. I co-authored two other analyses of the problem. Lott and Fremling describe the growth of government based upon the costs of voters evaluating the long term versus short term effects of government regulation, while Kenny and Lott interpret the growth of government as a result of women's emancipation. See John R. Lott, Jr. and Gertrud Fremling, "Time Dependent Information Costs, Price Controls, and Successive Government Intervention," *Journal of Law, Economics, and Organization*, vol. 5, no. 2, Fall 1989: 293-306, and John R. Lott, Jr. and Larry Kenny, "Did Women's Suffrage Change the Size and Scope of Government?," *Journal of Political Economy*, vol. 107, no. 6, part 1, December 1999: 1163-1198. Also see James Bennett and Manuel Johnson, *The Political Economy of Federal Government Growth: 1959-1978*, (College Station, Texas: Texas A&M University Press, 1980).

39.   Russell Hotten, "Paris Goes to War for Bigger Slice of Airbus," *Daily Telegraph* (UK), November 25, 2006.

40.   Michael Harrison, "Airbus may end up grounded if superjumbo fails to take off," *New Zealand Herald*, November 23, 2006.

41.     Hauser, Rolland K., The Interface Between Federal and Commercial
        Weather Services for Agricultural Industries—A Question of Policy, report
        prepared for the United States Department of Commerce, National Oceanic
        and Atmospheric Administration, Office of the Administrator, Washington,
        D.C. (November, 1985), 23. Jerome Ellig provides a list of other similar
        cases in Government and the Weather: The Privatization Option. Federal
        Privatization Project Issue Paper #109, Santa Monica, California: Reason
        Foundation (August, 1989a).

42.     Jerome Ellig, "For Better Weather, Privatize," *Wall Street Journal*, vol. 71
        (December 4, 1989b): A16. Hauser concludes that, "Current federal ag-
        weather policy, either advertently or inadvertently, has the effect of deter-
        ring investment by private meteorology in agricultural weather services."
        Hauser, ibid.

43.     Michael Stone, Executive Director of UCLA's, Marketing & Communica-
        tion Services, noted that for 2004-05, UCLA spent $3.35 billion, of which
        around $800 million was for research expenditures and $1.13 billion was
        for the medical school. Even excluding research spending, with over 37,000
        students, that comes to almost $40,000 per student. In-state tuition in 2006-
        07 was only $6,522. See http://www.admissions.ucla.edu/prospect/bud-
        get.htm. and Office of the President, University of California, 2006-07
        Budget for Current Operations, University of California, November 2005.
        The average tuition at public universities is $5,836 according to the College
        Board. See Jonathan Glater and Alan Finder, "In Twist on Tuition Game,
        Popularity Rises With Price," *New York Times*, December 12, 2006.

44.     In contrast, an elite private school like Swarthmore College spends slightly
        more per student ($73,690) but charges much higher tuition ($33,232). The
        public school tuition is only 20 percent of the private school's, but the per
        pupil costs of the public school are 57 percent of the private school's. Glater
        and Finder, "In Twist on Tuition Game." See also Melissa Bertosh, "2006-07
        Budget Calls for Tuition Hike," *The Phoenix* (Swarthmore College), March
        16, 2006 (http://phoenix.swarthmore.edu/2006-03-16/news/15931), and
        Jeanne Sahadi, "College Costs Spike Again," CNN/Money, October 19, 2004
        (http://money.cnn.com/2004/10/18/pf/college/college_costs/index.htm?postver
        sion=2004101910) for a breakdown of public versus private university
        tuitions by region of the U.S. Private school tuitions are 3.3 to 4.2 times
        greater than public school tuitions.

45.     See for example Steve Hill, "Merchants say A&M can hurt local business,"
        *Bryan-College Station Eagle* (Texas) (May 20, 1990a): A1, A4, and Steve

Hill, "Businesses learn to live with A&M competition," *Bryan-College Station Eagle* (Texas) (May 22, 1990b): A1, A3.

46.  Gary Wolfram, "Private College Under Seige" *USA Today*, January 1, 1999. See also Southern Regional Education Board, Total Enrollment in Higher Education. (Summary of NCES Data) (http://www.sreb.org/main/EdData/Data Library/03/highered/enrollment/FB22.xls); U.S. Department of Education, National Center for Education Statistics, 2003-04 and 2004-05 IPEDS, Table 314 (http://nces.ed.gov/programs/digest/d05/tables/dt05_314.asp); and U.S. Department of Education, National Center for Education Statistics, 2003-04 and 2004-05 IPEDS, Table 197 (http://nces.ed.gov/programs/digest/d05/tables/dt05_197.asp).

47.  Conversation with economics professor Isaac Ehrlich at the University of Buffalo.

48.  John R. Lott, "Predation by Public Enterprises," *Journal of Public Economics* no. 43 (1990): 237-251 and D. Daniel Sokol, "Express Delivery and the Postal Sector in the Context of Public Sector Anti-competitive Practices," *Northwestern Journal of International Law and Business*, (2003): 353-381.

49.  The German government still owned a majority of Deutsche Post AG at the time. For a detailed discussion of the Deutsche Post case in the context of trade liberalization, see Robert B. Cohen, "Trade and Competition Issues Raised by the Liberalization of State-Owned Monopolies: The Example of Deutsche Post's Cross-subsidization of Its Express Delivery Operations," (Washington, DC: Economic Strategy Institute) 2004. See also R. Richard Geddes, "Pricing by State-owned Enterprises," Cornell University working paper (2006).

50.  Geddes, "Pricing by State-owned Enterprises." A competitor brought similar charges against the Japanese Post, though it did not win the case. Editorial, "Japan's Postal Behemoth Digs In on Deregulation," *Wall Street Journal*, January 6, 2000, A14.

51.  US Postal Rate Commission, Domestic Mail Rate History (http://www.prc.gov/rates/stamphistory.htm) and 2006 Rate Source: USPS Express Mail Rate Table (http://pe.usps.com/text/dmm300/ratesandfees.htm#wp3804532). See also Lott, "Predation by Public Enterprises," 237-251.

52.  John R. Lott, "Predation by Public Enterprises," *Journal of Public Economics* no. 43 (1990): 237-251.

53.  NASA claims that it costs about $450 million to launch each shuttle, though other estimates are much higher. The cost of taking cargo into orbit is now over $20,000 per pound. NASA, Frequently Asked Questions, Kennedy

Space Center, http://www.nasa.gov/centers/kennedy/about/information/shuttle_faq.html#10. See also Milton R. Copulos, "Hearings before the House Committee on Science and Technology, subcommittee on Space Science and Applications," June 18, 1985,1-2, and Associated Press, "Critics scrutinize cost of shuttle," *USA Today*, February 4, 2003 (http://www.usatoday.com/news/nation/2003-02-04-shuttle-critics_x.htm).

54.     John M. Logsdon and Ray A. Williamson, "U.S. Access to Space," *Scientific American*, vol. 260, no. 3 (March, 1989): 34-40.

55.     See John R. Lott, Jr. and Tim Opler, "Testing Whether Predatory Commitments are Credible," *Journal of Business*, vol. 69, no. 3, (July 1996), 339–82 and Lott, *Are Predatory Commitments Credible?: Who Should the Courts Believe?* (Chicago: University of Chicago Press, 1999), Chapters 1 and 2.

56.     For more examples, see Lott, *Are Predatory Commitments Credible?*, University of Chicago Press, 1999.

57.     For a discussion of guilds in Paris and Genoa see Steven A. Epstein, *Wage and Labor Guilds in Medieval Europe*, (Chapel Hill: The University of North Carolina Press, 1991).

58.     Adam Smith, *An Inquiry into the Nature and Causes of the Wealth of Nations* [1774]. Edited by E. Canna, (Chicago: University of Chicago Press, 1974) 133, 136-7. Milton Friedman wrote his dissertation on how modern professional licenses restrict entry into a profession in order to drive up incomes. See Milton Friedman, "Income from Independent Professional Practice," Ph.D. Dissertation, Columbia University, 1946. Also published in: Milton Friedman and Simon Kuznets, *Income from Independent Professional Practice*, NBER Publications, (New York: National Bureau of Economic Research, 1954).

59.     Epstein, 1991, 106-09, 141-43. See also Richard MacKenney, Tradesmen and Traders: *The World of the Guilds in Venice and Europe, c. 1250- c. 1650*, (Totowa, New Jersey: Barnes & Noble Books, 1987).

60.     Robert J. Havighurst, study director, National Commission on Accrediting: *Commission on the Study of Optometric Education*, National Commission on Accreditation: Washington, D.C. (1973), and David P. Bianco, ed., *Professional and Occupational Licensing Directory: A Descriptive Guide to State and Federal Licensing, Registration, and Certification Requirements*, (Detroit: Gale Research Inc., 1993), 697-704.

61.     Helen Hofer Gee and E. Shepley Nourse, *Admission Requirements of American Medical Colleges Including Canada*, Association of American Medical Colleges, Washington, D.C., 1960. See also *Comprehensive Guide of Bar*

*Admission Requirements*, American Bar Association Section of Legal Education, 1989, and *AAMC Curriculum Directory*, Association of American Medical Colleges, Washington, D.C., 1972–1980.

62.  Bureau of Labor Statistics, "Training, Other Qualifications, and Advancement," U.S. Department of Labor, *Occupational Outlook Handbook* (http://www.bls.gov/oco/ocos169.htm#training).

63.  David P. Bianco, 1993, 155-190.

64.  Bianco, 1993.

65.  Association of Real Estate License Law Officials, 1991. Also based upon an interview with Joe McClary from the Association of Real Estate License Law Officials (334) 260-2928).

66.  Data are for the U.S. during the 2001-2002 academic year. Wendy Stock and John Siegfried, "Time-to-Degree for Economics Ph.D. Class of 2001-2002," *American Economic Review* (May 2006): 467-474. The ranges of time-to-degree were obtained by the author from Wendy Stock.

67.  Charlotte Tubbs, "Teacher Job Fair Attracts 1,500 Prospective Educators," *Arkansas Democrat-Gazette* (Little Rock), February 6, 2005.

68.  John R. Lott, Jr., "Why Does Professional Licensing Rely on Minimum Schooling Requirements," University of Chicago Working Paper, 1996.

69.  There are two types of tests that doctors take to practice: board and licensing exams. Doctors can in theory practice with just a license, but hospitals will rarely let a doctor perform surgery without the doctor being board certified. Board exams are different than the licensing exams and these tests do try to evaluate skills, such as a surgeon's ability to perform an operation. For information on licensing see G.F. Dillon, J.R. Boulet, R.E. Hawkins, and D.B. Swanson, "Simulations in the United States Medical Licensing Examination," *Quality & Safety in Health Care*, 2004:i41-i45 (http://qshc.bmj.com/cgi/content/full/13/suppl_1/i41); Kate Shatzkn, "Test for better bedside manner fulfills Melnick's mission," *Physician Executive*, July-August 2004 (http://www.findarticles.com/p/articles/mi_m0843/is_4_30/ai_n6133525) and Anthony M. Alleman and Al F. Al-Assaf, "Have you Wondered About Your Colleague's Surgical Skills?" *American Journal of Medical Quality* (March/April 2005): 78-82 (http://ajm.sagepub.com/cgi/reprint/20/2/78.pdf).

70.  This also explains why the length of the time requirements gradually increase over time. As a profession's overall quality falls, professionals keep expanding school requirements in order to discourage increasing numbers of ambitious aspirants from joining the profession. As the quality of existing professionals declines, hardworking, ambitious students become more

serious threats as potential competitors in the field. Of course, testing also plays an important role by maintaining a floor on the quality of entrants. Professions may run into trouble if the quality of new entrants declines too much.

71.  This discussion is based upon Robert G. Hansen and John R. Lott, Jr., "Regulating Indoor Air Quality: The Economist's View," *The EPA Journal*, vol. 19, no. 4 (October-December, 1993): 30-31.

72.  Http://miltonfriedman.blogspot.com.

## Chapter Four: Crime and Punishment

1.  Robert E. McCormick and Robert D. Tollison, "Crime on the Court," *Journal of Political Economy 1984*, 223-235.

2.  The original work on this point was done by Brian Goff, William Shughart, and Robert Tollison, "Batter Up!: Moral Hazard and the effects of the designated hitter rule on hit batsmen," *Economic Inquiry*, July 1997. See also John C. Bradbury and Douglas J. Drinen, "Crime and Punishment in Major League Baseball." *Economic Inquiry*, 2007.

3.  Michael E. Staten and John Umbeck, "Information Costs and Incentives to Shirk: Disability Compensation of Air Traffic Controllers," *American Economic Review*, December 1982, 1023-1037.

4.  Larry L. Bailey, David J. Schroeder, and Julia Pounds, "The Air Traffic Control Operation Error Severity Index: An Initial Evaluation," U.S. Department of Transportation, Federal Aviation Administration, April 2005. Http://www.faa.gov/library/reports/medical/oamtechreports/2000s/media/0 505.pdf.. See also Staten and Umbeck, "Information Costs," 1034-1035. The "Operation Error Severity Index" is based on a number of factors: vertical and horizontal separation distances, relative flight paths, cumulative closure rates, as well as the air traffic controller's awareness of the problem. If controllers want to increase their error rate without actually causing more accidents, errors should occur during relatively light traffic volumes, not primarily when the controller is "overloaded." And indeed, Staten and Umbeck cite evidence for this.

5.  Eric Ferkenhoff, Darnell Little and David Mendell, "Murders in Illinois jump by 10%," *Chicago Tribune*, June 30, 2002, C1.

6.  The data were obtained from the FBI UCR data: http://www.fbi.gov/ucr/ucr.htm.

7.  Lynette Clemetson, "The Gospel According to John," *Newsweek*, February 12, 2001, 25.

8. Valerie Pottie Bunge, Holly Johnson, and Theirno Balde, "Exploring Crime Patterns in Canada," Crime and Justice Research Paper Series, *Statistics Canada*, Ministry of Industry, 2005. Canada had a smaller percentage drop in its murder rate than did America in the 1990s, but it already had a lower murder rate when the decade began. Canada registered a lower murder rate despite the fact that its overall violent crime rate, surprisingly, is about 50 percent greater than America's. The International Crime Victimization Survey, http://www.unicri.it/wwd/analysis/icvs/pdf_files/key2000i/app4.pdf.

9. The information for these figures was obtained from: http://www.ojp.usdoj.gov/bjs/glance/tables/viortrdtab.htm, http://www.ojp.usdoj.gov/bjs/glance/tables/proptrdtab.htm, http://www.ojp.usdoj.gov/bjs/dtdata.htm#crime, and http://www.disastercenter.com/crime/uscrime.htm. The reported crime rate is obtained by dividing the number of crimes reported to police departments by the National Crime Victimization Survey that indicates the number of crimes people reported to the pollsters. The arrest rate is obtained by dividing the number of arrests by the National Crime Victimization Survey that indicates the number of crimes people reported to the pollsters.

10. FBI Uniform Crime Reports, Crime in the United States, September 2006. Http://0-www.fbi.gov.mill1.sjlibrary.org/ucr/05cius/data/table_07.html.

11. To understand the magnitude of this change, consider this: if the rate of reporting of violent crimes had remained constant after 1999, the violent crime rate in 2005 would have been 390 per 100,000 people, not 469. Since nearly all murders are reported, this adjustment also implies that the overall violent crime rate has fallen more than the murder rate since 1991.

12. "Findings," *Washington Post*, November 22, 2006.

13. "2006 Program Seeks to Fight Poverty by Building Family Ties," *New York Times*, July 20, 2006.

14. Levitt and Dubner, *Freakonomics*, 137-144 revised edition 2006, 129.

15. Daniel Callahan, *Abortion: Law, Choice, and Morality* (New York: MacMillan Publishers, 1970).

16. Rockefeller Commission, "Report of the Commission on Population Growth and the American Future" presented to the President and Congress in March of 1972. Http://www.population-security.org/rockefeller/011_human_reproduction.htm.

17. Hans Forssman and Inga Thuwe, "One hundred and twenty children born after application for therapeutic abortion refused," *Acta Psychiat. Scand.*, 1966, 71-78.

18. Henry Morgentaler, "Message from Henry," 1998. Online document available at: http://prochoice.about.com/newissues/prochoice/gi/dynamic/offiste.htm?sitehttp://www.morgentaler.ca.

19. Henry Morgantaler made this claim in the late 1960s. By 1979, opinion surveys showed that 61 percent of Americans believed that "many unwanted children end up being subject to child abuse, and it's a mistake to force unwanted children to be born." Roper Center at University of Connecticut Public Opinion Online, survey done from Februrary 8, 1979 to February 12, 1979.

20. David M. Alpern, "Abortion and the Law," *Newsweek*, March 3, 1975.

21. John Donohue and Steven Levitt, "The Impact of Legalizing Abortion on Crime Rates," *Quarterly Journal of Economics*, (2001): 379-420.

22. These were Alaska, California, Hawaii, New York, and Washington.

23. John Donohue and Steven Levitt, "Further Evidence that Legalizing Abortion Lowered Crime: A Reply to Joyce," *Journal of Human Resources* (2004): 29-49. See also Ted Joyce, "Did Legalizing Abortion Lower Crime?" *Journal of Human Resources* (2004): 1-28.

24. The data comes from the Centers for Disease Control. See Abortion Surveillance: Preliminary Analysis—United States, 1996, CDC, December 4, 1998, 1025-1028.

25. John R. Lott, Jr. and John Whitley, "Abortion and Crime: Unwanted Children and Out-of-Wedlock Births," *Economic Inquiry*, Advanced Access June 29, 2006, 3. Donohue and Levitt do examine the relevant CDC data for a few of their estimates that use their aggregate measure of abortion (their so-called "effective" abortion rate). However, they never do this for the estimates that break down the murder rates by the age of the murderer where it is possible to closely link the age of the murderer with whether abortions were legalized at the time of birth ("Further Evidence that Legalizing Abortion Lowered Crime: A Reply to Joyce," *Journal of Human Resources*, 2004, 29-49).

26. Abortion Surveillance: Preliminary Analysis – United States, 1996, Centers for Disease Control, December 4, 1998, 1025-1028, 1035. "Homicide Trends in the United States," Bureau of Justice Statistics (www.ojp.usdoj.gov/bjs/homicide), June 29, 2006.

27. The omission is curious, since it would have been easy to test a eugenics explanation, for example by measuring whether the drop in crime in the 1990s was still evident after accounting for the changing racial composition of the population. All my research on crime, including the link to abortion, controls for demographics.

28.  A range of economists have noted Donahue and Levitt's failure to test the eugenics approach. See Jonathan Klick, "Econometric Analyses of U.S. Abortion Policy: A Critical Review," *Fordham Urban Law Journal*, March 2004.

29.  George Akerloff, Janet Yellen, and Michael L. Katz, "An Analysis of Out-of-Wedlock Childbearing in the United States," *Quarterly Journal of Economics*, 1996, 277-317. See also Jonathan Klick and Thomas Stratmann, "The Effect of Abortion Legalization on Sexual Behavior: Evidence from Sexually Transmitted Diseases," *Journal of Legal Studies*, June 2003, 407-433. Klick and Stratmann find that "a large increase in gonorrhea and syphillis rates [occurred] due to changing sexual behavior" as a result of abortion (p. 431). See also George Akerloff and Janet Yellen, "An Analysis of Out-of-Wedlock Births in the United States," *Brookings Policy Brief*, August 1996 (http://www.heartland.org/pdf/24604a.pdf), 3.

30.  Alberto F. Alesina and Paola Giuliano, "Divorce, Fertility and the Shot Gun Marriage," Harvard University Institute for Economic Research Working Paper, No. 2117, June 2006. Alesina and Giuliano find that reducing restrictions on abortion increases out-of-wedlock births, but decreases births in two-parent families. See also Akerloff, Yellen, and Katz, "An Analysis of Out-of-Wedlock Childbearing," 277-317, and John R. Lott, Jr. And John Whitley, "Abortion and Crime: Unwanted Children and Out-of-Wedlock Births," *Economic Inquiry*, Advanced Access published June 29, 2006, 19-20.

31.  Akerloff, Yellen, and Katz, "An Analysis of Out-of-Wedlock Childrearing;" Akerloff and Yellen, "An Analysis of Out-of-Wedlock Births;" and Alesina and Giuliano, "Divorce, Fertility and the Shot Gun Marriage."

32.  Http://statistics.adoption.com/information/adoption-statistics-placing-children.htm. Interestingly, the peak year for adoptions was 1970, the year when abortion was granted unrestricted access in five states, including the two largest, California and New York. See George Akerloff, Janet Yellen, and Michael L. Katz, "An Analysis of Out-of-Wedlock Childbearing in the United States," *Quarterly Journal of Economics*, 1996, 277-317. For other evidence on these trends see Department of Health and Human Services, "Report to Congress on Out-of-Wedlock Childbearing," September 1995, p. 53 (http://www.cdc.gov/nchs/data/misc/wedlock.pdf).

33.  Jay D. Teachman, Jeffrey Thomas, Kathleen Paasch, "Legal Status and Stability of Corresidential Unions," *Demography*, 1991, 571-586. See also

Britta Hoem and Jan M. Hoem, "The Disruption of Marital and Non-Marital Unions in Contemporary Sweden," 61-93, in James Trussell, R. Hankinson, and J Tilton (eds.), *Demographic Applications of Event History Analysis*, (Oxford, England: Clarendon Press, 1992).

34.   A large portion of out-of-wedlock births are to teenage mothers. Without the increase in teenage births, the aggravated assault rate would have been about 20 percent lower than it was. See Jennifer Hunt, "Do Teen Births Keep American Crime High," *Journal of Law and Economics*, October 2006, 533-566. The increased criminality among children born outside of wedlock is borne out in many other studies, although much of the research fails to separate out whether it is single parent families that lead to more crime or something else that causes both more single parent families and more crime. Examples of this research include: report by the Social Exclusion Unit, "Reducing Re-Offending by Ex-Prisoners" (2002). Http:// scholar.google.com/scholar?hl=en&lr=&q=cache:DVVPgqNYQHsJ; www. renewal.net/Documents/Policy%2520Guidance/Reducingreoffendingexprisoners.pdf 1; Sampson, R. J. (1987), "Urban black violence: The effect of male joblessness and family disruption," *American Journal of Sociology 93*, 348–82; and Kellam, S. G., Adams, R. G., Brown, C. H., and Ensminger, M. E. (1982), "The long-term evolution of the family structure of teens and older mothers," *Journal of Marriage and the Family 44*, 539–54.

35.   Child Trends tabulations of data from the 2002 National Survey of America's Families. See also Laura Meckler, "How a U.S. Official Promotes Marriage to Help Poor Kids," *Wall Street Journal*, November 20, 2006.

36.   "Oops-onomics," *The Economist*, December 1, 2005. Levitt and Donohue thought they had accounted for whether states with low crime rates after the change in abortion laws already had low crime rates before the change. While Donohue and Levitt correctly described what test should be done, they carried out a different test. Another flaw is that they used changes in the abortion rate to explain changes in the total number of crimes in a state, not changes in the crime rate. For example, California and Louisiana may have had similar murder rates per 100,000 people in 1980 (14.5 and 15.7, respectively), but they had vastly different numbers of murder (3,411 and 661). The authors made a similar mistake in their arrest statistics, confusing the total number of arrests with the arrest rate.

37.   Christopher L. Foote and Christopher F. Goetz, "Testing Economic Hypotheses with State-Level Data: A Comment on Donohue and Levitt

(2001)," Federal Reserve Bank of Boston Working Paper No. 05-15, November 22, 2005. Their Table 1, row 1, shows that adding the state-year fixed effects implies that abortion increases violent crime, though it isn't statistically significant. Foote and Goetz accounted for the number of people in different states to measure the per capita rates of crime and abortion and they used the arrests per capita instead of the total number of arrests in a state. Doing so led to results implying a strong, statistically significant increase in violent crime from more abortion.

38. The study by Whitley and I tried to improve on Donohue and Levitt's methodology through steps such as using murder data that more closely linked the date of a murderer's arrest with the date of his crime and by accounting for abortions performed prior to *Roe v. Wade* and to the 1970 "legalization" in five states See John R. Lott, Jr. And John Whitley, "Abortion and Crime: Unwanted Children and Out-of-Wedlock Births," *Economic Inquiry*, Advanced Access published June 29, 2006, 14.

Donohue and Levitt responded to these criticisms by developing new estimates of abortion's effect on crime, estimates that they claimed accurately reflect whether a criminal was born before or after the legalization of abortion. The most accurate data, however, continue to show that legalized abortion increased crime. Furthermore, a new working paper by the pair does not use the most relevant data—the FBI's Supplemental Homicide Report (SHR). See Donohue and Levitt, "Measurement Error, Legalized Abortion, the Decline in Crime: A Response to Foote and Goetz (2005)," University of Chicago Working Paper, January 2006. One crucial advantage of the SHR is that it records information according to the date that crimes were committed, not the date of arrest. For crimes such as murder, many years can elapse between the crime and the perpetrator's arrest, thus skewing annual statistics. Based on SHR figures, my study with Whitley not only links dates of each criminal's birth with what the abortion law was at that time, but also takes into account cross-state mobility. Unfortunately, the FBI only directly linked a criminal's characteristics with when the crime occurred for the data regarding murder, not any other crime. Apparently, the only other study that uses the SHR is by Ted Joyce, who also found that the legalization of abortion implies more murders. See Ted Joyce, "The Inconsequential Association Between legalized Abortion and Age Specific Crime Rates," Baruch College Working Paper, March 2006.

39.  John R. Lott, Jr. And John Whitley, "Abortion and Crime: Unwanted Children and Out-of-Wedlock Births," *Economic Inquiry*, Advanced Access published June 29, 2006, 5-6.

40.  Abortion Law, History & Religion, The Canadian Health Network (http://www.cbctrust.com/history_law_religion.php#62). Although a 1969 Canadian abortion law loosened some restrictions on abortion, the law was nevertheless extremely strict. A committee of at least three doctors had to decide whether an abortion was necessary to protect the mother's health, and the mother had no right to appeal their decision. These conditions were as strict as the most restrictive U.S. state laws prior to 1970. Studies of other countries have also cast doubt on the theory that abortion reduces crime. See Leo Kahane, David Paton, and Rob Simmons, "The Abortion-Crime Link: Evidence from England and Wales," Department of Economics, California State University, East Bay Working paper, March 2006 and Christopher L. Foote and Christopher F. Goetz, "Testing Economic Hypotheses with State-Level Data: A Comment on Donohue and Levitt (2001)," Federal Reserve Bank of Boston Working Paper No. 05-15, November 22, 2005.

41.  However, as discussed later in this chapter, the impact of race on crime rates during the 1990s was very small. All the demographics for age, race, and sex accounted for only about 1 percent of the change in crime rates.

42.  John R. Lott, "Does a Helping Hand Put Others at Risk?," *Economic Inquiry*, April 2000, 241 and 242.

43.  The survey was conducted for the U.S. Department of Justice and Nassau County, New York. See Marvin Dunnetted, Joan G. Haworth, Leaetta Hough, James L. Outtz, Erich P. Prien, Neal Schmitt, Bernard Siskin, and Sheldon Zedeck, "Police Selection and Promotion Practices Survey Results," HRStrategies (April 1993), 18.

44.  Ibid.

45.  "Test Officials Question State's Move," *The Advocate* (Baton Rouge, La.), August 31, 1996.

46.  Spielman, Fran, "Mayor Defends Hiring Promotion Decisions on Police and Firefighters," *Chicago Sun-Times* (January 31, 1996): 16, and "U.S. Judge OKS Exam for Firefighting Hiring; Ruling Ends 2 Decades of Federal Oversight," *Chicago Tribune*, July 25, 1995.

47.  Flannery, Mary, "Fitness Standards Set Up Through 'Gender Norming,'" *Houston Chronicle*, September 11, 1995, 2.

48.   Frank J. Landy, Principal Investigator. Alternatives to Chronological Age in Determining Standards of Suitability for Public Safety Jobs, volume 1: *Technical Report*, Boulder, Colorado: Saville and Holdsworth, 31 (January 1992).

49.   Mary Ellen Synon, "Q. How do you help criminals get away? A. Easy, recruit women officers," *Mail on Sunday* (London), May 1, 2005, 59.

50.   The central part of my research examined the largest 189 cities in the U.S. According to the U.S. Department of Justice, nineteen of those cities had consent decrees with the US government. Those consent decrees restricted the cities' ability to include intelligence tests in hiring new employees.

51.   John R. Lott, Jr., "Does a Helping hand Put Others At Risk?: Affirmative Action, Police Departments, and Crime," *Economic Inquiry*, vol. 38, no. 2 (April 2000): 239-277.

52.   Ibid.

53.   A gun might not be as much of an equalizer for female officers as it is for women who use a gun defensively. Officers are frequently called upon to have physical contact with the criminals that they are pursuing, while women who use a gun defensively merely use the gun to keep a threatening person at bay.

54.   John R. Lott, Jr., "Does a Helping hand Put Others At Risk?: Affirmative Action, Police Departments, and Crime," Economic Inquiry, vol. 38, no. 2 (April 2000): 257-260.

55.   Bryan Hubbell and Randall Kramer, "An Empirical Bayes Approach to Combining Estimates of the Value of a Statistical Life for Environmental Policy Analysis," US Environmental Protection Agency National Center for Environmental Economics Working paper, November, 2001. W. Kip. Viscusi, Fatal Tradeoffs: Public and Private Responsibilities for Risk. (New York: Oxford University Press, 1992).

56.   Uniform Crime Report, "Law Enforcement Officers Killed and Assaulted, 2005," FBI, Department of Justice, October 2006 (http://www.fbi.gov/ucr/killed/2005/downloaddocs/feloniouslykilled.pdf). For information on accidental deaths of police see http://www.fbi.gov/ucr/killed/2005/table46.htm.

57.   This is a fairly typical year. Over the ten years from 1993 to 2002, there were on average 64 law enforcement officers murdered on the job each year (though the number of police officers rose over time). Source: "Law Enforcement Officers Killed and Assaulted, 2002," FBI, U.S. Department of Justice.

58.  Obtained via Bureau of Justice Statistics, Capital Punishment, 1985-2005,
     (http://www.ojp.usdoj.gov/bjs/pubalp2.htm#cp) and from FBI Uniform
     Crime Reports, 1976-2005, (http://www.ojp.usdoj.gov/bjs/homicide/tables/
     totalstab.htm).

59.  Not all murderers are eligible for the death penalty. To qualify, murders
     must have either killed multiple victims, children, or law enforcement offi-
     cers, or committed murder while committing another felony. The smaller
     group of criminals that meet this criteria face a 1 in 70 chance of being exe-
     cuted. From 1977 to 2003, about 25 percent of murders were eligible for
     the death penalty. This assumes that that ratio holds for 2005. See Jeffrey
     Fagan, Franklin E. Zimring, and Amanda Geller, "Capital Punishment and
     Capital Murder: Market Share and the Deterrent Effects of the Death
     Penalty," *Texas Law Review* (June 2006): 1819.

60.  Steven Levitt, "Understanding Why Crime Fell in the 1990s: Four Factors
     that Explain the Decline and Six that Do Not," *Journal of Economics Per-
     spectives* (2004): 175.

61.  For more on the role played by risk in criminal behavior, see W. Kip Viscusi,
     "The Risks and Rewards of Criminal Activity: A Comprehensive Test of
     Criminal Deterrence," *Journal of Labor Economics* (1986): 317-340, and
     Michael K. Block and Vernon E. Gerety, "Some Experimental Evidence on
     Differences Between Student and Prisoner Reactions to Monetary Penalties
     and Risk," *Journal of Legal Studies* (January 1995): 123-138.

62.  Raymond Bonner and Ford Fessenden, "States With No Death Penalty
     Share Lower Homicide Rates," *New York Times*, September 22, 2000, A1.

63.  These were Alaska, Hawaii, Iowa, Maine, Massachusetts, Michigan, Min-
     nesota, North Dakota, Rhode Island, West Virginia, Wisconsin, and Vermont.

64.  From 1977 to 1998, the population weighted drop in murder rates for the
     12 states that never instituted the death penalty fell by 21 percent. For the
     38 other states, their murder rate fell by 29 percent. Http://www.disaster-
     center.com/crime/uscrime.htm.

65.  Some analysts inexplicably date the end of capital punishment to the 1972
     Furman decision by the Supreme Court, even though executions had
     stopped in 1968. See John Donohue and Wolfers, "Uses and abuses of
     empirical evidence in the death penalty debate," *Stanford Law Review*,
     2006, 791-845. The graph I show uses the execution rate because it gives
     readers the best indication of the execution risk that criminals face by com-
     mitting murder.

66.    Paul G. Cassell and Richard Fowles, "Handcuffing the Cops? A Thirty-Year Perspective on Miranda's Harmful Effects on Law Enforcement," *Stanford Law Review* (April, 1998): 1055-1144. The Miranda decision may have affected crime rates, but it's precise effect is difficult to evaluate; since it was a Supreme Court decision, we can only evaluate it through time-series data for the entire United States. Furthermore, there were so many other Supreme Court decisions as well as other possible explanatory factors that it is simply impossible to disentangle all of them.

67.    The first serious cross-sectional tests using census data were in Isaac Ehrlich, "Capital Punishment and Deterrence: Some Further Thoughts and Additional Evidence," *Journal of Political Economy*, August 1977. The first time-series estimates were in Isaac Ehrlich, "The Deterrent Effect of Capital Punishment," *American Economic Review*, August 1975.

68.    Isaac Ehrlich, "Capital Punishment and Deterrence: Some Further Thoughts and Additional Evidence," *Journal of Political Economy* (August 1977): 779.

69.    Committee on Research on Law Enforcement and Criminal Justice, Understanding Crime—An Evaluation of the National Institute of Law Enforcement and Criminal Justice (National Academy of Science, Susan White and Samuel Krislow editors, 1977). See also Alfred Blumstein, Jacqueline Cohen and Daniel Nagin, *Deterrence and Incapacitation: Estimating the Effects of Criminal Sanctions on Crime Rates* (Washington, D.C.: National Academy of Science, 1978). Ehrlich co-authored another study responding to the National Academic of Sciences report. See Isaac Ehrlich and Mark Randall, "Fear of Deterrence," *Journal of Legal Studies* (1977): 293-316.

70.    The few studies that fail to find any deterrence from the death penalty either don't use all the data or measure the execution rate in strange ways. For example, ignoring data from individual states, Narayan and Smyth look only at national statistics through a data set that has only thirty-seven observations. Richard Berk, for his part, achieved his result by discarding data for entire states such as Texas. See Paresh Kumar Narayan and Russell Smyth, "Dead Man Walking: An Empirical Reassessment of the Deterrent Effect of Capital Punishment Using the Bounds Testing Approach to Cointegration," *Applied Economics*, 2006, and Richard Berk, "New Claims about Executions and General Deterrence," *Journal of Empirical Legal Studies*, 2005. Rather than analyzing the percent of murders that result in

execution, some researchers measure the number of executions per prisoner. It is not clear why anyone would believe that if jails are filled up with additional prisoners convicted of crimes like drug possession or car theft, the risk murderers face from execution would decline. Comparing two unrelated statistics, it is hardly surprising that this research cannot identify any benefit from the death penalty. See Lawrence Katz, Steven Levitt, Ellen Shustorovish, "Prison Conditions, Capital Punishment, and Deterrence," *American Law and Economics Review*, 2003, 318-343. Another paper by Donohue and Wolfers has used this approach uncritically. See John Donohue and Wolfers, "Uses and abuses of empirical evidence in the death penalty debate," *Stanford Law Review*, 2006, 791-845.

71. My work with Bill Landes finds a much larger benefit—implying that each execution saves hundreds of lives. We found that each one percentage point in execution rates lowered the murder rate by at least four percent. Lott, *The Bias Against Guns* (2003), Chapter. 6.

72. Lott and Landes in Lott, *The Bias Against Guns* (Regnery 2003), Chapter 6.

73. Lott, *More Guns, Less Crime* (University of Chicago Press, 2000), Chapter 9.

74. Prison wardens face a similar problem. If a prisoner is sentenced to death, it's hard to find an additional penalty that you can impose on him in order to control his behavior. You can take away some privileges, but without some additional penalty it is difficult for the warden to control the prisoner.

75. ABC News/*Washington Post* Poll. June 22-25, 2006 (http://www.pollingreport.com/crime.htm). A 2006 Gallup poll further found that 51 percent of respondents believed the death penalty is not used enough, compared to 25 percent who think it is used "about right" and 21 percent believing it is used "too often." Gallup Poll. May 8-11, 2006 (http://www.pollingreport.com/crime.htm.

76. Polls have found support for the death penalty at 60 percent among Eastern Europeans, 72 percent of South Africans, and 51 percent among Brazilians. See Craig Smith, " In Europe, It's East vs. West on the Death Penalty," *New York Times*, November 19, 2006, p. 4; David W. Moore, "Death Penalty Gets Less Support From Britons, Canadians Than Americans," Gallup Poll News Service, February 20, 2006; Datafolha / Folha de Sao Paulo, http://www.angus-reid.com/polls/index.cfm/fuseaction/viewItem/itemID/12893. See also http://www.angus-reid.com/polls/index.cfm/fuseaction/viewItem/itemID/11872, http://www.angus-reid.com/polls/index.cfm/

fuseaction/viewItem/itemID/9970, http://www.angus-reid.com/polls/index.cfm/fuseaction/viewItem/itemID/11639.

77.   49 percent of Britons support the death penalty (David W. Moore, "Death Penalty Gets Less Support From Britons, Canadians Than Americans," Gallup Poll News Service, February 20, 2006), For somewhat lower percentages, see http://www.angus-reid.com/polls/index.cfm/fuseaction/viewItem/itemID/10758.

78.   In a recent debate over the death penalty, Scalia declared:

> What nations are you talking about? You know, public opinion polls in both England and France, at least until very recently, showed that if they had as responsive a democracy as we do, they would still have the death penalty.
>
> I find it so hypocritical, not that the Europeans don't have the death penalty—fine; although its abolition was imposed by the Court of Human Rights, which said, "You cannot have the death penalty." So it's not as though all the Europeans voted to abolish it. It was judicially imposed, and that doesn't impress me very much.

Source: "ACLU Membership Conference Debate," Federal News Service, October 15, 2006.

79.   "Study Finds 2.6% Increase In U.S. Prison Population," New York Times, July 28, 2003.

80.   The Washington Post makes a similar argument: "It is one of the least-told stories in American crime-fighting. New York, the safest big city in the nation, achieved its now-legendary 70-percent drop in homicides even as it locked up fewer and fewer of its citizens during the past decade. The number of prisoners in the city has dropped from 21,449 in 1993 to 14,129 this past week. That runs counter to the national trend, in which prison admissions have jumped 72 percent during that time" (Michael Powell, "Despite Fewer Lockups, NYC Has Seen Big Drop in Crime," Washington Post, November 24, 2006; There is a simple explanation for why both prison population and crime can fall in New York. When murders fall by 70 percent, can you really keep on expanding the prison population? Note that the prison population has fallen by a third, but violent crime in the city has fallen by much more than that. The number of prisoners per crime has still gone up dramatically. Or take their example for Idaho. "Perhaps as intriguing is the experience in states where officials spent billions of dollars to build

prisons. From 1992 to 2002, Idaho's prison population grew by 174 percent. the largest percentage increase in the nation. Yet violent crime in that state rose by 14 percent." It would have been helpful if they had put the numbers in per capita rates, rather than comparing numbers 10 years apart. Idaho's population grew by more than 14 percent, though less than 174 percent. Thus their crime rate did fall as the prison population grew. Among the academic papers that find an increase in imprisonment leads to less crime, see Thomas Marvell and Carlisle Moody, "Prison Population Growth and Crime Reduction," *Journal of Quantitative Criminology*, 1994, 109–140.

81.   Gordon Tullock, "Does Punishment Deter Crime?" *The Public Interest 36* (Summer 1974), 103-11. James Q. Wilson, *Thinking About Crime*, (New York: Random House, 1985). See a more recent summary in my book, *More Guns, Less Crime* (2000).

82.   David B. Mustard, "Re-examining Criminal Behavior: The Importance of Omitted Variable Bias," *Review of Economics and Statistics*, vol. 84, no. 1, 2002.

83.   John R. Lott, Jr. and John Whitley, "Abortion and Crime: Unwanted Children and Out-of-Wedlock Births," *Economic Inquiry*, April 2001.

84.   There is a broad range of private law enforcement. Other papers look at everything from private security guards (see Bruce Benson and Brent D. Mast, "Privately Produced General Deterrence," *Journal of Law and Economics*, October 2001) to private enforcement catching those who jump bail (see Eric Helland and Alexander Tabarrok, "The Fugitive: Evidence on public verses private law enforcement form bail jumping," *Journal of Law and Economics*, April 2004, 93–122.)

85.   While it is difficult to compile precise national statistics for the number of outstanding concealed weapons permits, the following list relates the figures in some states: Florida (549,000) (http://licgweb.doacs.state.fl.us/stats/license-typecount.html); Pennsylvania (600,000) (http://www.argusleader.com/apps/pbcs.dll/article?AID=/20061217/NEWS/612170334/-1/DATABASE01); Washington (239,000) (http://seattletimes.nwsource.com/html/localnews/2003298710_shootingside11m.html); Ohio (82,144) (http://www.ag.state.oh.us/le/prevention/concealcarry/statistics.asp); Utah (80,000) (http://bci.utah.gov/CFP/Firearm%20Statistical%20Review/firearmrev_200603.pdf); Texas (247,000) (http://www.txdps.state.tx.us/administration/crime_records/chl/demographics.htm); Virginia (125,020) (Let's hunt for answers on gun use,

*Richmond Times-Dispatch*, February 15, 2006); Indiana (300,000) (http://www2.indystar.com/articles/1/161649-4651-092.html), Michigan (133,000) (http://www.michigan.gov/documents/msp/ccw_county_report_ approved_177644_7.pdf); North Carolina (59,597) (http://sbi2.jus.state. nc.us/crp/public/other/conceal/Sept302004stats.pdf); and South Dakota (41,000) (http://www.argusleader.com/apps/pbcs.dll/article?AID=/20061217/ NEWS/612170334/-1/DATABASE01).

86.   Permits are particularly popular among celebrities who face a variety of potential security threats: in 2006, Donald Trump, Robert De Niro, Harvey Keitel, Howard Stern, and Don Imus were among those holding right-to-carry permits just in New York City. A high rate of permits is also held by professional athletes, including NBA stars Shaquille O'Neal, Paul Pierce, and Vince Carter, and NFL players like Edgerrin James, Marvin Harrison, Santana Moss, Jason Taylor, Bob Sanders, Cato June, Jeff Saturday, and Daunte Culpepper. Even famous coaches such as Barry Switzer and Bobby Knight have carried concealed handguns. See Bob Hohler, "Many players regard firearm as a necessity: Concealed weapon licenses common," *Boston Globe*, November 10, 2006; Kenneth Lovett, "Mike to Gun-Permit Holders: 'Pack' It in," *New York Post*, November 1, 2006; and John R. Lott Jr., "Athletes and Guns," Foxnews.com, January 28, 2004 (http://www. foxnews.com/story/0,2933,109670,00.html).

87.   Some gun control advocates, however, continue to deny this. For example, Douglas Weil, while he was with Handgun Control (now called the Brady Campaign), claimed: "In states with lax CCW [Concealed Carry Weapons] laws, hundreds of licensees have committed crimes both before and after their licensure. For example, in Texas, which weakened its CCW law in 1996, the Department of Public Safety reported that felony and misdemeanor cases involving CCW permit holders rose 54.4% between 1996 and 1997." (Douglas Weil, "Carrying Concealed Guns is Not the Solution," Intellectualcapital.com, March 26, 1998). This is indeed true, but Weil fails to mention that the number of permits also increased by 50 percent between those two years, thus keeping the rate at which permit holders were arrested virtually unchanged. Texas permit holders actually tend to be quite law-abiding compared to the rest of the population, with just 180 out of 225,000 convicted of a misdemeanor or felony in 2001 (http://www. txdps.state.tx.us/administration/crime_records/chl/convrates.htm). For a more extensive debunking of these and other faulty claims of gun control

advocates, see Chapter 9 of my book, *More Guns, Less Crime* (2000).

88.    Florida Department of Agricultural and Consumer Services, Concealed Weapon / Firearm Summary Report, October 1, 1987 - November 30, 2006 (http://licgweb.doacs.state.fl.us/stats/cw_monthly.html). See also *More Guns, Less Crime* (2000), 221.

89.    Telephone interview with Ms. Mary Kennedy of the Florida Department of Agricultural and Consumer Services, Concealed Weapon / Firearm Division during February 2007.

90.    Jonathan Rauch, "And Don't Forget Your Gun," *National Journal*, March 20, 1999.

91.    Http://www.ojp.usdoj.gov/bjs/cvict.htm.

92.    Brian Blasé, "The National Crime Victimization Survey," November 27, 2005, http://johnrlott.tripod.com/other/NCVS.html.

93.    Stephen Bronars and John R. Lott, Jr., "Deterrence, Right-to-Carry Concealed Handgun Laws, and the Geographic Displacement of Crime," *American Economic Review*, May 1998, 475-479.

94.    Lott, *More Guns, Less Crime*, Ch. 9.

95.    See Lott, *More Guns, Less Crime*, 110–113.

96.    Mark Duggan, "More Guns, More Crime," *Journal of Political Economy*, 2001, 1110.

97.    Carlisle E. Moody and Thomas B. Marvel, "Guns and Crime," *Southern Economic Journal*, 2005, 720-736. Duggan uses some creative methods to reach his conclusion that lawful gun ownership increases crime. For example, he estimates gun ownership by measuring sales of *Guns&Ammo*, the fourth biggest-selling gun magazine. Unfortunately, his result only holds true for a single magazine whose unusual sales practices skew the resultes. Skip Johnson, a vice president for *Guns&Ammo's* and *Handguns Magazine's* parent company, *Primedia*, told me that between 5 and 20 percent of *Guns&Ammo's* national sales in a particular year were purchases by his own company to meet its guaranteed sales to advertisers. These copies were given away for free in places like dentists' and doctors' offices. Because the purchases were meant to offset any unexpected national declines in sales, Johnson said that his own purchases were very selective and produced very large swings in a relatively small number of counties. More importantly, while a precise breakdown of how these free samples are counted toward the sales in different counties is not available, these self-purchases were apparently related to factors that helped explain why people might purchase

guns, and these factors included changing crime rates. Johnson indicated that the issue of self-purchases is particularly important for *Guns&Ammo* because the magazine had declining sales over part of this period. See also Peter Kennedy's example 20. Peter E. Kennedy, "Oh No! I Got the Wrong Sign: What Should I Do?" *Journal of Economic Education*, 36(1) (Winter 2005): 77–92.

98.    Another skeptical study by Dan Black and Dan Nagin disregarded all counties with fewer than 100,000 people, as well as the entire state of Florida, but still found drops in robberies and aggravated assaults attributable to right-to-carry laws. See Dan A. Black and Daniel S. Nagin, "Do Right-to-Carry Laws Deter Violent Crime?" *Journal of Legal Studies* (January 1998): 212. The drop in robbery was statistically significant at 6 percent.

Jens Ludwig dismissed as an anomaly his own findings of decreasing crime rates connected to the passage of right-to-carry laws because crime fell against both juveniles and adults, even though only adults are allowed to carry concealed handguns. An earlier study I co-authored with David Mustard explained this same result by noting that both age groups benefit when the passage of right-to-carry laws results in criminals leaving an area, or in the protection of juveniles by adults with right-to-carry permits.See David Mustard and I found the same result (*Journal of Legal Studies*, 1997, 51), but we also offered explanations for it that Ludwig never investigated. See Jens Ludwig, "Concealed Gun Carrying Laws and Violent Crime: Evidence from State Panel Data," *International Review of Law and Economics*, November 1998, and John Lott and David Mustard, "Crime, Deterrence, and Right-to-carry Concealed Handguns," *Journal of Legal Studies* (1997): 51. Similar problems are found in the other major studies denying that right-to-carry laws reduce crime rates. Duwe, Kovandzic, and Moody claim to find no statistically significant impact of right-to-carry laws on multiple victim public shootings, though they only examine the very small set of cases where four or more people were killed in attacks. Indeed, while the original work that I did with Bill Landes found significant drops in crime when we examined two or more people killed or three or more people killed, we also did not find a statistically significant result for one type of specification when we looked at only four or more people killed (Lott, *The Bias Against Guns*, 307, fn. 61). See Grant Duwe, Tomislave Kovandzic, and Carlisle E. Moody, "The Impact of Right-to-Carry Concealed Firearm Laws on Mass Public Shootings," *Homicide Studies*, (November 2002): 271-

296. The work by Dezhbakhsh and Rubin is discussed in my book *More Guns, Less Crime* (302, and 304). See also Hashem Dezhbakhsh and Paul H. Rubin, "The Effect of Concealed Handgun Laws on Crime: Going Beyond the Dummy Variables," *International Review of Law and Economics*, 23, 2003, 199-216, and Dezhbakhsh, Rubin, and Shepherd, *American Law and Economics Review*, 2003.

Finally, there are several unrefereed papers by Ian Ayres and John Donohue. For a response to their 1999 paper, see my book *More Guns, Less Crime*, Chapter 9. For their 2003 *Stanford Law Review* paper, see Plassmann and Whitlely's piece in the same law review. Plassmann and Whitley point to a number of misleading figures from Ayres and Donohue (there was no increase in crime for in the fifteenth, sixteenth, and seventeenth years after the right-to-carry laws were in effect, and the only appearance of an increase was an artifact of them dropping states out of their sample). Also in the Ayres and Donohue paper state by state regression results are an artifact of them limiting the time period to five years and fitting a line and an intercept shift to non-linear data. See Ian Ayres and John Donohue, "Nondiscretionary Concealed Weapons Laws," *American Law and Economics Review*, Fall 1999, 436-470. Florenz Plassmann and John Whitley Confirming 'More Guns, Less Crime,'" *Stanford Law Review*, 2003, 1313-1369, http://johnrlott.tripod.com/Plassmann_Whitley.pdf. Ian Ayres and John Donohue, "Shooting Down the More Guns, Less Crime Hypothesis," *Stanford Law Review*, 2003. While their *American Law and Economics Review* piece simply argues that the evidence that right-to-carry laws reduce crime is weak, the final conclusion of their other paper is more ambiguous. I am relying on Donohue's statement that "his own research shows that concealed carry laws have a negligible effect on crime either way. 'We're still not sure what the true impact is. It's very easy to get it wrong.'" See Erin Grace, "Concealed-carry absolutes are a moving target," *Omaha World-Herald* (Nebraska), July 16, 2006.

99.  Another quarter of the drop in crime is explained by changing economic factors such as the male unemployment rate, non-college educated male wages, and family income. See Eric Gould, Bruce Weinberg, and David Mustard, "Crime Rates and Local Labor Market Opportunities in the United States: 1979-1997," *Review of Economics and Statistics*, February 2002: 57, fn. 35.

100. For the very oldest ages the graph is affected somewhat because there are fewer people in those age categories. This really doesn't make much difference until you get to around 60 years of age, and the number of criminals

in that age group is so small that making the adjustments would not make much of a difference.

101. One of the more important, politically incorrect books on crime is Wilson and Hernstein's *Crime and Human Nature*, New York: Simon and Schuster, 1985. The book postulated and provided evidence that certain broad groups of people are more likely to engage in crime.

102. See Table 2.7 in "Murder – Crime in the United States, 2004," Department of Justice, Federal Bureau of Investigation, February 17, 2006 (http://www.fbi.gov/ucr/cius_04/offenses_reported/violent_crime/murder.html).

103. Transcript from CNN's *American Morning*, September 8, 2004 (http://transcripts.cnn.com/TRANSCRIPTS/0409/08/ltm.05.html).

104. John R. Lott, Jr., "Hype and Reality," *Washington Times*, October 28, 2005.

105. In contrast, during the same months in 2003 the murder rate fell only 1 percent.

106. Christopher S. Koper and Jeffrey A. Roth. 2002, *An Updated Assessment of the Federal Assault Weapons Ban: Impacts on Gun Markets, 1994-2000*. Unpublished interim report to the National Institute of Justice, U.S. Department of Justice. Washington, DC: The Urban Institute. See also Christopher S. Koper, 2004. *An Updated Assessment of the Federal Assault Weapons Ban: Impacts on Gun Markets and Gun Violence, 1994-2003*. Report NCJ-204431 to the National Institute of Justice, U.S. Department of Justice. Philadelphia: Jerry Lee Center of Criminology, University of Pennsylvania. Available electronically from the Jerry Lee Center (www.sas.upenn.edu/jerrylee/research.htm) and the National Criminal Justice Reference Service (www.ncjrs.org/pdffiles1/nij/grants/204431.pdf).

107. James Q. Wilson and George L. Kelling, "Broken Windows," *The Atlantic Monthly*, March 1982.

108. Brian A. Reaves and Matthew Hickman, "Police Departments in Large Cities, 1990-2000," Bureau of Justice Statistics, Department of Justice, May 2002 (http://www.ojp.usdoj.gov/bjs/pub/pdf/pdlc00.pdf).

109. Bureau of Justice Statistics, "1985-1997 Homicide and population data for cities with population of 100,000 and over in 1997," FBI, Uniform Crime Reports (http://www.hopemcc.org/data/lgcithom.htm) and FBI Uniform Crime Reports for 2000 (http://www.fbi.gov/ucr/00cius.htm).

110. Reaves and Hickman, 5 and 13-14.

111.   Patrick A. Langan and Matthew Durose, "The Remarkable Drop in Crime in
       New York City," Bureau of Justice Statistics, U.S. Department of Justice,
       October 21, 2004, Appendix table 3. The number of police in New York City
       peaked in 1999 at 41,791. Earlier numbers underreported the change in the
       number of sworn full-time police officers. See Brian A. Reaves and Matthew
       Hickman, "Police Departments in Large Cities, 1990-2000," Bureau of Jus-
       tice Statistics, Department of Justice, May 2002. Large cities are defined as
       those with over 250,000 people (http://www.ojp.usdoj.gov/bjs/pub/pdf/pdlc00.
       pdf). See also Bruce Frankel, "Ex-NYC officer tells stark tale of cops gone
       bad," *USA Today*, September 28, 1993, 3A.

112.   Reaves and Hickman. If I used the NYPD numbers provided by Reaves and
       Hickman showing that the number of sworn full-time police officers went
       from 31,236 in 1990 to 40,435 by 2000, the per capita increase in New
       York's police force is still almost three times greater than that for other large
       cities.

113.   John R. Lott, Jr., "Does a Helping hand Put Others At Risk?: Affirmative
       Action, Police Departments, and Crime," *Economic Inquiry*, vol. 38, no. 2
       (April 2000): 241.

114.   John Marzulli and David L. Lewis, "Cop Hopefuls Face Chase Test to
       Mimic Run After Suspect," *New York Daily News*, March 12, 1997, 7.

115.   Ibid.

116.   Stephen Bronars and John R. Lott, Jr., "Deterrence, Right-to-Carry Con-
       cealed Handgun Laws, and the Geographic Displacement of Crime," *Amer-
       ican Economic Review* (May 1998): 475-479.

117.   Lance Lochner, "Perceptions of the Criminal Justice System," University of
       Western Ontario Working Paper, January 2003.

118.   John Lott, *More Guns, Less Crime* (University of Chicago Press, 2000),
       Chapter 9, 190-4. Other policies analyzed in this study included problem-
       orientated or community-orientated policing programs. Other work exam-
       ining a much smaller sample has confirmed this research. See Bernard
       Hacourt and Jens Ludwig, "Broken Windows: New Evidence from New
       York City and a Five-city Social Experiment," *University of Chicago Law
       Review*, vol. 73, 2006).

119.   John R. Lott, Jr. and Russell Roberts, "Why Comply: The One-Sided
       Enforcement of Price Controls and Victimless Crime Laws," *Journal of
       Legal Studies*, vol. 18, no. 2 (June 1989): 403-414.

120. John R. Lott, Jr. and Russell Roberts, "The Expected Penalty for Committing a Crime: An Analysis of Minimum Wage Violations," *Journal of Human Resources*, vol. 30, no. 2, Spring 1995: 397-408.

121. Rich Schleif, "Project ChildSafe Begins Second Phase of Nationwide Firearm Safety Tour," Project ChildSafe, September 1, 2004 (http://www.projectchildsafe.org/news/092004.cfm).

122. John R. Lott, Jr., "A False Safety," *Washington Times*, July 6, 2006.

123. Public Health News Center, "Gun Laws Requiring Safe Storage Prevent Some Youth Suicides," Johns Hopkins Bloomberg School of Public Health, August 3, 2004.

124. Sam Peltzman, "The Effects of Automobile Safety Regulation," *Journal of Political Economy*, August 1975; W. Kip Viscusi, "The Lulling Effect: The Impact of Child-Resistant Packaging on Aspirin and Analgestic Ingestion," *American Economic Review*, May 1984; and John R. Lott, Jr. and John Whitley, "Safe Storage Gun Laws: Accidental Deaths, Suicides, and Crime," *Journal of Law and Economics*, vol. 44, no. 2, part 2, October 2001, 659-689.

125. John A. C. Conybeare, "Evaluation of automobile safety regulations," *Policy Sciences*, June, 1980, 27-39. While they did not examine pedestrian deaths, other research has found that "improved automobile safety results in more accidents but fewer total injuries both in NASCAR and on the street." Russell S. Sobel and Todd M. Nesbit, "Automobile Safety Regulation and the Incentive to Drive Recklessly: Evidence from NASCAR," *Southern Economic Journal*, forthcoming (accepted August 2006). This idea was discovered by Sam Peltzman, "The Effects of Automobile Safety Regulation," *Journal of Political Economy*, 1975, 677-725. Peltzman's research found no net change in the number of deaths.

126. W. Kip Viscusi, "The Lulling Effect."

127. Paula Spencer, "We Protect Kids from Everything But Fear," *Newsweek*, April 2, 2007. Http://www.msn.com/id/17770831/site/newsweek/.

128. See the National Center for Injury Prevention and Control (http://webappa.cdc.gov/sasweb/ncipc/mortrate10_sy.html).

129. Ibid.

130. Ibid.

131. John R. Lott, Jr., *The Bias Against Guns*, Chapter 7.

132. Ibid.

133. Ibid.

134. Ibid.

135.   Ibid. See also John R. Lott, Jr. and John Whitley, "Safe Storage Gun Laws: Accidental Deaths, Suicides, and Crime," *Journal of Law and Economics*, vol. 44, no. 2, part 2, (October 2001): 659-689. Webster et al. find evidence of a change in suicides for 14- to 17-year-olds. My work in my book and with Whitley examined those under age 15 and those between ages 15 and 19. While there were a few regression estimates that found some drop in suicides for 15- to 19-year-olds, the effects for most regressions did not show statistically significant effects. Daniel W. Webster, Jon S. Vernick, April M. Zeoli, and Jennifer A. Manganello, "Association Between Youth-Focused Firearm Laws and Youth Suicides," *Journal of the American Medical Association*, August 4, 2004.

136.   For the period from 1977 to 1998 see John R. Lott, Jr., *The Bias Against Guns*, 170-171. For earlier research for the period from 1977 to 1996 see John R. Lott, Jr. and John Whitley, "Safe Storage Gun Laws: Accidental Deaths, Suicides, and Crime," *Journal of Law and Economics*, vol. 44, no. 2, part 2, (October 2001): 682.

## Chapter Five: Voting Rights and Voting Wrongs

1.   The most notable exception to this rule is Chile during the Pinoche regime. Some might also include Singapore or even modern day China.

2.   The gender gap was 14 points in 1980, 16 in 1984, 15 in 1988, 5 in 1992, 17 in 1996, 22 in 2000, and 14 in 2004.

3.   Republicans still would have lost the 1992 election, in which Bill Clinton received 41 percent of the men's vote compared to 38 percent for George H. W. Bush. See Karlyn H. Bowman, "Election Results from A to Z," AEI Online, January 1, 2001 (http://www.aei.org/publications/pubID.12234/pub_detail.asp); Ruy Teixeira, "A Tour of the 2004 Exit Poll,"The Century Foundation, November 9, 2004 (http://www.tcf.org/list.asp?type=NC&pubid=767); and Gary Langer, "The Gender Gap Makes a Difference," ABCNews.com, November 8, 1996.

4.   For more examples of issues with evident gender gaps, see the 1996 Voter News Service General Election Exit Poll Survey (http://www.icpsr.umich.edu/cgi-bin/bob/archive2?study=6989&path=ICPSR&docsonly=yes).

5.   Kingsley Browne, "Sex and Temperament in Modern Society: A Darwinian View of the Glass Ceiling and the Gender Gap," *Arizona Law Review*, 1995, 980.

6.  Wyoming and Utah were ahead of their time internationally. Outside the United States, women's suffrage was first gained in New Zealand in 1893 and in various Australian states beginning in 1895. In those Australian states, as in the U.S., women were first given the vote in somewhat out-of-the-way places where relatively few women lived. By granting women's suffrage, these states hoped to attract more women to settle the areas. Additionally, women's suffrage was not viewed as much of a threat, since the small number of women living there meant that their vote initially did not have much of an impact on election outcomes. In 1869, Britain began allowing some women to vote strictly in local elections. Sweden had also granted limited women's suffrage for some local elections in 1862-63. By contrast, Wyoming and Utah granted suffrage to all women for all elections. (http://womenshistory.about.com/od/suffrage/a/intl_timeline.htm).

7.  Unfortunately, no data exists on voting by men and women separately.

8.  To the extent that voting by women reduces the return to men of voting, the simple increase in the percent of the population voting underestimates the number of women who vote.

9.  Because state expenditures and revenues were missing for some years, the changes in the average state's values between years were calculated for those states which had values in both adjacent years. When a state is missing no more than one consecutive year of data, the change between the two years for which the data is available is calculated and then divided by 2. These changes were linked to the average expenditure and revenue levels in the eleventh year after suffrage was enacted. Graphing the means for the observed state expenditures and revenues in each year produces a very similar graph.

10. Figure 2 shows the raw data, but there are other factors that are also changing over time. While giving women the right to vote was the main factor, other factors included the manufacturing wage, fraction of the population over 65, percent of population living in rural areas, total population, percent of workers that were females, percent of workers in manufacturing, and voting regulations.

11. Real per capita expenditures grew from $101 to $208. By comparison, 1994 per capita state government expenditures in 1996 dollars averaged $3,177. See John R. Lott, Jr. and Lawrence Kenny, "Did Women's Suffrage Change the Size and Scope of Government?," *Journal of Political Economy*, vol. 107, no. 6, part 1, December 1999: 1163–98.

12. Ibid.

13. Immigrants experienced the same delay – between 1870 and 1940, for each 10 percent of Americans who were foreign born, the voter turnout rate was reduced another 5 percentage points. The younger people were when they arrived in America, the smaller the decline in voter turnout. As we shall see, a similar delay was evident among African Americans as well.

14. John R. Lott, Jr. and Lawrence Kenny, "Did Women's Suffrage Change the Size and Scope of Government?," *Journal of Political Economy*, vol. 107, no. 6, part 1, December 1999: 1183.

15. Ibid. Interestingly, men raising children on their own are only three percent more likely to vote Democratic than single men without children.

16. The poll tax also made Prohibition more likely by reducing the political influence of the poor, who generally opposed prohibition.

17. While the original thirteen U.S. states had some type of property or tax requirement to vote, all of them had cancelled the requirement by 1856. See Stanley Engerman and Kenneth Sokoloff, "The Evolution of Suffrage Institutions in the New World," National Bureau of Economic Research working paper 8512.

18. Much of this discussion is based upon John R. Lott, Jr., "Evidence of Voter Fraud and the Impact that Regulations to Reduce Fraud have on Voter Participation Rates," SUNY Binghamton working paper (http://ssrn.com/abstract=925611).

19. The Twenty-Fourth Amendment to the Constitution banned poll taxes for federal elections, while the Voting Rights Act abolished them in state elections.

20. John E. Filer, Lawrence W. Kenny, and Rebecca Morton, "Voting Laws, Educational Policies, and Minority Turnout," *Journal of Law and Economics*, vol. 34, October 1991: 371-393.

21. A $1-2 fee in 1940 is roughly equivalent to $14-28 today. Larry Kenny and I set up an extensive empirical analysis to test the impact of these fees and other voting rules. Data on up to 36 biennial elections from 1870 to 1940 were obtained for the 48 states. Infrequent elections and recent statehood reduced the sample to 1,215 elections. The dependent variable is defined as the fraction of the total population aged 21 or older who voted in the state's gubernatorial election. This variable ranges from 2 to 83 percent, with a mean of 37 percent. The socioeconomic and voting law variables that are used to explain changes in voter participation rates include: fixed year and

state effects, fraction of population age 65 and older, fraction of population that is illiterate, relative manufacturing wage, real manufacturing wage, female workers, rural population, rural population squared, fraction of the population that is foreign born, winning governor vote share, dummy for a Senate election, and dummy for a presidential election, as well as variables for female suffrage, poll tax, literacy test, and secret ballot. For a more extensive discussion see Lott and Kenny, "Did Women's Suffrage Change the Size and Scope of Government?" 1163-1198, and Filer, Kenny, and Morton, "Voting Laws, Educational Policies, and Minority Turnout," 371-93.

22.   However, there were only three statewide elections from the late 1970s to 1984 where Republicans won by less than one percentage point and the outcome would thus have been affected (Texas U.S. Senate and Governor races in 1978 and Virginia U.S. Senate 1978). There is also the Arkansas U.S. Presidential race in 1980, but Reagan's landslide would not have been altered by the Arkansas vote. See John R. Lott, Jr., "Evidence of Voter Fraud and the Impact that Regulations to Reduce Fraud have on Voter Participation Rates," SUNY Binghamton working paper (http://ssrn.com/abstract=925611).

23.   "Citizens vote by secret ballot so that they can vote without fear of how others will react" (http://www.voteutah.org/learning/elections/voting.html).

24.   This occurred when states introduced secret ballots during the 1882–1950 period. This 4 or 5 percentage point drop in turnout is equivalent to an 8-12 percent drop. See Lott and Kenny, "Did Women's Suffrage Change the Size and Scope of Government?," 1196.

25.   Frederic Charles Schaffer, "Might Cleaning Up Elections Keep People Away from the Polls? Historical and Comparative Perspectives," *International Political Science Review*, vol 23, no. 1, 2002: 69–84.

26.   Mark Lawrence Kornbluh, *Why America Stopped Voting: The Decline of Participatory Democracy and the Emergence of Modern American Politics* (New York: New York University Press, 2000).

27.   John R. Lott, Jr., "Why is Education Publicly Provided?: A Critical Survey," *Cato Journal*, Fall 1987, 475-501. My study with Kenny, as well as many others, found that higher income individuals are more likely to vote. See Lott and Kenny, "Did Women's Suffrage Change the Size and Scope of Government?," 1175.

28.   Jac C. Heckelman, "The effect of the secret ballot on voter turnout rates," *Public Choice*, volume 82, numbers 1- 2, January 1995: 107-124.

29.    Some literacy tests also asked factual questions about the constitution and current events. Take the questions from Alabama's test at the time that the 1965 Voting Rights Act was passed:

> 1.What body can try impeachments of the president of the United States?
>
> 2. Check the applicable definition for responsibility: ___ a duty, ___ a speech, ___ a failure
>
> 3. Name the attorney general of the United States.
>
> 4. May women now serve on juries in Alabama State courts?
>
> 5. If a person charged with treason denies his guilt, how many persons must testify against him before he can be convicted?
>
> 6. At what time of day on January 20 each four years does the term of the president of the United States end?
>
> 7. If the president does not wish to sign a bill, how many days is he allowed in which to return it to Congress for reconsideration?
>
> 8. If a bill is passed by Congress and the President refuses to sign it and does not send it back to Congress in session within the specified period of time, is the bill defeated or does it become law?

The answers in order: 1. The Senate; 2. a duty; 3. Nicholas Katzenbach; 4. Yes; 5. two; 6. 12 noon; 7. ten; 8. it becomes law unless Congress adjourns before the expiration of 10 days. The number of correct answers required to pass the test was left up to each county election board. See http://www.crmvet.org/info/litques.htm.

30.    See Lott and Kenny, "Did Women's Suffrage Change the Size and Scope of Government?" For an interesting discussion on literacy test voting requirements in North and South America, see Stanley Engerman and Kenneth Sokoloff, "The Evolution of Suffrage Institutions in the New World," National Bureau of Economic Research working paper 8512.

31.    Literacy tests became less effective over time, reducing turnout by only 1 percentage point by 1960. See John Filer, Lawrence Kenny, and Rebecca Morton, "Voting Laws, Education Policies, and Minority Turnout," *Journal of Law and Economics*, October 1991, 383.

32.    Scott Farmelant, "Dead Men Can Vote: Vote Fraud is Alive and Well in Philadelphia," *Philadelphia City Paper*, October 12-19, 1995.

33.    Ibid., and Mark Fazlollah, "Workers Apparently Broke Residency Rules," *Philadelphia Inquirer*, May 17, 1995.

34. Jingle Davis, "Even death can't stop some voters," *Atlanta Journal and Constitution*, November 6, 2000.

35. Jim Boulet Jr., "Commission Creation," *National Review*, February 26, 2002.

36. Deborah M. Phillips, Testimony on Election Issues, Senate Rules and Administration, March 14, 2001.

37. Tim Collie, "Florida's Flawed Election Process," *Sun-Sentinel* (Fort Lauderdale, Florida), December 10, 2000.

38. John Fund, *Stealing Elections* (San Francisco: Encounter Books, 2004), 62–64. Nearly a third of jurisdictions in Missouri have more registered voters than people. See Bill Lambrecht and Virginia Young, "U.S. Sues Missouri over Voter Lists," *St. Louis Post Dispatch*, November 23, 2005. See also Jeremy Hagen, "Photo IDs protect one-person, one-vote ideal," *Springfield News-Leader* (Missouri), April 5, 2006, and "Inflated voter rolls complicate election turnout percentages," *Fairbanks Daily News-Miner*, October 4, 2005.

39. John Fund interviewed on the Dennis Prager radio show on November 8, 2006, first hour (http://boss.streamos.com/download/Townhall/audio/mp3/7d23b263-65b5-4c19-9ac8-67ebd7cdc3f6.mp3?siteid=PodCast).

40. Editorial, "Voter Suppression in Missouri," *New York Times*, August 10, 2006.

41. Chuck McCutcheon, "Absentee Voting Fosters Trickery, Trend's Foes Say," *Times-Picayune*, October 24, 2006.

42. Fund, *Stealing Elections*, 44.

43. John Fund, "Absent Without Leave," OpinionJournal.com, October 30, 2006 (http://www.opinionjournal.com/diary/?id=110009167).

44. Rick Montgomery, "Questions abound in voter push," *Kansas City Star*, October 12, 2006, and Jeff Douglas, "Voter Registration Fraud Alleged in St. Louis," *Kansas City Star*, October 11, 2006.

45. Both these measures were supported by the bipartisan Carter-Baker Commission on election reform. Such rules are also supported by an overwhelming majority of Americans. A survey by Rasmussen Research indicated that 82 percent of all Americans, including 75 percent of Democrats, agree with the statement that "people should be required to show a driver's license or some other form of photo ID before they are allowed to vote." See Fund, *Stealing Elections*, 5.

46. Deroy Murdock, "Cleaning up America's Election System," Scripps Howard News Service, September 28, 2006.

47.  David Lieb, "Missouri Voter ID Law Latest in National Test Cases," Associated Press, August 20, 2006 (http://www.belleville.com/mld/belleville/news/state/15320528.htm) and "Supreme Court Allows Arizona Voter ID Law," Reuters News Wire, October 20, 2006 (http://www.washingtonpost.com/wp-dyn/content/article/2006/10/20/AR2006102001203.html).

48.  "Mexican Senate approves mail-in absentee ballots for Mexicans living abroad," Associated Press, April 28, 2005 (http://www.azcentral.com/specials/special03/articles/0428mexicovote-ON.html). Absentee ballots are the source of fraud in many different countries. The United Kingdom also faced claims of widespread vote fraud from "postal votes" during the 2005 parliamentary election. See Zoe Hughes, "Reform call after postal votes row," *The Journal* (Newcastle, UK), May 21, 2005.

49.  Curiously, however, the election reforms resulted in only a trivial increase in voting rates for Mexican congressional elections. Comparing the four congressional elections prior to the reforms with the four afterward produces only a one percent increase, from 56 to 57 percent. For the turnout data up through the 2003 elections see Joseph L Klesner., "The Not-So-New Electoral Landscape in Mexico," Working Paper, Department of Political Science, Kenyon College, September 15-16, 2003.

50.  John R. Lott, Jr., "Evidence of Voter Fraud and the Impact that Regulations to Reduce Fraud Have on Voter Participation Rates," SUNY Binghamton Working Paper, July 29, 2006.

51.  Provisional ballots allow people to vote even if their names do not appear on voter rolls, while no excuse absentee ballots allow any registered voter to receive an absentee ballot without having to provide a reason for needing one.

52.  John R. Lott, Jr., "Evidence of Voter Fraud and the Impact that Regulations to Reduce Frand have on Voter Participation Rates," SUNY Binghamton Working Paper, July 29, 2006.

53.  "Vote Fraud, Intimidation, and Suppression in the 2004 Presidential Election," American Center for Voting Rights Legislative Fund, Washington, D.C., August 2, 2005. If there is another report, I haven't been able to find it.

54.  John R. Lott, Jr., "Evidence of Voter Fraud."

55.  Since the study follows states both before and after they either adopt or stop the practice, the result can't simply be attributed to low voter participation in states adopting the rule.

56. Much of this discussion is based on John R. Lott, Jr., "Non-voted Ballots, The Cost of Voting, and Race," *Public Choice*, forthcoming.

57. *"Poll: Voter Interest Highest in Decade*," Associated Press, October 11, 2006 (http://www.cnn.com/2006/POLITICS/10/11/motivated.voters.ap/index.html). Nor are these concerns new. Nationally, as many as 18 percent of African Americans and 20 percent of 18- to 24-year-olds claim they don't believe their votes are counted accurately. See Rad Sallee, "Voters lose some faith in election accuracy," *Houston Chronicle*, July 9, 2004.

58. Kimball Brace, "69 Million Voters will use Optical Scan Ballots in 2006," Election Data Services, February 6, 2006 (http://www.electiondataservices.com/EDSInc_VEStudy2006.pdf#search=%22PUnch%20card%20machines%20million%20voters%22), and US Census Bureau, "Voting and Registration in the Election of November 2000," US Census Bureau, February 2002 (http://www.census.gov/prod/2002pubs/p20-542.pdf).

59. These data are for presidential elections from 1988 to 2000. See "Residual Votes Attributable to Technology," Caltech/MIT Voting Technology Project, March 30, 2001.

60. John R. Lott, Jr., "Non-voted Ballots."

61. This pattern has held true for decades. Even an expert hired by the ACLU, Professor Herb Asher at Ohio State University, found that punch card machines overall had much lower rates of non-voted ballots than other machines during the 1978 election. After this became clear, the ACLU declined to call on Asher to testify in a voter fraud court case.

62. Susan King Roth, "Human Factors Research on Voting Machines and Ballot Design: An Exploratory Study," Virginia Commonwealth University working paper, undated. See also Bederson, Benjamin B. Bongshin Lee, Robert M. Sherman, Paul S. Herrnson, and Richard G. Niemi, "Electronic Voting System Usability Issues," University of Maryland working paper (ftp://ftp.cs.umd.edu/pub/hcil/Reports-Abstracts-Bibliography/2002-23html/2002-23.html).

63. Ibid. Bradley Smith, then chairman of the Federal Election Commission, suggested to me in a telephone interview that older people's eyes may have a harder time focusing on computer screens, especially for longer periods of time.

64. And even then, the race of voters only explains 0.4 percent to 3 percent of the variation in non-voted ballot rates, itself an already small number.

65. This compares voters in households making under $15,000 annually with those in households with income of over $500,000.

66. John R. Lott, Jr., "Hacker Hysteria," *Washington Times*, May 11, 2004.

67. Michael I. Shamos, Testimony before the Maryland General Assembly House Ways & Means Committee, December 7, 2004 (http://euro.ecom. cmu.edu/people/faculty/mshamos/WaysMeansTestimony.htm). Shamos went so far as to wager a bet at 2 to 1 odds that such tampering could not occur (http://www.votingmachinesprocon.org/tamperingchallenge.pdf).

68. Michael I. Shamos, Testimony before the Environment, Technology, and Standards Subcommittee of the U.S. House of Representatives' Committee on Science, June 24, 2004 (http://euro.ecom.cmu.edu/people/faculty/mshamos/ HouseScience.htm).

69. Zev Chafets, "Florida Got Bad Rap in Vote Mess," *New York Daily News*, June 10, 2001.

70. By comparison, it took an additional 125 African Americans of all party affiliations in the average precinct to generate one spoiled vote. All these results control for a wide range of factors that influence spoiled-ballot rates, including education, gender, income, age, number of absentee votes, voting-machine type, ballot type, and whether votes are counted at the precinct or centrally. In other words, it is the isolated fact of being a Republican that makes an African American vastly more likely to have his or her ballot declared as not showing a vote. John R. Lott, Jr., "Non-Voted Ballots and Discrimination in Florida," *Journal of Legal Studies*, vol. 32, no. 1, January 2003: 181-220.

71. Ibid.

72. For example, listing the candidates' names in a straight line produces fewer problems than printing them on different pages or in separate columns.

73. The discussion in this section is based upon John R. Lott, Jr., "Documenting Unusual Declines in Republican Voting Rates in Florida's Western Panhandle Counties in 2000," *Public Choice*, vol. 123, June 2005: 349-361.

74. Reagan Coast-To-Coast, *Time*, Nov. 17, 1980.

75. A Field Institute survey indicated that 10 percent of Democratic voters blamed the media projections for their failure to vote. U.S. Representative Billy Tauzin, House Energy and Commerce Committee Hearing on Election Night 2000, February 14, 2001.

76. There was even one congressional race that spanned the two time zones, so half the district still had polls open when the Senate and presidential elections

were called for the Democrats. After the early call, turnout dropped by several percentage points in the precincts that remained open.

77. Lott, "Documenting Unusual Declines," 349-361.

78. Ibid.

79. Ibid.

80. Throughout election day, Florida counties report to the State Secretary of State on the voter turnout rate in their counties. It was only during the last part of the day that the turnout fell in the Western Panhandle counties relative to the rest of the state.

81. Lott, "Documenting Unusual Declines," 349-361.

82. John Stossel and Bill Ritter, "Where the Boys are," ABC News, March 16, 2001; Robert J. Vickers, "Tinsel Town's Glitter Factor a Challege for Delegates," *Plain Dealer*, August 18, 2000; Jim Hopkins, "More Women Flex Muscles in Politics," *USA Today*, September 16, 2003; "Interview with Bill Maher," CNN Larry King Live, January 20, 2004; Editorial, "The Angry Left," *Calgary Herald*, January 8, 2004; and http://www.newsmeat.com/billionaire_political_donations/.

83. Ryan S. King, "A Decade of Reform: Felony Disenfranchisement Policy in the United States," The Sentencing Project, October 2006 (http://www.sentencingproject.org/pdfs/FVR_Decade_Reform.pdf).

84. Michelle Chen, "Felon Voting Rights Conflict Hits Federal Courts," *The New Standard*, June 24, 2005.

85. John R. Lott, Jr. and James K. Glassman, "The Felon Vote," *New York Post*, March 1, 2005.

86. Dick Gordon, "Voting Rights for Felons." April 7, 2004.

87. Interview with the Assistant for Clemency for the Governor of Virginia for 1994 and 1995 (Voting Rights for Felons, National Public Radio's *The Connection*, April 7, 2004).

88. Ibid.

89. The implications for Senate races after the mid-1990s are based upon extrapolating their results. See Jeff Mana, Christopher Uggen, and Marcus Britton, "The Truly Disfranchised: Felon Voting Rights and American Politics," University of Minnesota working paper, January 3, 2001 (http://www.northwestern.edu/ipr/publications/papers/manza.pdf).

90. Survey conducted in Washington State by Venture Data L.L.C. on May 22-23, 2005 for Public Opinion Strategies.

91. While the effect isn't statistically significant for Hispanics, non-felon Hispanics fall between "independent" and "a few more Democrats than

Republicans," while felon Hispanics fall between "a few more Democrats than Republicans" and "mostly Democrats."

92. Brian Faler, "Election Turnout in 2004 Was Highest Since 1968," *Washington Post*, January 15, 2005.

93. Pauline Jelinek, "Election Turnout Rate Tops 40 Percent," Associated Press, November 8, 2006 (http://hosted.ap.org/dynamic/stories/E/ELN_TURNOUT? SITE=7219&SECTION=HOME&TEMPLATE=DEFAULT&CTME=2006- 11-08-18-54-03).

94. John R. Lott, Jr., "A Review Article on Donald Wittman's The Myth of Democratic Failure," *Public Choice*, vol. 92, no. 1-2 (July 1997): 1-13.

95. Http://www.worldnetdaily.com/news/article.asp?ARTICLE_ID=40862.

96. For example, in 2004, 55 percent of journalists at national media outlets claimed that the media was "not critical enough" of President Bush, while only 8 percent believed that the media has been "too critical." By contrast, a similar poll during 1995 found that 48 percent of the press believed that "too little" coverage had been given to President Clinton's accomplishments, while only 2 percent thought that "too much" coverage went to his achievements. See the Times Mirror Survey, see MRC's June, 1995 edition of MediaWatch. Pew Research Center for the People and the press, Survey of Journalists, March 10 – April 20, 2004. Patterson and Donsbach's survey of journalists lead them to conclude that "there is . . . a perceptual gap between journalists' self-image and their actions, and it leads them to reject any suggestion that they are politically biased." Thomas Patterson and Donsbach Wolfgang, "News Decisions: Journalists as Partisan Actors," *Political Communication* (1996): 466.

97. This discussion is based upon John R. Lott, Jr. and Kevin Hassett, "Is Newspaper Coverage of Economic Events Politically Biased?: Reagan to Bush II," AEI working paper 2004 (http://ssrn.com/abstract=588453). Hassett and I assembled a list of dates on which important economic news was released for most newspapers from 1991 to 2004. We also followed four major papers and the Associated Press for a slightly longer period—from 1985 onward. We then used Nexis—a computer database of news stories from 389 newspapers—to gather all 12,620 headlines that ran in America's newspapers covering economic news stories on those dates. We looked at headlines the day of and the day after the data were announced but excluded follow-up and feature stories in order to link the headlines directly with the economic numbers.

98. For example, unemployment fell by 2 percentage points during Reagan's second term and by 1.5 percentage points during Clinton's second term,

while GDP growth was similar (3.8 and 4.0 respectively) during both periods. Yet, Reagan received 7 percent fewer positive headlines than Clinton even after accounting for the slight differences in economic conditions. Unsurprisingly, during Reagan's second term, those who believed the economy was getting worse exceeded those who thought it was improving. The difference was almost 17 percentage points. During Clinton's second term, the reverse was true – optimists about the economy outnumbered pessimists by 6 percentage points.

99.    There have been a few other attempts to measure systematically media bias. One interesting paper by Groseclose and Milyo developed an index of how conservative or liberal media coverage was by counting the number of times that a media outlet cited various think tanks and comparing that with the number of times that members of Congress cited the same think tanks in speeches on the floor of the House and Senate. By comparing the citation patterns between politicians and media, they constructed an Americans for Democratic Action score for each media outlet, and thus ranked it on the same scale that politicians are ranked from liberal to conservative. They found that "Most of the mainstream media outlets that we examined . . . were closer to the average Democrat in Congress than they were to the median member of the House." This may indicate bias, but since an article may also quote an academic or a business, government, or union official, examining only think tanks could give a mistaken picture of any bias. Most reporters interview both sides for a story (though the vast majority of news stories in their data set only mention one of the 200 think tanks that they categorize as conservative or liberal), and any bias is likely to be much more subtle.

Another paper by DellaVigna and Kaplan claims that FOX News is conservative because people in particular areas tended to vote more conservatively after their cable systems started carrying FOX News. Even if one accepts their test and results, this does not constitute evidence that FOX is "conservative," only that it is not as liberal as the other media that it was replacing. See Tim Groseclose and Jeff Milyo, "A Measure of Media Bias," *Quarterly Journal of Economics*, 2005, 1191-1237, and Stefano DellaVigna and Ethan Kaplan, "The FOX News Effect: Media Bias and Voting," University of California at Berkeley, March 30, 2006.

100.    The discussion in this section is based upon: John R. Lott, Jr., "Public Schooling, Indoctrination, and Totalitarianism," *Journal of Political Econ-*

*omy*, vol. 107, no. 6, part 2, December 1999: S127-S157; John R. Lott, Jr.,"An Explanation for Public Provision of Schooling: The Importance of Indoctrination," *Journal of Law and Economics*, vol. 33, no.1, April 1990: 199-231; John R. Lott, Jr.,"Why is Education Publicly Provided?: A Critical Survey," *Cato Journal*, vol. 7, no. 2, Fall 1987: 475-501; John R. Lott, Jr., "The Institutional Arrangement of Public Education: The Puzzle of Exclusive Territories," *Public Choice*, vol. 54, no. 1, 1987: 89-96; and John R. Lott, Jr.,"Alternative Explanations for Public Provision of Education," UCLA Dissertation, 1984.

101.  J. Bruce Amstutz, *Afghanistan: The First Five Years of Soviet Occupation*, (Washington, DC: National Defense University Press, 1986). Another example of Soviet opposition to the family is the official propagation of the tale of Pavlik Morozov in the 1930s. According to the story, the twelve-year-old Morozov denounced his own father to the authorities for allegedly assisting efforts by private farmers to resist the state's collectivization of their farms. Pavlik, who was later killed by his own family members, was immortalized as a martyr for communism in songs and stories taught to Soviet children until the regime's collapse. The moral of Morozov's story was to trust the state, not one's own family.

102.  Charles Glenn, *Educational Freedom in Eastern Europe*, (Washington, D.C.: Cato Institute, 1995) 52.

103.  Carlsson was later Sweden's Prime Minister. See Roland Huntford, *The New Totalitarians*(New York: Stein and Day, 1972), 222 and 233.

104.  Huntford, 1972, 222. See also Sherwin Rosen, "Public Employment and the Welfare State in Sweden," *Journal of Economic Literature* (June 1996): 729-740.

105.  John R. Lott, Jr., "Public Schooling, Indoctrination, and Totalitarianism," *Journal of Political Economy*, vol. 107, no. 6, part 2 (December 1999): S127-S157.

106.  Robert Kaiser, *Russia: The People and the Power* (New York: Secker & W, 1976), 484.

107.  Edward Taborsky, *Communism in Czechoslovakia* (Princeton, NJ: Princeton University Press), 1961, 542.

108.  David K. Shipler, *Russia: Broken Idols, Solemn Dreams* (New York: Times Books, 1983): 116.

109.  Quote from John Loftus, former federal prosecutor, "Obsession: The Threat of Radical Islam," FOX News, November 5, 2006, 5 p.m. to 6 p.m.

(http://www.foxnews.com/video2/player06.html?103106/103106_Obses-sion2&FNL&Watch%20a%20Preview%20of%20%27Obses-sion%27&acc&World&320&News&422&&&new#).

110. Discussion from Wayne Kopping on "Obsession: The Threat of Radical Islam," FOX News, November 5, 2006, 5 p.m. to 6 p.m. (http://www.foxnews.com/video2/player06.html?103106/103106_Obsession2&FNL&Watch%20a%20Preview%20of%20%27Obsession%27&acc&World&32 0&News&422&&&new#).

111. West argues that education in New York was essentially universal prior to government subsidies. "The term 'universal' is intended to mean, something like, 'most,' 'nearly everybody,' of 'over 90 percent' then we lack firm evidence to show that education was not already universal prior to the establishment of laws to provide a schooling which was both compulsory and free." E.G. West, "The Political Economy of American Public School Legislation," *Journal of Law and Economics*, 1967, 127.

112. John R. Lott, Jr., "Alternative Explanations for Public Provision of Education," UCLA Economics Ph.D. Dissertation, May 1984.

113. E.G. West, "The Political Economy of American Public School Legislation," *Journal of Law and Economics* (1967): 105.

114. The argument here is not that there is a mistake being made here, but simply that teachers incentives are set up to reflect the desires of those who want to have larger government. This argument also applies to public ownership of the media—National Public Radio employees likely have the same type of incentives as pubic school teachers.

115. Like the previous example, this compares totalitarian and free countries of the same total income.

116. John R. Lott, Jr., "Public Schooling, Indoctrination, and Totalitarianism," *Journal of Political Economy*, vol. 107, no. 6, part 2 (December 1999): S144-S146.

117. A survey of 10 countries (Canada, England, France, Italy, New Zealand, Portugal, South Korea, Soviet Union, Sweden, and West Germany) found that citizens have much more choice in selecting between public doctors or different public hospitals than in selecting the public school or teacher for their child. Unlike schooling, customers of public medical care do not bear the large cost of changing their residence in order to change doctors. While public doctors and hospitals do not compete for patients on the basis of price, they do compete on the basis of quality, and doctors and administra-

tors' salaries vary depending on the number of patients served. Forbidding salaries to vary on this basis or stopping patients from choosing among doctors would seem to lower the quality of care produced. See John R. Lott, Jr., "The Institutional Arrangement of Public Education: The Puzzle of Exclusive Territories," *Public Choice*, vol. 54, no. 1 (1987): 89-96.

## Conclusion: Parting Thoughts

1. F. A. Hayek, "The Use of Knowledge in Society," *American Economic Review* (September 1945): 519-530.

# Index

FDA. *See* Food and Drug Administration

Federal Bureau of Investigation (FBI), 58, 115, 116, 148

Federal Election Campaign Act, 61

Federal Trade Commission, 199n2

FedEx, 100

527 groups, 68–69

527 Reform Act of 2005, 69

Fletcher, Ernie, 198n2

flood insurance, 89

Florida, 140; Election 2000 and, 169, 177–79, 181–82; voter fraud in, 169–70

Food and Drug Administration (FDA), 76

football helmets, liability and, 205n58

Foote, Christopher, 125

Forssman, Hans, 118–19, 226n17

FOX News, 180, 186

France, 97

fraud: corporate, 49, 79–82; voting, 169–74

*Freakonomics* (Levitt and Dubner): abortion and crime and, 5, 117-127; campaign finance and, 64-65; corporate crime and, 79; free market, distrust of and, 2, 39; lemon thesis and, 35; real estate agents and, 37-43

free competition. *See* free market

freedom: academic, 11; economic, 12–13

free market: academia and, 11; central planning vs., 1, 12–13, 93; distrust of, 2–3; economic self-interest and, 1–2, 193; failure of,

5; failures of, 34–44; incentives and, 5; reputation and, 3–4, 49; success of, 1, 1–2; wealth and, 6

free-riding problems, 86–88

Free Schools Act of 1867, 191

Friedman, Milton, 12, 85–86, 109, 198n8, 217n7, 223n58, 225n72

Fund, John, 170

*Furman v. Georgia*, 233n65

# G

Gallup Poll, 187

Gandhi, Mohandas, 141

gas: full- vs. self-service, 30–32, 201n28, 201n29; price of, 3; shortages of, 12, 19, 20. *See also* oil prices

gas stations, franchising of, 81–82

GEICO insurance, 44

gender gap, 160–61, 165

Genuardi's, 200–201n19

George Mason University, 64

George Mason University School of Law, 99

Georgia, 171

Germany, 98, 100

Ginsburg, Ruth Bader, 54

Giuliani, Rudolph, 53, 65

Goetz, Christopher, 125, 229n37, 230n38, 231n40

Goff, Donald, 214n56

Goldberg, Bernie, 185

Gordon, James, 153

Gordon, Slade, 182

Gore, Al, 53, 53–54, 177–78, 180–81

Gould, Jay, 33–34